Right to the Edge

Also by Charley Boorman

Race to Dakar
By Any Means: From Wicklow to Sydney

Right to the Edge

Sydney to Tokyo
By Any Means

CHARLEY BOORMAN

with **JEFF GULVIN**

sphere

SPHERE

First published in Great Britain in 2009 by Sphere

A CIP catalogue record for this book
is available from the British Library.

ISBN 978-1-84744-351-9

Typeset in Times by M Rules
Printed and bound in Great Britain by
Clays Ltd, St Ives plc

Papers used by Sphere are natural, renewable and recyclable products
sourced from well-managed forests and certified in accordance with the
rules of the Forest Stewardship Council.

Mixed Sources
Product group from well-managed
forests and other controlled sources
www.fsc.org Cert no. SGS-COC-004081
© 1996 Forest Stewardship Council
FSC

Sphere
An imprint of
Little, Brown Book Group
100 Victoria Embankment
London EC4Y 0DY

An Hachette UK Company
www.hachette.co.uk

www.littlebrown.co.uk

To Olivia, Doone and Kinvara, for always being there.

And to Ewan – thanks for everything.

Contents

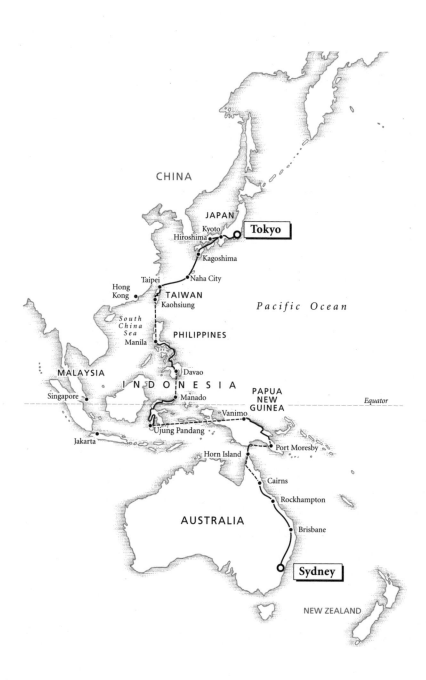

1

The Juice

ON 13 MAY 2009, I felt the wheels of our plane touch the tarmac at Sydney airport. We'd arrived. I felt a rush of exhilaration and relief. All the months of planning and dreaming had come together at last. But my excitement didn't quite hide the nerves that had been building since long before we set off from London twenty-four hours earlier. I settled back in my seat and tried to relax. Best not to think about all the challenges that lay ahead. My mind drifted back to my last visit to Sydney – and the end of my previous adventure . . .

Just ten months earlier I'd ridden through the Sydney Harbour Tunnel at the end of another mammoth journey. Starting from my dad's house in County Wicklow, I had crossed Eastern Europe before travelling the length of Iran using any means of transport I could find. I'd been through India, Nepal and China. I'd island-hopped across Indonesia before enduring a dramatic sea voyage from Timor to Darwin on a boat made from Kalimantan ironwood. When we at last stepped ashore, I remember kissing the harbour wall in gratitude.

But that had only been half the journey. I'd always dreamed of pushing on even further – right on through Australia with Japan our final destination. And now that dream was coming true at last. We would begin by heading up the east coast of Australia to Brisbane before continuing north to Cairns. From there it was on to Papua New Guinea, where there had been reports of recent trouble. That was as far ahead as I wanted to think right now.

The week before I left, just as I started thinking about saying goodbye to my wife Olly and the kids, I began to realise that, despite all my travels, I had learned almost nothing about the business of leaving. Since 2004 I'd ridden a motorbike from London to New York via Russia; I'd raced the Dakar Rally and ridden from John O'Groats to Cape Town. Then last year I'd taken advantage of just about every type of vehicle you could think of during the trip from Ireland to Sydney. But as usual, the week of departure dawned and nothing was ready.

The preparation for this expedition had been fraught with difficulties, not least the onset of a global recession. We had a *sort of* budget and I had a rucksack that was *sort of* packed and that was about it. And there was an added pressure on me this time round, or at least *I* felt there was. On previous trips I had always had either my friend Ewan McGregor or our producer, Russ Malkin, at my side. But Ewan was very busy with his film work, and this time Russ was needed back in London to coordinate the TV series. It's true that producer Sam Simons and cameraman Robin Shek were flying out with me. And Claudio von Planta – who had joined Ewan and me on our *Long Way* . . . trips, and filmed my Dakar challenge – would be meeting up with us shortly, which I was really pleased about. But there was no getting away from the fact that on this trip, more than any other, the buck stopped with me. If anything went wrong, it would be down to me to sort it out. And while that was exciting in some ways, it was also bloody terrifying . . . I'd spoken to my dad, John, about my worries the last time I saw him. His sister, my aunt Wendy, died recently and my sisters and I went down to the funeral in Cornwall. Dad and I had a bit of time together and I voiced my fears about undertaking this project on my own. Dad pointed out that he was about to begin another massive project himself, and after all his years in the film business he was still suffering from the same kind of nerves.

I knew I was lucky to have Sam and Robin on board. Sam is a really passionate producer/director with a fantastic background in high-quality documentaries, and Robin had worked tirelessly on *Long Way Down*, *Race to Dakar* and *By Any Means*. And as for Claudio – he was, of course, the unsung hero of the two *Long Way* . . . trips, matching his expertise with the camera with an excellent general knowledge of the countries we were travelling through. He has a serious mind, old Claudio, and given my *somewhat* justified reputation for talking bullshit, you could say he's the ideal foil. It was good to have him back on board.

I'd started the trip envying Claudio, who was flying out after the rest of us and therefore missed seeing his equipment being swabbed for explosives at Heathrow and testing positive. I couldn't believe it – every item had to be taken out and searched and then we had to go through the incredibly laborious task of putting it all back again. At least they let us fly – to my endless embarrassment I'd been kicked off an aeroplane at the start of *Long Way Down*. I'd never have lived down a repeat performance.

I soon stopped envying Claudio when I saw him arrive, bleary-eyed, at the hotel a couple of days later. He told me he'd hardly slept on the journey at all and there was no time to recover – it was hit the ground running. To my delight we were doing the first leg of the journey on bikes, and Claudio would spend the first day filming from the back of a BMW.

By Any Means had been a fantastic expedition: 112 forms of transport covering 25 countries in 102 days. As far as I was concerned, the only downside was that I'd have liked more motorbikes. This time I would still be taking different forms of transport, but it wasn't the means of travel that was important so much as the people I was hoping to meet along the way.

Suddenly it was all go and the fear really started to kick in. I had an attack of the colly-wobbles, the butterflies I always seem to suffer from as we're about to set out. It never seems to get any easier. I have the same dreams, the same worries. Will people welcome us? Will anything go wrong? Will I be able to fix it if it does? Originally we were just going to slip quietly north on a couple of motorbikes, but we kept getting hits on the website from bikers suggesting a convoy. I have a love/hate relationship with convoys – I love the feeling of everyone riding together, but I always worry that no one will show up. Every time I do it, I pray that there will be at least a few motorbikes to meet us. So far it's worked out well, and fortunately this time we'd had some air time on Australia's morning TV show, *Today*, so I was able to let people know I would be leaving from the Freshwater Reserve in Manly.

I would be riding a customised flat tracker built by Deus Ex Machina, a motorcycle outlet on Parramatta Road and just about the coolest place imaginable. It truly is one of a kind, a large showroom with a workshop where they specialise in taking Kawasaki W650s and turning them into street trackers – an homage to the racing bikes they used back in the 1950s and 1960s. The company is run by Dare Jennings, a tall, extremely laid-back man with an easy smile and very dry sense of humour. Dare is a mad-keen biker and ex 'big-wave rider'.

Dare's place is different from any bike shop I've been in. There are so many amazing machines, and not just Deus creations, but ancient Harleys, an original Indian, a fully restored Indian . . . the imagination his team has put into the place is visible. Everyone is really into what they do and they produce some seriously impressive bikes. The one they had for me was a Kawasaki based on an old BSA. The Japanese designer was an ardent fan of British bikes and had bought the patent and copied the style – the W650 could have been a badged BSA complete with jam-pot cylinder heads, the works. One of the mechanics explained to me that the Deus principle is to simplify the bike Kawasaki put out – they take the weight off and stand the back end up a bit so that the bike turns nicely into the corners. They work on the suspension – the exhaust is invariably a burbling two-into-one – and the tail had been cut down and flared to give it a sort of 'bobber' look. Mine had a red and pale blue paint job and the seat was fibreglass, padded and covered with studded leather. After being stuck on a plane for twenty-four hours and with the heebie-jeebies gnawing, I just wanted to throw my leg over and go for a blat.

Dare is a really nice guy; I noticed that when he's socialising he's extremely good at including everyone, which is an endearing quality. He used to run a surf business called Mambo but sold that in the 1990s. One wall in the Deus showroom is devoted to a massive black-and-white photo of a guy on a motorbike with a side rack designed to carry a surfboard. Dare told us that a couple of years ago they built some bikes for a bunch of guys who wanted to cruise the coast with their boards without the hassle of a van. That was the perfect kind of challenge and something about the romance of bikes and boards caught the public's imagination.

The literal translation of Deus Ex Machina is 'God from the machine'. In books and movies it's a plot device where something is introduced into the story to help a character overcome what otherwise would be an insoluble problem. That's Dare all over: his life is about the fun of making the difficult doable, and a bike racked for a surfboard sums it up. His great hero is the Australian bike racer Herbie Jefferson, who was not only a racer but a big-wave rider. 'It's all the same juice,' Herbie would say.

On the morning of 18 May we all woke up early, praying that a decent crowd of people would be there to see us off. At least this time I knew there would definitely be a few of us riding out together. We'd met Terry, Chris, Steve and Jack last year on *By Any Means* in a tiny town called Daly Waters. Old school mates who were now retired, they had been on a mammoth road trip and had talked fondly about a fifth member of their gang who should have been with them. His name was also Chris and he was suffering from leukaemia. At the time we met the guys, Chris was home in Canberra waiting for a bone-marrow transplant and I had spoken to him on the phone. Since then he had had the treatment and today I would finally get to meet him.

So that was five at least. Then there was my mate Wayne Gardner, the ex-racer who won the World 500 cc Championship on a Honda back in 1987. Wayne is a legend, an awesome rider from the days of two-strokes: no traction control and no engine braking. During his championship year he clocked up seven race wins. In 1982 he'd been TT world champion and in 1985 and 1986 he won the Suzuka 8 Hour. That made six, then; in addition to myself and Claudio. It would be fine.

But I still woke up feeling nervous as hell. We met downstairs and jumped in a taxi to take us back to Parramatta Road. Sitting beside me, Claudio was looking both pale and weary.

'Clouds,' I said. 'This is the fifth project I've done in six years, you know that?'

He gave me a sort of sidelong glance, as he often does. 'So what went wrong that you got me on board again?'

'No one else wanted to do it.'

I was really glad he was with us. Knackered or not, you can rely on Claudio absolutely. He has an instinct for the shot, the camera is like an extension of his psyche. I remember him in the market town of Bati, Ethiopia, standing on top of a ruined building with the tripod before Ewan and I even realised he'd gone. That's no reflection on anyone else – Mungo was terrific on the last trip – but this time I needed the experience Claudio brings just by us having worked together so often. And he's a cult hero, of course, even if he isn't aware of it.

I had spoken to Ewan a couple of days previously and he wished me luck with the trip. He's based in LA at the moment so I've not seen so much of him lately, but we're in touch and always talking about potential biking projects. He's been a great friend and I never forget that if it wasn't for him I probably wouldn't be doing what I'm doing.

At around 10 a.m, with my nerves just about intact, we were on the bikes and riding through the streets of Sydney with the rain holding off and people waving as we passed. I really did have the butterflies now; I'd had them in England a year ago when we set off from Coventry and the same words rattled through my head. Let there be bikes, I thought. Please God, let there be bikes.

Bikes. My God, there were hundreds of them. It was Monday morning, with a bad weather forecast, and yet there must have been three or four hundred motorcyclists gathered at the Freshwater Reserve. I pulled into the car park and gave everyone a wave and a few people cheered. Moments later Claudio arrived with the camera rolling and, as he took his helmet off, a huge cheer went up. Instant recognition for the master of the little red bike; the man who'd survived the Road of Bones and Charley tailgating him in South Africa. Before he knew what was happening people were cramming around him, begging for his autograph.

I was delighted for him. Being the unassuming bloke he is, he was a little taken aback, but it brought home to me that it's the camaraderie of what we do that people identify with. There had been three of us on the bikes for *Long Way Round* and *Long Way Down*, and without Claudio, Ewan and I would've been hopelessly lost.

It wasn't just bikers there to see us off either; loads of people had come down who weren't on bikes at all. I had photos taken, I signed books and DVDs – I even had babies thrust into my arms. Claudio was trying to film but he found himself swamped by fans he didn't know he had and spent most of the time signing jackets, fuel tanks, body parts and anything else someone had a pen for.

Wayne Gardner was there, of course: he only lives down the road and was riding a Honda Fireblade. Then there were the guys from Daly Waters and finally I was able to shake hands with Chris.

The introductions completed, we got back on the bikes – all three hundred-odd of us – and rode north from Manly to Fraser Beach. It was one great swarm of motorbikes and as soon as I'd topped the rise and glimpsed them all gathered in the car park, my fears had evaporated. The nerves had been replaced by sheer excitement. There were so many of us it took twenty minutes to get everyone out of the car park. It was just fantastic, better than I could ever have hoped for. There was one guy riding beside me on a yellow bike whose left hand didn't work and he had it pressed into his pocket. He had thumb brakes and the clutch had been switched to the right handlebar and he rode along popping second-gear wheelies.

The cops in Australia can be a bit of a pain in the arse, though. No offence, boys, but you were all over us! We had to stop completely at one point because the convoy wasn't orderly enough for their liking (they wanted us in two neat lines all the way). As Wayne said later, the ride was fun, if a little slow.

We made it to the beach finally, an hour and a half's ride north of Sydney. Claudio, who was riding pillion with a local guy called Matt, managed to get lost – they stopped for fuel and lost touch with the rest of the bikes and then they went the wrong way. They eventually showed up with Claudio on the back trying to appear professional and Matt looking especially sheepish.

'No, we weren't lost,' Claudio insisted. 'We were just checking out a little of Australia.'

No wonder the poor guy got lost; he was still exhausted from the flight and had spent the morning on the back of a motorbike trying to film me waffling away as I rode through the streets of Sydney. Olly and I lived in Sydney for a while back in our twenties. We had a place in Five Ways, Paddington; Olly worked as a PA and a waitress while I was a barman as well as a labourer on the Harbour Bridge. They were great days with great memories and here I was again. For all my fears we had had the perfect start and when I spoke to Olly later I was full of enthusiasm about it all.

It did rain, though. It rained hard and it was dark when we got to Wingham, a small town close to Taree. It was only Dare and me now, with Robin filming from the back of Matt's bike. Claudio had had it; eyes closing, he had curled up in the back of the support truck and fallen asleep.

The boys from Daly Waters met us at the pub. Steve and Chris, Jack and Terry and the other Chris, of course, whom I now got to speak to properly. He was an amazing guy, so breezy and cheerful – he put it down to the steroids. Seriously though, he told me that when I'd spoken to him on the phone he'd been anxious about finding a donor. Thankfully he did get the marrow that would keep him alive, from a thrity-eight-year-old woman in the UK. He was very grateful to her.

We stood outside the pub and drank beer. The first time I'd met these guys had been in that wonderful little blink-and-miss-it town of theirs between Darwin and Alice Springs. I'd been considering a ramshackle little shop with a helicopter buried in the roof when a bike pulled up and this older-looking bloke peered at me.

'Charley,' he said, 'what're you doing here? Loved the series, mate. Is Ewan with you?'

That was Steve McGrath and here we were almost a year later shooting the breeze again.

'It's great to see you guys,' I said. 'A nice little full circle story.'

'Full circle's good for me,' Chris piped up. 'It could've been a dead end.'

We fell about laughing.

'I tell you,' he went on, 'when I got that call last year, I didn't know what was going on. Chris said: "There's someone wants to talk to you," and then this little pommie voice comes on the line and I thought, Is it some bloody backpacker they've picked up?' He grinned broadly. 'It was a moment, a real little boost, the kind you need when you're where I was back then.' He raised his glass and we drank. 'I tell you, I'm just glad to be alive. Every day's a gift, mate; every healthy day.'

We slept the night in the Australia Inn at Wingham. I was really tired but I'd read in the paper that there had been riots in Lae, Papua New Guinea, which was a little unnerving. We would be travelling through Lae, and I had to think, What is it about us and riots? Last time it had been football fans in Istanbul, then Russians invading Georgia and China closing the Tibetan border. Oh well, we'd see how it was when we got there. In the meantime it had been an exhilarating first day and all I wanted now was a shower, some food and some sleep.

It was still dark outside when the sound of rain rattling off tin roofs woke me. I went to the window and stared into the gloom. There were a few lights glowing here and there but the glass was pretty opaque and the balcony slick with rain. My heart sank. This morning I was riding with Dare and the last thing we needed was this kind of weather. It was a bummer, but it was all part of the adventure I suppose, and it's not as if I can't ride in the rain. Last year it seemed like every time we got on a motorbike it was pouring with bloody rain. There were still a couple of hours before we were due to leave and, ever the optimist, I thought it might clear up.

It didn't. It was still coming down when we said goodbye to the guys from Daly Waters, who were riding south to Canberra. It had been great to meet Chris at last. He told me he owed a lot to the Leukaemia Foundation and planned to go to the UK so he could look up the woman who had donated the bone marrow that saved his life. He said that if he made it he'd give me a call, but between you and me, I think he really wanted to meet my wife. I'm a nice guy apparently, but Chris reckoned that was down to Olly . . .

Dare and I jumped back on the bikes and this time he rode the flat tracker while I was on the rat-style Triumph Thruxton he'd been riding yesterday. It's a café racer he put together and it has awesome power. I'd ridden it for a few miles last night and was really looking forward to a good day, even if the rain was bucketing down. I was wearing an open-face helmet though, and as we hit the highway the wind was rushing past my ears. Little did I know just how deaf I would be by the time we stopped again that evening.

Wingham was a nice place, if a little wet. It was incredibly green, with palms that were dripping water as we headed north. We were on good tarmac to begin with – two-lane blacktop – and the road was bordered by trees and fields, single-storey houses with red-tiled roofs dotted here and there. Then we hit some dirt, red cinder, which on the right bike would've been excellent, but on the rat-style I took it a little easy. After that it was tarmac again and seventy-odd clicks later we pulled into the driveway of Mark Johnson's house in Wauchope, where a massive bull-nosed truck was waiting. It was gorgeous, a brilliant blue with chrome grille and bumper, twin chrome exhausts rising behind the doors. It reminded me of my favourite book when I was a kid. The book had no words, just pictures of a big Mack truck with pullout drawings of the engine and everything. I loved it.

But this wasn't a Mack; it was a Diamond T* that, until thirteen years ago, had been carrying cotton gins in Western Australia. Mark was a panel beater by trade, and came out to greet us wearing only a pair of shorts and bomber jacket against the rain. We shook hands and he told me the truck was owned by a friend of his and the two of them had spent a couple of years restoring it.

It was time to say goodbye to Dare and I was sad to see him go. He's such a great guy and we're like-minded. I tried to persuade him to join me and the family for a holiday when the trip was over. 'I'll see what I can do, Charley,' he said. 'But in the meantime thanks for letting me come along.' He gestured to where Mark was already in the truck and pressing his fist to the horn. 'You'd better go,' he said. 'Your chariot awaits.'

*

---

* I'd always thought the 'T' in Diamond T was the designer's initial, but Mark reckoned it stood for the forward tilt-style bonnet.

As I climbed into the cab Mark looked sideways at me with a mischievous grin on his face, and we were pulling away before I'd even closed the door. He was in his late fifties, maybe early sixties, it was hard to tell. Short grey hair and a pair of wraparound shades that made him look a little menacing. He ground the gears as we turned out of his driveway.

'How long since you drove this truck, Mark?' I asked him.

He showed his teeth. 'Thirteen years.'

The truck was the noisiest vehicle I think I've ever been in. We left Mark's place in Wauchope and drove 100 kilometres up the coast with the two-stroke ringing in my ears. This was the 653 American edition, with the GM engine rather than one made in Australia under licence. The main difference is the twin air cleaners, like a pair of blue milk churns attached to the wings – apparently the air was inducted back through the body, whereas on the Aussie version it was through the bonnet. It was fabulous, but as I say, incredibly loud: a two-stroke diesel V6 with what they call a thirteen-spread ranger gearbox. It had been built in 1962 and was known as a 'screamer' – that scream really was unbelievable, even Mark thought so. I take my hat off to anyone who could have driven one of these trucks for a living.

Anyway, we were on the road heading north and having to shout across the cab to each other. Above the brain-numbing din I managed to work out that Mark ran a mobile paint shop and had sign-written many of the trucks that passed us on the highway. He was married to an English woman he met when he was travelling around Australia.

The way their trucks looked was always as important to Diamond T as how they functioned, and the chrome was everywhere – a sort of Harley Davidson of the commercial vehicle family. 'Dad's Pride' was emblazoned on the front bumper of this one, the interior was pale studded upholstery, the gear knob a piston head and the steering wheel white with four spokes. I loved it, apart from the noise anyway. By the time we got to our next stop, Stan's place in Macksville, I was deaf as a post.

*

Stan was another Aussie good old boy. He was older than Mark, tall and lean and wearing a faded baseball cap. His great passion was trucks – big, old trucks – and he was going to give us a ride in an Oshkosh as far as Coffs Harbour.

I thought the Diamond T was big, but this thing was colossal. A bright yellow tow truck with a powder-coated towing rig – Stan told me it weighed thirteen tonnes. He had restored it after it went out of service. He was a member of the Heritage Vehicle Association and without people like him these old trucks would vanish from the roads altogether. His wife was equally involved. Stan said that she was getting used to the gears now and if he was away she would clean the Oshkosh in readiness for a show. There was one every year in Alice Springs and a really massive one every five years. Stan's father had always been into trucks too. Back in the 1940s he drove for the forest service before buying a bus route and settling in Macksville. Over the years he had restored lots of vehicles and that was where Stan got the bug.

Oshkosh is a city in Wisconsin. The trucks all come from there – not just tow trucks like Stan's, but army vehicles too. This was a left-hand drive that had been brought over and converted – Stan pointed out the shaft that ran under the dash from left to right. Oshkosh was an American Indian chief: the word means 'claw' and considering the massive power of this thing, that seemed apt somehow. Its GCM (Given Concentration Mass) was 120 tonnes, which means that it can pull anything up to 107 tonnes (as its own weight was the 13 tonnes Stan had mentioned). So it was strong enough to pull the massive road trains I'd driven the last time I was over here.

I was keen to drive it myself, so halfway to Coffs Harbour I suggested to Stan that we swap places.

'You've got a truck licence, right?' he asked as I slipped behind the wheel.

'Oh yeah,' I lied. 'I drove an International S Line over at Coober Pedy.'

'Great, away we go then.'

I ground the gears, that horrific screeching sound of synchromesh not meshing, and with a smile I squinted at him. 'You know the old saying, Stan: if you can't find it – grind it.'

Then we were off down the freeway with sweat rolling off my brow and my palms wringing wet.

'Are you all right, mate?' Stan asked. 'Your hands are sweating.'

'I'm fine.'

I was, actually. Even though it was huge, the truck wasn't that hard to manoeuvre, although because of its age the steering felt a little vague and I found myself over-correcting. But it was great fun and immensely powerful and I loved being that high up, looking down on what appeared to be miniature cars trundling by. We were on the move. I'd been riding bikes, I was in my second truck and the juice Herbie Jefferson talked about was flowing.

2

Spitting Fire in the Rain

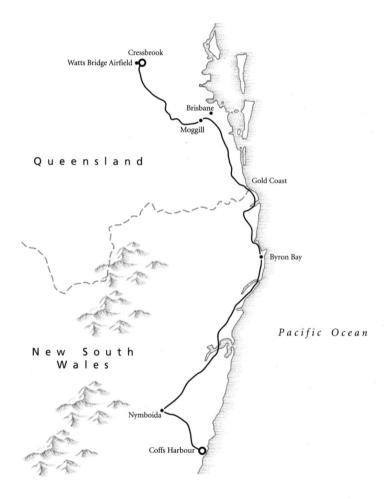

LEAVING STAN SOUTH of the harbour, we carried on to the Coaching Station Inn at Nymboida. It was still wet outside but there was a fire in the grate and I could smell food being cooked. Feeling pretty exhausted, I slumped down at a table.

The only other guests seemed to be a young couple sitting across the way and I got talking to them. Joel and his wife Tatum had been married a year and were spending their first anniversary at Coffs Harbour. We spent the evening chatting and at one point Joel suggested we go for a swim in the river before breakfast. I wasn't much up for it but I was looking for a lift in the morning so I agreed.

'I'll be there,' I said. 'I used to swim in the river that ran through my dad's place in Ireland. Listen, Joel: I've got to meet a guy with an electric car at a petrol station tomorrow. It's about twenty kilometres up the road. Is there any chance of you two giving me a lift?'

'Sure,' he said. 'We could do that, yeah.'

I woke to the smell of eucalyptus, more rain and a grey mist that coated the hills. This was a beautiful spot, log-cabin-style rooms with great views across an evergreen valley with the river coursing through it. And I mean *coursing*: from where I was standing it looked pretty fast-flowing and pretty cold. Suddenly I was having second thoughts about this morning's 'refreshing' dip. But Joel came by, and having made a commitment the night before, I followed him down to the shore. It was bloody freezing and the swim was brief to say the least, but we did manage to find a section where the rapids weren't roaring. And for those of you who complained about the quality of my underpants the last time you saw me in a river, I had a proper pair of swimming shorts this time, all right?

The weather was really grim still: not cold but the rain

appeared to have set in. It was as if a great grey blanket had been thrown across this section of the Australian coast and there was no way out from under it. In a couple of days we were due to fly up the coast in a Spitfire and I really hoped the weather wouldn't get in the way. I'd had a few flying lessons – I could take off and land – but a Spitfire . . . it reminded me of my dad's film *Hope and Glory*, where I'd played a German pilot who crashed his plane. I did not want to miss out.

In the meantime the weather would do what weather does. Joel and Tatum gave me a ride in their Holden.

'So what do you think about the idea of electric cars then?' I asked Joel. 'There's a bit of a love affair with the V8 in this country, isn't there?'

He looked sideways at me. 'Take someone's V8 off them and give them an electric car? Yeah, I'm not sure how well that would go down.'

The electric car was bright green and looked like a small Mazda. I'm not sure what I'd been expecting but I'd driven a fairly outlandish-looking solar-powered car the last time I was here, and this looked like a normal compact.

Turned out it *was* a normal compact, based on a Mazda but with a bunch of boxes and computers under the bonnet instead of a petrol or diesel engine. The car was called an evMe and had been built by Phil Coop and his company, Energetique. To all intents and purposes it looked and felt like any other car. There was an ignition key, though no gears as such: just a 'Drive' position and, of course, reverse. It easily coped with 130 kmph. I was amazed; it was so quiet, and after the trucks yesterday that was wonderful.

Phil is a committed and enthusiastic guy who isn't trying to solve the environmental problems of the world, just do his bit. Not only is he involved with the car company; he also run a cattle farm where everything is sustainable and organic. The battery-powered car is his passion, however, and he explained that trying to develop something for everyday use was like trying to wade through treacle.

'I'm not one for conspiracy theories,' he said, 'but even the smallest problem in this business becomes a major challenge. In the past it was politicians and fossil-fuel companies who would try to block us. More recently it's been computer and technology companies. For example, just this last year we tried to buy a piece of important equipment from the States and were blocked completely.' He shrugged his shoulders. 'I can't tell you why, maybe these people just don't want us to move forward, but that bit of equipment suddenly became unavailable.'

He told us that things were changing, though. For years battery technology had lagged behind other areas in terms of what he called 'the electrification of society'. Then with the development of nanotech batteries, they made a huge leap forward. The battery in the evMe would last ten years and even then it would still work at 80 per cent of its original capacity. The new breed that would be available in only a couple of years' time would last fifty years and have other applications long after the life of the car was over. This little car ran for two hundred kilometres on one charge; the charge took only seven minutes and cost about three quid. It wasn't the only solution for future clean fuelling, but it was certainly one of them.

I for one was impressed. The evMe was great to drive, it had good pick-up, lots of torque and it ate up the miles to Byron Bay. The car was simple and so quiet, and in many ways so much better than a normal version.

The evMe was a million miles away from the next car we'd be driving. Brendan's clapped-out old Mitsubishi estate had been given to him by his mate Declan and it's fair to say that it was significantly less environmentally friendly than Phil's car. We met Brendan at the Arts Factory in Byron Bay, a cool town on the coast that has an American feel to it, with wide roads and diagonal parking, and palm trees that today were bent almost horizontal by the wind and rain. It really was kicking up a storm. We stopped at the beach and the waves were massive, rolling whitecaps. I'd been hoping to go surfing tomorrow but there was no chance of a novice like me venturing out in this. There was also an ever-diminishing chance that we would be up in that plane. Sam phoned the Spitfire people and they told him the weather was just as bad in Brisbane and that as things stood there was only about a 40 per cent likelihood we'd be flying.

It was a bummer. Not only did it mean we'd miss out on an incredible experience, but it would add time to the journey and we'd have to find another way of moving up the coast.

As if to really piss us off, when we came through town the rain seemed to get even worse, the wipers working nineteen to the dozen and the road all but flooded. We made it to the Arts Factory, and ducked inside to keep dry. This was the backpackers' hostel where we would be spending the night. It's very famous and one of the most used in Australia, with over three hundred and fifty beds. There are loads of little rooms called cubes, and there is also a tented village, as well as a number of different-sized communal tepees.

The manager, Peggy, greeted us. She came hobbling round from behind the counter on a pair of crutches, her right leg plastered to the knee.

'So what happened to you?' I asked her.

'Too many tequila slammers: stiletto slipped on the table and off I went.'

'You broke your foot dancing on a table?'

'Yeah.'

'Oh well, I suppose if you're going to do it at all, that's got to be the way.'

Peggy showed us to a large tepee that looked like a hospital dormitory inside, with six or seven metal-framed beds lining the walls. I could hear rain on the canvas and thought it would be a pretty cool place to spend the night, just so long as it didn't leak.

'Look, Peggy,' I said. 'Tomorrow we have to get up to Brisbane where we're supposed to be hitching a ride in a Spitfire. I know it's a couple of hundred kilometres but do you reckon there's anyone here who might give us a lift?'

'I'm sure there is,' she told me. 'Ask around, Charley. Word of mouth is the way here. Just ask around.'

Claudio and I went off to do just that and about thirty seconds later we bumped into Brendan, a tall, barefoot English guy with a few days' stubble on his chin, wearing a baseball hat with the peak hugging the back of his neck.

'Sure, I can take you,' he told us. Then he showed us his Mitsubishi. 'What do you think? She's got a little more character than the car you arrived in, hasn't she?' He nodded to the bright green evMe. 'But you might have to push.' He paused, then added with a grin, 'I'm joking. We'll be fine if we park on a hill.'

Brendan's Irish mate Declan had given him the car just a couple of weeks ago. He told us it was like that at the Factory: people moved on and left things behind for other people, and Declan had left his car. Brendan had come to the hostel for a couple of days, and ended up staying for three and a half months. He lived in a tent, the flysheet reinforced with a blue plastic tarp to help keep the rain out. In fact, the whole of the tented village was a mass of blue tarps – it was reminiscent of some South American shanty town seen through the murk of the day.

Peggy told us that Brendan staying for as long as he had was not unusual, it was that kind of place. The Jungle Hut personified the spirit of the Factory – a sort of tented bar/recreation area packed with people drinking, playing music and sorting through belongings that had been left by other backpackers. I reckoned the average age was about nineteen and it made me feel like some old granddad or something at forty-two. When I was younger I'd not really been into the backpacking scene, but here there was a real community feel and I could see the attraction. We had a good night, drinking a few beers and listening to music, playing a bit of table tennis and praying the weather would change.

Later on, Peggy came by to tell us it wasn't safe to sleep in the tepee after all. There was a severe weather warning and when it rained as hard as this the water dribbled onto the electrics. It was a pity because I had been looking forward to it, but there was no choice so we opted for cubes instead: a room each with wooden walls that shook a little when you leaned on them. Peggy reckoned the weather would keep us at Byron Bay for tomorrow at least, though we would not be surfing. That was all right; we had a day's grace if we needed it and things might be brighter come Friday. I really wanted to be on that plane, though. I mean, a Spitfire is always iconic, even if it is a replica built in Brisbane.

But an hour or so later my hopes seemed to be dashed completely, when a slightly drunk-looking girl with wild hair told us the road to Brisbane was flooded.

The storm that night was as bad as any I've experienced. It poured with rain and the wind howled and in the morning we discovered that some of the backpackers had been flooded out completely. There didn't look to be any let-up in the rain either, but overnight I had decided I really wanted to try to make it to the Spitfire place. Sam phoned them early to see what the situation was and they told him the weather up there was getting better, though they had had to dig trenches around their hangar to stop it flooding. They could not afford to get any moisture into the alloy they used for the aircraft because it would corrode. If anything got even the slightest bit damp they had no choice but to dump it.

It was much better news than we'd hoped for and after all the stories of disaster we'd heard last night, I had a sneaking feeling this was going to come off. Down here the rain was still torrential, mind you, and although it was warm enough for shorts and flip flops, when we left the Arts Factory in Brendan's Mitsubishi we had the headlights on. The car was called the Millennium Pigeon. Brendan's mate Declan had driven up from Melbourne with a whole bunch of people, one of whom was a dead ringer for Han Solo apparently. According to Brendan, Declan had enough body hair to resemble Chewbacca, so you can see how the car got its name.

The weather was foul, every bit as bad as yesterday, and Brendan told us his tent had all but washed away. He was pretty relaxed about it though, just one of life's little hazards. He was that kind of guy, good company, and for a couple of hundred kilometres we chatted away like old friends. He told me he had been travelling for a year or so, making his way through South America before coming to Australia. He was a photographer and had left college about six years ago, and then worked as an art director for a firm that made wood-burning stoves. He loved the job but one day he just decided to quit. He left the house he was renting and bought an old caravan on a strip of land outside Exeter in Devon. Looking for a simpler existence, he worked at various jobs, saved his money, then bought a plane ticket and eventually ended up here. He was doing his thing and I admired him for it.

The closer we got to Brisbane, the better the weather became. When I finally spotted blue sky I was yelping with excitement. South of Brisbane we had to divert because the road disappeared into a flood plain that extended as far as the eye could see. The water level was gradually going down but it had been a metre deep at one point and the only vehicles getting through were big trucks and jacked-up utes. Brendan was great: he hadn't planned to go to Brisbane that day, but he took us all the way to the hangar. We had to detour a few times because of the flooding, before eventually turning into a country lane that led beyond some soggy-looking mobile homes to the Supermarine Aircraft Company at Moggill.

'Brendan,' I said. 'Thank you so much, you've been terrific.'

'No worries. If you see me by the side of the road with my thumb out you'll stop, right?'

'No,' I said, 'we'll drive right past you.'

The hangar was open and I could see a Spitfire with a kangaroo wearing a pair of boxing gloves painted on the fuselage. Oh my God, I was tingling. I know it sounds obvious, but it really did look like a *proper* Spitfire. The sun was out and there was no wind – with any luck tomorrow I would be flying up the coast to Maryborough.

A guy in his late twenties was sitting at a desk in the back office with some blueprints spread before him. This was Clint, the bloke we'd been speaking to on the phone. He worked for the owner of the company, Mike O'Sullivan, who had been making these planes for the last nine years now.

'Clint,' I said pointing to the plane and stating the obvious again, 'it looks like a Spitfire.'

'It does, doesn't it?' We shook hands. 'That's the Mark 26B, Charley, ninety per cent of the original.'

'You mean in size?'

'That's right, yeah, ninety per cent of the original size. We started with a Mark 25, which was only seventy per cent and a single-seater, but a lot of the customers wanted to take someone up with them, so we made it bigger to accommodate a passenger.'

I took a closer look at where I would be perched in the morning, a tiny little seat behind the pilot; barely enough room to squat. I could feel a rush of nervous excitement: a replica of a Second World War icon, the plane that stopped Hitler. I slid my hand across the surface of the wing, almost stroking it. 'How long did it take to build?' I asked him.

'This one, eight months from when Mike walked out of the office with the spec until it was in the air. When he came down from the maiden flight he reckoned it was as good as it got and we've not touched the design since.'

Clint explained that the company supplies these aircraft in kits; they include the complete fuselage, the wings, the undercarriage and everything bar the propeller, paint and instrumentation. They ship the kits to enthusiasts all over the world who assemble them like giant Meccano sets. Everything is prefabricated, right down to the rivet holes and the nuts and bolts. It's packed in a massive wooden crate then sent to the customer along with the engine. There are three engines you can choose from: a pair of Isuzu V6s, one normally aspirated and the other supercharged, or if you want a 450 bhp V8.

Clint showed me a second-generation Griffin engine that was used in the Spitfires in the latter part of the war. Built by Rolls Royce, it was an enormous 37-litre V12 with a supercharger that produced 2000 bhp. Of course, with all the armaments the original plane was much heavier than the one I would be in, and the Isuzu V8 produced the same amount of power. They had an engine ready for testing now and Clint told me I could start it up.

'The birth of an engine,' I said. 'I can't believe I'm here at the birth of a Spitfire engine.'

God knows what it weighed but it was sitting well off the ground on a special jig. The propeller was in place and the engine linked to a switchboard and laptop. Clint handed me a set of ear plugs. 'There you go, Charley,' he said, 'you'll need those.' I checked that the circuit breakers were in place, flicked four switches, gave it a little throttle and hit the starter. The engine grunted and groaned for a few moments, just about turning over.

'OK,' Clint said, 'at least we know the test battery is flat.'

With another battery fitted, I made sure the prop was clear and tried again. This time it fired, and as the engine coughed into life the gust of wind from the propeller was so fierce it tore at the roots of my hair.

'It will tick over around 800 rpm,' Clint yelled above the noise. 'Maximum revs about 5000; you need 4800 for take-off.'

The company checks everything on the engine before it goes out: the timing, oil pressure, water pressure, temperature, etc. Once they are satisfied, the ECU is locked in and that is it. According to Clint, you don't need to touch it again.

'Wow,' I said when I'd switched the motor off. 'And I thought I had a good job.'

It was late afternoon now and we had another hundred kilometres to go to get to Cressbrook, north of Brisbane, and Watts Bridge airfield. I was sleeping in the hangar tonight because, if all went to plan, we had a big day tomorrow and would be away early.

Jumping into Clint's ute we drove north. By the time we got to the airfield it was gloomy, the sun going down and a rainbow in the sky. We picked our way across the field to another hangar, where light spilled onto the grass and a second Spitfire was sitting grinning at anyone who walked by. And I mean literally: the paint job was a shark's mouth complete with lots of white teeth. Clint pointed out a guy in his forties sitting in the cockpit, checking the instruments. This was Bruce, another of Mike O'Sullivan's crew. He'd painted the shark's mouth. This plane took my breath away. The teeth around the fuselage were complemented by zebra stripes on the wings and it looked every bit the Second World War fighter.

'It's wonderful that you're still making them,' I told Bruce. 'It keeps the whole spirit of the Spitfire alive.'

Climbing into the cockpit was no mean feat. It was pretty cramped and all I could see from the pilot's seat were the tips of the prop at the end of the nose that lifted at quite an angle. I wondered how the hell the pilot saw to take off . . . but maybe it was best not to dwell on that too much.

The fuselage was what I would call up close and personal, barely any elbow room, and when the canopy was closed it really felt like I was in a fighter. The joystick was an original, complete with the central firing mechanism and its three-position trigger. The top part was for machine guns, the bottom for cannon, and if you wanted them both you pressed the middle. The recoil on that would stop the plane in the air.

'Jesus,' I muttered, 'that's incredible.'

'All they had was eight seconds of machine-gun time,' Bruce told me. 'Eight seconds and the ammo was out. What they'd do is get within three hundred yards of the German planes and zut-zut' – he made a firing sound – 'just a little burst. Hold it for the full eight seconds and you'd be out completely.'

I looked sideways at him. 'That's not how it is in the films, Bruce.'

'Right.'

We went into Cressbrook for some food and Claudio and I took a moment to get some air. It was calm now, almost balmy and a really nice temperature. The town was pretty old and I loved the layout of the streets. The pavements were made of wood with the balconies from the upper floors extending right across to the kerb: it created a wonderful ambience.

'How're you feeling?' Claudio asked me.

'I'm a bit nervous actually. I think we're going to do some barrel rolls and loop-the-loops, so I'd better take a plastic bag with me. I did this once before, Clouds, years ago in Africa when I was making a film. I went up in an American trainer plane and when I came down my face was just ashen.'

After dinner we went back to the airfield where Rick, the guy who would be piloting tomorrow, had arrived on his BMW.

'There are so many pilots who ride, Rick,' I said, shaking hands. 'But then I guess it's the same juice.'

'I want you to teach me to wheelie,' he laughed. 'That's why I rode down.'

He was maybe sixty-five (he told me that only that week he had received his senior citizen's card) and British, a gentle guy who immediately put me at ease and told me that tomorrow we wouldn't do anything that my body would not take. 'I'm afraid there's no stick in the back,' he said, 'so I'll have to do all the flying. Unless of course you want me to sit in the back.'

'Well, I have done eight hours . . .'

Rick tests the planes for Supermarine. He's flown these Spitfires in England and at shows in America, and he said that even the Americans acknowledge that the Supermarine kit is one of the best in the world.

'Sometimes the customers are a little nervous about flying for the first time,' he said, 'especially when they've put the kit together themselves. If they ask then I'll go over and sit in the back. They're easy enough to fly though, soft and gentle planes really. They can be a bit of a bugger to land, mind you, because of the length of the nose.'

'How long have you been flying them?' I asked, trying not to think of that last comment.

'Since Mike started building them. He asked me to test the original Mark 25 and I've been there for the Mark 26A and B. This one', he said, waving at old sharky, 'is superb. It's the biggest and fastest Mike has built. It climbs at 3500 feet a minute, and when you consider the weight difference, the 450 brake horse power is equivalent to the output they had from the old Griffins during the war. It's quick, Charley, a real hot one.'

Rick had joined the RAF when he was seventeen. He flew fighters until 1981, then left the RAF, moved out here and joined the Australian Air Force. He flew Mirages and when he retired he slowed down a little and became a balloon pilot. He lived locally and Mike O'Sullivan had heard about him, so he asked if he would test the Mark 25.

Rick is a grandfather and his son and three grandsons have their own manufacturing business that supplies over seventy different parts for the Spitfire. I liked him a lot: he had that pilot's confidence, the kind of ease I'd seen in Ewan's brother Colin, who flew Tornados in the Gulf.

Rick said he would happily fly me up the coast as far as Maryborough, where we could skim the beaches at five hundred feet, and he would put down at an airfield, from where we could be on our way. A little later I laid out my sleeping bag. As it was getting chilly now, I decided to sleep in my clothes. The others settled down and as the lights went out, I lay for a moment thinking about the next day. I couldn't quite believe I was lying in a moonlit hangar north of Brisbane, gazing at the silhouette of a Spitfire.

3
Lunch at Loco Lobo

Mossman

Cairns

G r e a t

B a r r i e r

R e e f

Pacific Ocean

Mackay

Rockhampton

Q u e e n s l a n d

Maryborough

Cressbrook

Brisbane

I THINK RICK WAS a little bit disappointed in me. I mean, there I was, a veteran of the Dakar and all those expeditions, and within twenty minutes of being in the air I was all but throwing up.

We woke to thick fog but he was confident it would clear, and so it did, although it took a little longer than he thought. Sam had gone ahead to Maryborough to make sure we had seats on the Tilt Train that ran from Brisbane to Cairns – the next leg of our journey. We were going as far as Rockhampton and, assuming we were on time for the train, we would cover some serious ground today.

We ate breakfast cooked on a barbecue in the hangar then pushed the Spitfire outside.

The fog hung around for another hour or so but finally it cleared and I was in the back of the plane, cramped and sweating, an old-style helmet on my head and the fuselage almost like a cage around me. I only realised just how small it was when Rick got in too, and I was hunched behind him with my elbows at my sides and my hands between my knees.

It was fantastic, though. This was a replica of the most historic fighter in British aviation history and I was about to fly up the coast. When my dad was making *Hope and Glory*, I remember reading about the Battle of Britain pilots, how they had been quite happy to get on with the job once they were in the planes; it was the waiting around for the call to scramble that set their nerves jangling.

Finally we were up and away, with Claudio filming from the open door of the chase plane. Rick was super-cool, so confident and very experienced. He told me that it was usually after about twenty minutes that people started to feel sick. He was not wrong. Even so, I don't think he expected me to fail quite so spectacularly. There was another forty minutes to go and there I was with a hand to my mouth and my face beginning to resemble the emerald forests below. I didn't actually puke, but cold sweat was dripping from the ends of my hair onto the nape of my clammy neck.

The chase plane flew in a straight line while we climbed and dived, with the odd barrel roll and one almighty loop-the-loop thrown in for good measure. We were flying over towns and farms, rivers and forests, and at one point we banked steeply across the side of a mountain before scything around it, like taking a corner on a motorbike with your knee down, only much, much faster.

I was feeling really crook now, and to be honest it was hard to appreciate just how lucky I was, and how fabulous the world looked from a fighter aircraft. I had to take my helmet off because it felt like it was pressing my skull into my brain. I realised that the last time I'd felt this ill was when I went to a funfair as a kid and ate mountains of candy floss before being whirled around on a waltzer. When the thing finally stopped, I stumbled off and threw up everywhere.

But that was a waltzer and this was a plane and I couldn't just get off. We flew over Rainbow Beach with the waves breaking in white rollers only five hundred feet below. An hour or so in the air and I have to admit that, much as I loved it, I was not sorry to see the airstrip at Maryborough.

The TV must have broadcast where we were because when we taxied to a halt and I climbed out, there was quite a crowd to meet us. I signed a few autographs, still feeling pretty green, and then thanked Rick before jumping into a replica of a 1952 MG-TD driven by a wonderful old guy called Ron Stephenson. He was wearing a straw cowboy hat and handed me a black one, and like a couple of old desperadoes we drove four or five kilometres to the Maryborough Museum where John Meyers had an armoured car waiting.

Yep, an armoured car. It was a Ferret Scout and the steering was sort of up and under with the wheel horizontal to your knees rather than perpendicular. It came complete with machine guns and what they called a pre-select gearbox where you chose the gear you wanted then stamped on the clutch and it clicked in. The car was fifty years old, green and camouflaged, and was driven by a guy called Graeme Knoll. He actually had to drive it out of the museum and from there it was fifteen minutes to the station and the Tilt Train. I have to say I was looking forward to a bit of trainage. After being up in the plane for five hundred kilometres with my stomach in my mouth, I would be more than happy to sit for a few hours and let it settle.

I played machine-gunner as we drove up Maryborough High Street, then Graeme let me drive for part of the way. Of course I stalled the thing before we got going, but then it's not every day you drive an armoured car. Anyway, I eventually got the hang of it and we made it to the railway station with six minutes to spare.

The people operating the train (which is the fastest in Australia) were really accommodating. As soon as we got on board they told us they had arranged for me to be up at the front with the driver. The train is powered by electricity and very quiet; so quiet, in fact, that the driver told me it sneaks up on you before you know it and people at level crossings have to be careful. It can clock 160 kmph and sucks the juice from the tracks as it accelerates, then puts some of it back again when it slows down. I could just about take it all in, but I was still feeling pretty queasy, and after half an hour or so I went back to our compartment and, closing my eyes, dozed for half an hour. By the time we made Rockhampton I was feeling much better, and with almost a thousand kilometres covered since we left Watts Bridge airfield, we'd made quite a leap up the Australian coastline.

We were heading for Cairns to hook up with the flying doctors, which I was really excited about. Our plans beyond that had changed a tad, though. Apparently there was a big festival taking place in Papua New Guinea and we wanted to try to make it across to Port Moresby a day earlier. But first we had to get to Cairns.

Some time ago I'd heard about the ute culture that is so popular in Australia. Utes are pick-up trucks, many of them styled like cars only with truck beds, tailgates and fibreglass covers. Their owners like to customise them by lowering the suspension, changing the wheels and supercharging the engines. We thought it might be fun to travel some of the way in a customised ute, so we had been in touch with the website Utez.com before we left London. Three guys had agreed to meet us at the Old Station, a cattle ranch which was fifteen minutes by plane from Rockhampton.

The Old Station is exactly what it sounds like, one of the oldest cattle ranches in this part of Australia. It was first established 140 years ago and is home to a nice guy called Rob, who runs it with his wife Helen and their two kids Samantha and Matthew. We'd been invited to breakfast with them, having spent the night in Rockhampton, and drove up to the Aero Club to meet Rob and his Cessna 185.

'G'day, Charley,' he said as he came round from the pilot's door. 'How you going?'

He was in his thirties, lean and sinewy, wearing a baseball cap and jeans. I'd flown in a few planes that were not dissimilar to this and I have to say it was much more my kind of flying: six-seater, with me alongside the pilot instead of being crammed in the back like I had been in the fighter.

Rob loved to fly, but this wasn't just a hobby. His plane was a working vehicle on the cattle station – he said the place was so vast there was no more efficient way to cover the distances.

'How big is it then exactly?' I asked him when we were up in the air.

'We own twenty-six thousand acres and run about three thousand head of cattle.'

'Wow, that's enormous.'

'Yeah,' he said. 'You can see why we need the plane.'

The property was gorgeous, surrounded by scrub hills and situated in the middle of a stunning basin, fed by a creek that flowed even during the summer. The station had five separate irrigation licences which meant its pastures had water all year round, which was vital. Australia is the driest continent in the world, and when we were here the last time, we had seen what happens to a cattle station when there is no water.

Interestingly, from above the land looked quite wet: great swampy areas and tributaries seemed to drift out from the river. Crossing a line of hills, Rob told me that the Old Station covered the entire valley below; it was lovely country with good grazing and ragged hills covered with spindly trees.

'This Cessna's a tail-dragger,' he told me. 'You saw that just now, right? You want the two-wheels configuration at the front because it makes it easier to land in the bush.'

We put down on a rough strip close to a clutch of single-storey houses; Rob and his family lived in one and there was another for his parents and brother and a third for Rob's best mate, Kiwi, and his wife Lee. Kiwi had come to Australia from New Zealand when he was nineteen, and had been on the station for seven years. Apart from him and Lee it was pretty much just family. I couldn't believe that that was enough people for three thousand head of cattle.

The cows looked similar to the kind Ewan and I had seen in Africa: russet-coloured with smallish heads and long drooping ears. We got acquainted with one in particular, an orphan Helen had reared by hand and called Sausage – because that was almost certainly how part of him would end up.

Kiwi cooked the breakfast in a massive outbuilding; it was a bit like the barbecue we'd had in the Spitfire hangar. We ate on the veranda with the sun beating down. It was so warm, even though it was still winter – I shuddered to think what the heat would be like in the dry season.

After breakfast Helen asked me to help her muster a couple of hundred 'weaners' – young cattle that had been away from their mothers for a few weeks and were in the process of being 'educated' before they were shipped out to various paddocks across the station.

'We teach them how to muster,' Helen told me. 'We put them into corrals then use the dogs to get them to move from one side to the other. Cows are quick learners and they like routine. Once they know what the dogs want them to do, it's quite easy. After a week or so moving them from paddock to paddock they understand, and one person on a horse can easily lead two hundred.'

This was ranching Australian-style, and it was amazingly efficient. Helen and Rob had a big place but like most ranchers they were hardly cash rich and could not afford to employ lots of stockmen. Sometimes when I'm travelling I come across people living a way of life that, when I catch a glimpse of it, is so appealing I can see myself doing it. It's happened a few times, and it's the tranquillity, maybe, the security of knowing what you're going to be doing tomorrow. Perhaps that's particularly appealing when I'm on the road, rarely staying in a place for more than one night at a time.

Anyway, I climbed onto the back of a beautiful chestnut horse to help Helen muster the weaners. 'OK,' I said to my mount. 'Here we go. I haven't done this for ages, my love, so look after me.'

'It's a boy, Charley,' Helen called out, 'a gelding.'

'Boy,' I said, 'right.' I patted the horse's neck. 'OK, we'll have a few beers together or something, buddy, shall we?'

We rode through long grass with hills bordering the paddocks and the clear waters of the creek running by. It was a beautiful morning. Helen led the cattle with me trailing behind them and three dogs keeping the little herd together. It *was* easy; once the cows saw the dogs they knew what was expected and we moved them from one paddock to another. The only bit of hassle was when they were spooked by Claudio's camera.

After lunch the boys showed up in their utes. They came trailing up the dirt road, three shining examples of the kind of custom-car culture I'd heard about. We're talking chrome and alloy, metallic paint and the rumble of V8s. Utez.com has something like two thousand active members, people who buy a Holden or a Ford maybe, and do it up. I suppose it's a bit like Harley culture or sports-bike culture in the UK.

They had come to drive us up to Cairns, these three young guys in T-shirts and dark shades: Cameron, Ronnie and Ben, or Camshaft, Rocket and Big Ben, as I decided to dub them. Cameron was driving a Ford BF XLS, Ronnie an HSV Maloo and Ben a VZ 55 Holden.

We showed them where we wanted to get to on the map, and Ben reckoned we ought to be able to make Mackay that night, while another eight hours tomorrow should see us in Cairns. Saying our goodbyes to the Old Station, we took off along a dirt road heading for the main A1. We were planning to camp that night, so we stopped at a supermarket to buy ice boxes and food. It was after three o'clock now and we still had three hundred kilometres to go before we got to Mackay, and over a thousand to Cairns. We didn't make it to Mackay; in fact, as it began to get dark we were only half way there, so we pulled off into a rest area close to the Waverly Creek Reserve. We had no stove and no barbecue and I'd been hoping there would be fixed gas barbecues so we could cook the steaks and ribs Claudio and I had picked up. But no such luck.

There was lots of dust, a couple of camper vans and the sound of road trains thundering up and down the coast. Sam was moaning – he claimed that I'd forgotten to pack his sleeping bag and although he had an Aussie swag (a bedroll with built-in mattress and waterproof base), he had nothing more than a child's blanket to go on it.

'The stuff was all there,' he told me. He was talking about the last day in London when the kit was laid out with each pack.

'I asked you if it was yours, Sam,' I said.

'Yes, but you didn't check what it was. What you thought was a sleeping bag was only a pillow.' He held up the blanket – pink and blue with those little woolly holes in it, you know the kind of thing. 'This is all I've got, Charley. You've got your sleeping bag, Robin's got his and Claudio's got that really warm one filled with goose down.'

'I used it in Africa,' Claudio said matter-of-factly. 'It was very good in the cold.'

'Terrific.' Again Sam held up the blanket.

'You'll be fine,' I assured him. 'Some hot food and a couple of beers, you'll sleep like a baby.'

Hot food? Right. We still had nothing to cook on. It was dark now and with my head torch in place I wandered over to the camper vans where two elderly couples were sitting at a table laid with a chequered cloth, eating the dinner they had cooked on an open fire. It was burning brightly a few yards from the table.

'Sorry to interrupt your dinner,' I said, 'but you wouldn't have any spare wood we could use by any chance?'

'No, sorry,' the man sitting closest to me answered as he shovelled steak and potatoes into his mouth.

'Did you find the wood here?' I asked.

'No,' his wife said. 'We brought our own.'

Oh dear. They introduced themselves as Keith and Joy Bailey and together with their friends Trevor and Sorrell they were on a road trip, and unlike us they were fully prepared with wood and a fire complete with hot plate for cooking.

'I tell you what,' Keith said. 'Why don't you cook your food on our fire?'

'Can we?'

'Sure, why not?'

It was typical Australian hospitality. I remember when we ran out of diesel the last time I was here, we found a lovely couple in another camper who gave us their spare can. Grabbing the food, I set about preparing the meal while the others gathered round the fire and opened a few tinnies.

'Hey, Charley,' Keith called from the table. 'I've got something for those steaks.' He produced a bottle of his own recipe Worcestershire sauce. 'There you go,' he said. 'The main ingredient is treacle, and there's a little vinegar and herbs. You're supposed to put peppers in it too, but it makes it too hot. Slather it on the meat, it tastes great.'

'Thanks very much,' I said, taking the bottle.

'The only thing is what it does to your stomach.'

'Oh I see. So if we spend all night running to the toilet we'll know why, eh?'

He laughed. 'No, mate. That sauce will *stop* you running to the toilet. That's the point. It's that effective, if you poured it over Niagara Falls the water would stop flowing.'

The next day, the ute boys got us to Cairns and we took a day off from the travelling to do some essential housekeeping. I was running very short of underpants (though the least said about that the better) so we found a much-needed launderette. The following morning, the ninth day out since we left Sydney, we hitched a ride with the flying doctors.

I was up just after six and it was dark and wet. I sometimes forget that it's winter here, so it's darker in the mornings of course, but I hadn't thought we would see so much rain. The bad weather seemed to be following us up the coast and I have to admit it was beginning to affect my mood. It was at times like this when the responsibility started to weigh heavily on me, and I began to worry about the trip and all the logistical problems surrounding it.

But nothing matters when I'm on a motorbike and hopefully tomorrow, once we'd hooked up with David Williams, everything would be fine. David runs a company called Fair Dinkum Tours and we were planning to ride the forest roads to a place called Cooktown, a few hundred miles up the coast.

Today, however, I would be on another plane, only this time in the company of the flying doctors as they made a primary-healthcare visit to an Aboriginal community at a place called Pormpuraaw.

The Royal Flying Doctor Service was started back in 1928 by a guy named John Flynn, a Presbyterian minister who wanted to bring healthcare to people in remote areas of the country. It was no more than an experiment to begin with; in fact, it was only supposed to be in operation for a year. Eighty-one years later the service has grown to a point where there is coverage for the entire outback, and the Cairns operation looks after not just the Cape area, but the whole of Queensland, which is just a little bit larger than Western Europe.

At the airfield we met a girl called Gil who explained that although most people think of the flying doctors as landing in the bush in the middle of the night, their main function is to provide primary healthcare. There were three planes in the hangar; one was always on standby and the others were rotated between primary healthcare and what Gil called 'aero medical retrieval' – heart attacks, accidents and other incidents that required a swift response. In other words, the rescue missions.

It was hosing down again and I was getting sick of it, but the pilot, Emma, was going to fly us up to Pormpuraaw in the rain. As we settled in the back, the wipers were working nineteen to the dozen and I was thinking of tomorrow and what the dirt roads in the bush were going to be like.

Fortunately, as we left Cairns the weather began to improve, and by the time we landed at Pormpuraaw the sky was clear and the sun shining. We'd flown some four hundred nautical miles and were deep into the bush, a beautiful but wild part of the country. The airstrip was close to a stretch of fresh water where all kinds of birds were nesting. Pormpuraaw is an autonomous Aboriginal community that has proven to be one of the most successful in the country. Alcohol abuse, and the kind of domestic violence that can be a by-product of it, has been an issue among the Aboriginal population for some time. This was a self-managed town where the strict drinking rules had a beneficial impact. Some of these towns in the Cape are completely dry, but this one still had a bar. Only low- to medium-strength beers are sold, however, and the bar only opens between 5.30 p.m. and 8 p.m., five days a week.

I spoke to a guy called Kurt who was the director of the corporation that oversaw the Women's Resource Centre, a broad social programme that began life as a shelter for the victims of domestic violence. The town had a population of 720, and Kurt explained that since they introduced the drinking legislation, the attacks on women had been reduced significantly, in both frequency and intensity.

Kurt was a cool guy, very knowledgeable about his people. He told me about the stolen generation, when the Australian authorities (partially guided by the church) believed that the quickest way to assimilate the indigenous people into Australian society was to remove their children and place them in dormitories in different parts of the country. Often the children never saw their families again.

The practice started in 1869 and Kurt told me it was still going on as late as 1970. It is similar to what was done to Native Americans, and it caused untold problems and suffering. Generations were lost, children grew up with no link to family or their past and the repercussions went on for years and years. Even today you get the feeling that there is still a huge divide between the whites and the Aborigines in Australia.

Standing there in a remote little town, watching pelicans on the lake and listening to Kurt speak about a culture that is fifty thousand years old, was extremely moving. Around us the bush all but swallowed up the tin-roofed buildings, and beyond them mountains dominated in a dusty kind of grey.

The town has its own council, hospital and police force – two Queensland cops who are based there permanently. We were given a lift to the council buildings in a police car. Sliding into the passenger seat alongside a guy called Tim White, I glanced back at Claudio. 'This is the first time I've been in a police car voluntarily,' I whispered.

'Why am I not surprised?' he replied.

Tim turned out to be the Queensland police psychologist. I had no idea such jobs existed, but as we drove he told me it was vital that the police officers who worked in these kinds of areas were of sound enough mind to do so.

'Think about it, Charley,' he said. 'You take a twenty-two-year-old police officer from Brisbane who has lived in the city all his life and bring him up here. There are no creature comforts, no McDonald's or anything like that. Eighty per cent of the Australian population knows nothing about the indigenous culture, so the parallel to that is eighty per cent of the police officers don't either. There are only two of you up here and you're rotating shifts all the time. You're permanently the potential target of an assault and you're permanently armed. When you're not working there is nothing to do except fish and hunt. You need to be able to cope with those kinds of pressures emotionally.'

He was right of course and I tried to imagine being a copper in a place like this – beautiful but remote and both small enough and yet big enough to cause you all sorts of problems. At the council buildings we met Edward, the Deputy Mayor. He was a thoughtful-looking man, softly spoken, and when he heard where we were heading next, he gave me a card with his sister's phone number in Papua New Guinea. 'She'll put you up if you need a place to stay,' he told me.

Gil was keen to show us the Primary Healthcare Centre, a grey building half hidden among the trees. Inside she introduced us to Natalie, who basically runs the place. She loves her job; I mean really loves it. Every new day brings a different challenge. With no doctor permanently assigned, she has to think on her feet, not just in terms of patients' needs but also the logistics. The hospital was state-of-the-art – they had a crash unit, digital x-ray, a visiting dentist and enough drugs and dressings to last six months. They had to cater for the rainy season when the planes could still get in but could not carry heavy cargoes, so everything the hospital needed had to be in stock before the weather turned.

It was a humbling place to visit, reminiscent of the sort of facilities I've been to with UNICEF, and the people have the same dedication. Natalie had been there seven years and was not planning to leave. In fact, everyone we spoke to, including the police officers, loved Pormpuraaw. Some said that when they first arrived it had been a bit of a culture shock, but after a couple of months they were settled in and nobody wanted to leave.

I was feeling much better. There's nothing like a place like Pormpuraaw to make you realise that sometimes the things you stress about don't really matter at all. All the stuff I'd been fretting over was back in its proper perspective, and even more so as we landed back in Cairns. Another of the RFDS planes had just flown in with a man who'd had a heart attack. The aero retrieval plane is basically a flying intensive care unit. There was a doctor on board and the chap they wheeled to the ambulance had been in expert care ever since the pilot landed.

The following morning, 27 May, I woke up early. It was raining. Again. We had had a little respite up in the bush yesterday but this morning it was dark and overcast, and the clouds just seemed to dribble over the city. After a short drive north I was feeling much more positive. First there was David Williams, a cheerful soul with cropped hair and the kind of granite-like features I'd seen in Mark, the Diamond T driver. David was younger, though – in his thirties. He'd ridden with some serious dirt-bike riders and one wall of his house was devoted to newspaper cuttings of their exploits. He greeted us warmly and, better still, he had three motorbikes all ready and waiting – a pair of Suzuki DR Z400Es and a KTM 640 that he had borrowed from a mate of his. I'll come to the KTM later but suffice to say I think I put the hex on it.

Originally the plan had been for Claudio to ride on the back of David's bike, but with all this rain the dirt roads would be like an oil slick and with two up it would be very awkward. We decided the best thing to do was rig up a helmet camera for Claudio to use on his own bike.

'So when was the last time you rode on the dirt, Clouds?' I asked him.

'*Long Way Down*,' he said. 'Two years ago.'

'And how were you on the mud? I can't remember.'

'I was shit, Charley. I kept falling off.' He peered at me over the top of the camera. 'Have you got any tips for me?'

'Yes,' I said. 'Hold on tight.'

We were planning to get as far north as Mossman by nightfall, where we would sleep over at my great friend Diane's house. Diane is the mother of one of my oldest friends, Jason, who is godfather to my daughter Doone. I'd spoken to Diane on the phone and she had told me we were all welcome at the 'Playhouse', as she calls Karnak Farm. The Playhouse is a little home away from home – I'd been there many times before, the first time some twenty-four years previously. We had to make sure we made it for dinner – Diane was putting on a spread involving roast lamb and champagne. I assured her we would. Then, kitted up, at last I was on a motorbike.

'We're riding about twenty Ks on the coast road,' David explained as we got the cameras sorted out and the bikes going. 'After that we'll cut inland and take the Black Mountain Road as far as Mount Molloy. It's a forest road but it is public and people live up there, so make sure you stay on the left.' He looked at his watch. 'We ought to be in Molloy around twelve-thirty, maybe one o'clock, and there's a neat little café called the Loco Lobo where they serve the biggest hamburgers I reckon you'll have ever seen.' He nodded to the two yellow Suzukis. 'You've got brand-new rubber on those and with this rain the tarmac will be greasy. Watch the roundabouts, they can be treacherous.'

We headed up the coast to a sign for the Black Mountain Road. Then after crossing a soaking bridge at Duggan's Creek we were on the dirt and I was up on the foot pegs. At last, some off-road riding. Don't get me wrong, I love the tarmac and I love sports bikes, but the dirt . . . the dirt is fun, fun, fun.

Within minutes we were deep into the rainforest and the surface was alternating between mushy stuff, a little cindery clay and patches of hard baked dirt where the falling water had created just a few millimetres of mud. Those few millimetres were like sheet ice, and ahead of me on the orange KTM, David lost the back and was down.

'Are you all right?' I asked as Claudio and I pulled up.

'No worries. I'm all good,' he said, dusting himself down. He squinted at the bike. 'First time I've done that in . . . must be two years.'

We crossed bridges, we rode through great forests of soaking trees and across the slippery clay. We rode high into the mountains where the views of the valleys were breathtaking. In the dips the road was flooded and in one spot we passed a ruined Mitsubishi van that someone had long since abandoned. It was way down deep in a forested gulch, and the water was so high that if I'd not been up on the foot pegs, it would've been over my knees. I loved it. I was relaxed again and excited. Maybe I'd finally woken up and taken a sniff of the coffee. I'm in my element on a bike, and with the bush so close to the road we really were in the middle of nowhere. This was croc country – swamp land and swollen creeks where trees were down and pockets of floating islands massed under fallen leaves.

Claudio and David decided to swap bikes. Maybe that was just a silly mistake, but I reckon it's where I put the hex on. The KTM had already been down once and now Clouds was riding it – it was a recipe for disaster.

We were blatting along quite happily when the KTM started to cough and splutter as if it was running out of petrol. Then the thing just packed up completely. No matter what we tried we could not get it to go, and in the end David decided there was a problem with the vacuum pump that feeds the fuel to the carburettor.

'It's buggered,' he said. 'We can't fix it here. You'd better give me a tow.'

I'd never towed a bike before and it was some forty kilometres back to the tarmac and on to Mount Molloy.

'It's easy,' he told me. 'You tie this end of the rope to the back of your bike and I pass the other end under the steering head.' Sitting astride the KTM, he then wound the rope around the handlebars and held on to the loose end. 'That way I can just let go,' he said, 'so if there's any drama you don't drag me and the bike down the road.'

It made sense and I suppose I should've known that. When we went downhill I didn't use the brakes but behind me David did; that way the rope stayed taut, and with no further incident we made it for lunch at the Loco Lobo in Mount Molloy. David was right, the Mexican burgers were about two storeys high. Now we needed to figure out how to complete the last stage of today's journey, with one bike down. Thankfully David's brother-in-law was able to bring a spare bike. When we had finished eating, we left the KTM and Claudio rode with me while David flagged down the support truck and picked up his brother-in-law's Suzuki once we reached Mossman. I'd already phoned Diane and explained we'd be a little late.

It had been a long and tiring day but a bloody good one and we had covered some miles in the best way possible. Now I was itching to see Diane, sip a little champagne and, as David said later, eat a meal fit for a king.

4
No Fear (or Not Much, Anyway)

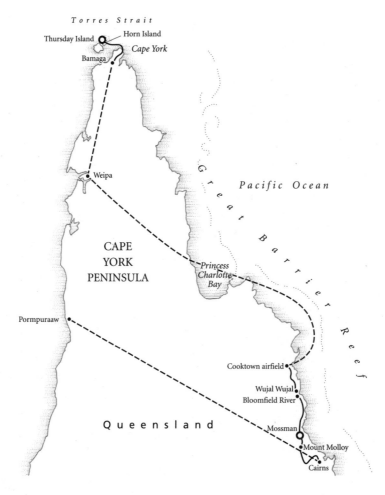

KARNAK FARM IS KNOWN as the Playhouse because Diane has a five-hundred-seat theatre in the grounds. It really is something, accessed by a beautiful wooden staircase – the stage is part of her garden and the backdrop is a lake. I remember years ago taking a strimmer to the weeds before the lake was sunk. Diane Cilento is semi-retired now, but in her day she was a very successful actress and back in 1963 she was nominated for an Oscar. She has never lost her love of the business, and she has all sorts of theatre groups performing at Karnak.

It's a gorgeous property. The main house is built among palm trees with sculpted lawns that fall away in terraces. It's a shame we could only stay for one night, but now we were heading for Cooktown where Claudio and I were hitching a lift with a boat surveyor in a light aircraft. Tonight we'd be staying at a famous old pub called the Lions Den, near the Aboriginal community of Wujal Wujal. We'd be riding all day, though not just on the dirt bikes David had provided. This afternoon I'd been asked to cast my eye over a battery-powered motorbike built by a company called Zero.

The Australian arm of Zero is based in Melbourne, but the bikes themselves come from the factory in Santa Cruz in California. Having already driven and been impressed by an electric car, I couldn't wait to see what someone had done with an off-road motorbike.

This morning we had David's mate Max with us. He'd recently taken over the Lions Den, and drove down to meet us in a ute with a KTM strapped in the back – his plan was to ride with us back up to his pub. It's an icon of the Cape York Peninsula, having been established back in 1875 when tin was discovered and miners flocked from all over.

Max was a good rider, and as we left Karnak we both pulled a pair of pretty decent wheelies, then proceeded to spend much of the morning messing about. It was a brilliant ride; we were in the middle of the rainforest and yet at the same time we were right on the coast. We pulled over at a spot called Rocky Point. 'It really is tropical,' I said to David as I gazed beyond the palm trees to the beach.

'Here it is, yeah,' he agreed, 'but not too far north it begins to dry out.'

It was wonderful country and they were wonderful roads too. We had a mix of narrow tarmac, good dirt and plenty of flooded creeks. The vegetation was soaking and there was a mist over the mountains, almost like steam, when the sun came out.

Australians are, by and large, a laid-back bunch. But as we'd found out with the overbearing police at our convoy in Sydney, Aussie officials can be really in your face – it is incongruous and doesn't seem in keeping with the rest of the country. They are so hung up on health and safety. We'd experienced some of this on the last trip, when Russ was pulled over when we were hauling the motorbike sculpture in the back of a ute. They were pretty aggressive, but I tell you, they had nothing on the Bloomfield River ferrymen.

We rode hard and fast along a narrow track between fields of sugar cane. Max was still popping wheelies and sliding his bike here, there and everywhere, and I was showing off a little bit myself. I noticed a set of train tracks that the cane farmers used to load cut cane for the factory, and me being me, I thought it would be great fun to race my bike between them. So leaving the others on the tarmac, I rode down the grass berm and hopped my bike between the rails. I really went for it, standing on the pegs and winding on the power, and raced between the fields of sugar cane. After a few hundred yards, I decided to rejoin the others. I got the front wheel clear again, but the back wheel caught in the rails. The bike snapped sideways and my stomach caught on the handlebars before I was sent flying over the high side. I landed on my left shoulder and, Jesus, I had a vision of popping a collar bone just as I'd done before the Dakar. Tumbling over and over I came to a stop in the rows of sugar cane.

Thankfully it wasn't my collar bone that was broken, but the Suzuki's throttle return cable. Still pretty bad news though. On top of that I'd bent the bars and mashed up the back brake pedal. My shoulder was throbbing and I could already feel stiffness gathering down my left side. Inspecting my stomach, I discovered a serious graze, the skin around it beginning to yellow with bruising.

Max was watching me, Claudio had the camera and David surveyed the damage to the bike.

'Are you OK?' Clouds asked me.

'Yes, it's just a graze.'

'You're sure it's nothing internal, Charley?'

'No, I don't think so.' I was holding my stomach, trying to see how badly I'd carved it up. 'That's not fat by the way,' I said, quickly. 'It's just swollen.'

I felt a right idiot. If you ride a dirt bike you're going to fall off, that's a given. But I had been messing about and showing off, and with the trip barely a week old, it was a dumb thing to do. On top of that I had damaged David's bike for no good reason.

We patched up the bike and I rode on with my confidence a little rocked and feeling annoyed with myself for being so foolish. It didn't get any better when a couple of hours later we arrived at the Bloomfield River car ferry. We wanted the truck to drive on first so we could film the bikes as we rode on. It wasn't an outrageous request, but the crew were having none of it. They told us we couldn't do that – the bikes had to go first, because those were the rules and rules were not to be broken. Up in his wheelhouse the driver had a loudspeaker and all the way over he kept chirping away at everyone.

'Stay with your vehicle. Do not get out of your vehicle. Stay with your vehicle.'

Claudio walked a few yards from his bike to get a shot of the river and all I could hear was the whine of the fucking Tannoy. 'Stay with your vehicle. You there: stay with your vehicle.'

I thought the whole thing was ridiculous. I mean, this wasn't the *Titanic*, it was a tiny little car ferry and all we were doing was crossing a bloody river.

Then I crashed again. I couldn't believe it – it's years since I came off twice in the same day. I don't know what happened really. I took a tight bend on some pretty glassy mud and the next thing I know I'm picking myself up, having lost the front this time. Of course the others got to me before I'd got the bike fully upright, so I couldn't even get away with pretending it hadn't happened. David slithered to a halt and cast an anxious glance across his machinery. 'Charley,' he said, 'you keep on like this, mate, and you'll own that bike before the day's out.'

Eventually we made it to Wujal Wujal without any further incident and parked the bikes at the Lion's Den. Max had bought the place just a few months previously and, together with his wife and two children, he was determined to make a success of it. It was a beautiful spot, close to Black Mountain, very tropical and very green. The pub itself backed on to farm land owned by an Aussie snake charmer called Jim. OK, not a charmer as such, but a guy with some land who liked snakes. The pub itself reminded me of the one in Daly Waters: inside it was covered in memorabilia, T-shirts, newspaper cuttings, bras and panties . . . Apparently it was a regular haunt for the 4×4 enthusiasts who took on the kinds of Cape York roads we'd just been riding.

The guys from Zero had got there ahead of us. They had two bikes which Phil (who ran the Melbourne-based operation) told me had come all the way from California.

'Yeah,' he said, 'all for you, mate. Seeing as how you're the icon of world motorcycling right now, we wanted your opinion.'

Me, an icon. Hmm . . . He'd got the wrong guy, hadn't he? But then again . . . Puffing out my chest I shot Claudio a glance that said: keep your mouth shut about the two spills I had on the way up here, while I impress this gentleman, OK? God bless him, Claudio said nothing.

The bike was brilliant. It looked like a mountain bike, only bigger . . . which I suppose is pretty much what it was. On the dirt track in the snake charmer's field, it performed every bit as well as the bikes we'd been riding all day. You could limit the speed to 30 mph if you wanted but it would hit 60. Phil explained that it ran on a lithium-ion battery and each charge lasted around two hours. It gave out zero emissions and was easy on the eye. As with the car I'd driven, I am sure that if

In Manly, Australia, at the start of my trip. As ever I was thrilled and relieved so many had turned up to ride convoy with me for the first leg.

Riding to Fraser Beach with Dare Jennings beside me.

Stan's handsome Oshkosh
in Macksville.

Left to right: Robin, me, Sam in his Deus Ex Machina top, and the legendary Claudio far right.
Dare Jennings and Dare's colleague Ben behind.

Caught in floods near Brisbane.

Posing for Britain! (In Australia.) Perched
on a Ferret Scout in Maryborough.

A Brisbane Spitfire . . . Just about to take off, with pilot Rick.

In the cockpit – equally excited and bricking it, as you can see!

At the Women's Resource Centre in Pormpuraaw. And yes, the beards give away the fact that a couple of us aren't women!

With Helen, the owner of the Old Station cattle ranch, on our way to muster some cattle.

'Just a graze . . .' About to ride the ZERO bike, powered by electricity.

Throw another shrimp on the barbie! With John Hone from Pearl Island Seafood.

Off-roading in Queensland.

Sailing a tinny boat to Thursday Island.

No Worries! A happy team on Thursday Island – Robin, Sam, me and Claudio.

you're going to put forward an alternative to conventional vehicles, it has to look like something a customer is familiar with. And this one did.

We took them for a spin, Phil tearing ahead of me, sliding the thing across the dirt like a supermotard. He caught some air at the top of the rise while in the fields next door the horses went on eating. The bike wasn't silent, it gave out a slight clattering sound, but that was it. On normal dirt bikes those horses would have been at the other end of the field by now, frightened away by the noise. The Zero was nimble and quick, and it felt like a 125 or a 250 maybe. It offered 100 per cent torque, had no gears, no clutch and no foot controls. There was a back and front brake on the handlebars, just like on a mountain bike.

I was seriously impressed. Phil told me they made a street version, and I would happily use one of those at home in London. We made a point of sharing the dirt track with Max and David on the regular bikes and, I have to say, there was very little to choose between the levels of performance.

Jim the snake charmer came out to watch. He looked like some old drover in a beat-up cowboy hat with a sweat-stained rim.

'G'day, Charley,' he said when we pulled up. 'Your mate Claudio here tells me you'd like to see some snakes.'

'Snakes?!' I squawked. What was he talking about? I hate snakes. Claudio knows that.

'For the programme, Charley, for the BBC,' said Claudio. 'Jim told me he keeps more than thirty.'

'Does he?' I said. 'Just as long as he doesn't release them all at the same time then.' Reluctantly I followed the farmer into a large shed where he had various glass cages, one of which was secured by a chipboard lid. It was screwed down and Jim had to undo it with his drill and screwdriver bit.

'The fellow in this one is pretty venomous,' he explained. 'People get drunk in the pub next door and sometimes they wander in here. Wouldn't want them putting their hand into the cage now, would I?' He made a face. 'I suppose I could put a lock on the bloody thing, but I'd only lose the key.'

In the bottom of the cage was a particularly vicious-looking snake that Jim called a speckled brown. 'He can be pretty nasty,' he said, giving the snake a prod. 'When he gets pissed off he'll flatten out . . . see there he goes now.'

The snake had lowered his head as if to strike and I was less than impressed. I really do not like snakes.

'Yeah, you want to commit suicide? Just put your hand in there,' Jim went on. 'Won't cost you nothing, he'll do it for free.'

He also had a coastal taipan, the third most venomous snake in the world. It was a pale brown colour and could grow up to twelve feet long.

'I've got a new one,' he told Max, 'a fear snake, caught her just the other day.' He showed us another cabinet where a thin, black snake was lying on a patch of shingle. Opening the lid, Jim took his long-stemmed snake-catching device and went to move it. 'Very fast striking,' he said. 'I'll give her a prod, Charley, and you can touch the scales.'

I looked at him as if he was mad. 'Absolutely not,' I said.

'You'll be all right. I'll catch her behind the head and you can see what she feels like.'

'All right, go on then.' It was for the show, I was telling myself. It was for the TV show.

'There you go.' Jerking the stick, he hoiked the snake from the glass case and tossed it right at me.

I nearly died of fright. A venomous snake hurled by a grizzled old Cape farmer, who clearly thought it was hilarious. It hit me in the chest and I leapt back, yelling out and expecting to be bitten any minute. But I wasn't . . . the snake lay in the dirt where it had fallen, and the others were doubled up with laughter. It wasn't real. It was rubber! They had set me up, the bastards.

The following morning, Max drove me and Claudio to a little airfield at Cooktown, where we were due to meet Graeme Normington, the guy from the Queensland Ship Surveyors. He landed at eight-thirty in a twin-engine Beechcraft Duchess.

'There's something about two engines,' I said to Claudio as Graeme taxied along the runway. 'I'm happier knowing there are two engines when you're flying over the middle of nowhere. Do you know what I mean?'

'I know *exactly* what you mean.'

It was a great little plane, each engine producing 180 bhp; the tail was set quite high, which made it stable and fast, and the undercarriage was retractable.

And talking of retractable undercarriages, mine had retracted pretty sharply on those cane tracks yesterday. The bruise on my stomach was almost black now and it had spread right across my middle. There was bruising on my shoulder too and I couldn't move my left arm properly. My own stupid fault, but I was suffering, I can tell you.

Graeme flew us from Cooktown out over the Great Barrier Reef. We were on the eastern side of the Cape York Peninsula and he said we couldn't be in the air without seeing the reef. After that we would cut across Princess Charlotte Bay and the mountains, then fly the width of the Cape to a place called Weipa on the west coast.

The land in this area is traditionally owned, by which I mean Aboriginal. Weipa is a town built around an open-cast aluminium mine – they call it the Oasis in the Wilderness, and the Barramundi Capital of Queensland. The barramundi is a sport fish that can live in both salt- and freshwater, and one of the great delights of the Weipa community is catching it.

Graeme was going to inspect three boats in the area and would be back in the morning to fly us up to the northern tip at Bamaga. His remit covers any kind of marine situation, from assessing the amount of fuel on a massive cargo ship, to litigation, insurance claims, hull inspection, you name it.

He dropped us at the airfield in Weipa, where a lady called Bianca Graham was waiting to meet us. She had organised a trip to the mine and her parents, John and Chana, had very kindly offered to put us up for the night.

Both John and Bianca worked for Rio Tinto, the aluminium mining company that for the past forty years has been skimming ore from the red dust in this part of Queensland. They mine a total area of four thousand square kilometres on two separate leases, which were negotiated with the traditional owners when the aluminium ore was discovered. They pay for the privilege, of course. The money goes into a trust fund which the tribal government distributes throughout the community.

The whole thing seemed to have been planned around conservation. When the miners finished in one area they only moved on to another after restoring the land to how it had been before. Aluminium ore is found close to the surface, so they skim the topsoil, lift the ore and put the topsoil back. Then they replant.

Lynn Olsen showed me the process. Lynn is a truck driver, and when I say 'truck' I mean a massive Caterpillar dumper. It is enormous – the cab is situated over the front wheel on the left, and you have to climb a fixed iron stairway to get to it. The top of the wheel rim is taller than I am and Lynn told me that when she first started driving one of these trucks seventeen years ago, it was a little daunting. Now it's second nature. She took me up the dirt roads to the ore fields where the dust was loaded. Then we returned to the plant, drove up a ramp with a grille cut through it and the truck drained its cargo. The dust was then scooped up and taken to be washed. After that the loose ore was transported by train to storage facilities before being shipped to processing plants all over the world.

The Caterpillar itself was quite easy to operate, and although it wasn't the case when Lynn started, now something like half the drivers are women. She reckoned they were better at it than the men. 'The truck gets smaller,' she told me. 'It's huge when you start out, of course, but over the years it just seems to get smaller and smaller.'

When the shift ended we drove out to the Grahams' house in a quiet suburb, a stone's throw from a gorgeous tropical beach. It was beautiful and so tranquil, flat water and white sand with palm trees that were fairly dripping with coconuts.

'We love the view,' Bianca told me, 'but you can't really use the beach. You can't swim because there are box jellyfish and sharks, of course, and then there are the salties – crocs who like to bask on the sand.'

We spent a very relaxing evening eating a barbecue with them and John explained more about the running of the mine. His role was in community relations, so he dealt with the traditional owners. Weipa was a good, if quiet, place to live, but it was isolated. For four months of the year it rained and the only way in or out was to fly. But there was plenty of outdoor stuff to do – fishing, hunting and camping – and he and his family loved it.

In the morning we went back to the airfield, where Graeme had the plane ready. Having completed his work in Weipa, he was heading to Bamaga to look at some more boats. Sam and Robin were already there, having flown up from Cairns in order to try to sort out what was going to happen when we got to Papua New Guinea. Together again, the four of us would take a small boat, what they call a tinny, to Thursday Island across the Torres Strait.

It's funny. For years now I've had this thing about flying, this romantic notion that I can get my pilot's licence and fly off wherever I want. The reality, however, is that I get airsick. Even yesterday in the twin-engine Beechcraft, it only had to be a little bumpy and I started to feel nauseous.

It's just one of those things, I suppose, and it's the same with boats. I get sick on small boats. Actually I'm crap around boats altogether. Whenever I go near a boat something goes wrong. I call it the Charley Factor. In Vietnam we were on a speedboat that conked out between two massive rocks and I thought we were going to drown. Then there was an abortive sea crossing from Nikoi Island to Borneo, where an hour into the voyage the *Pinisi* started taking on water. Then there was an overloaded ferry when we island-hopped through Indonesia on the last trip that listed so badly I thought it might capsize at any time. Not to mention a three-and-a-half-day crossing to Darwin that took six and a half days because the sea was so rough. I should avoid boats, I really should. It's a bit like KTMs – I seem to put the hex on them.

Graeme dropped us off at the airfield in Bamaga where we had arranged to hook up with a young guy called Brett, who worked on Horn Island teaching youngsters how to drive the small tinnies, and his mate Jeff, who lived in Bamaga. Tinnies were the traditional method of getting around up here, and Brett had borrowed one to ferry us on the next leg of our journey, first to Horn Island and then on to Thursday Island. But, of course, the boat was playing up – on the way over they had had a bit of engine trouble and while Brett came to pick us up, another mate was trying to fix it.

The boat wasn't big enough to take all of us so Brett suggested he make two trips. It was only twenty minutes from Seisa Beach, where it was moored, to Horn Island and back. Now the boat was working again, we agreed that Robin and Sam would go first.

It was a beautiful day and while we waited for Brett to return, I went for a paddle in a warm sea. Winter at the top of the Cape, I could get used to it. Brett's friend Jeff – a cool, very tall and laid-back guy with chipped front teeth and a thick, gold band in his ear – had hung around with Claudio and me to wait for the boat. As the sun got hotter we sat under a shelter made out of palm leaves where it was more comfortable.

We waited and we waited. A twenty-minute round trip, Brett had said, but an hour and twenty minutes later there was still no sign of him. Jeff tried to get hold of him on his mobile phone but could not get a connection.

'It's funny,' he said. 'He really ought to be back by now.'

'What could've happened?' I asked him.

'I don't know.' He was gazing out to sea. 'Brett reckoned it was pretty choppy coming over this morning, but look at her now. She looks as flat as, Charley, doesn't she?' He scratched his shaven head under his baseball cap. 'I suppose they could've tipped over, hit something maybe. You have to watch it, there're plenty of rocks under the water.' He looked at me briefly. 'A couple of years ago I was fishing for turtle with a few mates. Being locals we're allowed to fish for the turtles. Anyway, we caught this big old boy and it took the four of us to haul him over the side. Trouble was we were all on the one side of the boat when a wave hit and we capsized.'

I was staring at him.

'You don't really want to do that out there, you don't want to do it in any of the waters round here – you've got sharks and sea wasps, you bloody name it.' He pursed his lips. 'Anyway we lost the turtle and we were four hours in the water before we could right the boat and get her going again. By then we'd drifted for miles, could've been in real trouble now I come to think about it.'

He showed me the chips in his teeth. 'No worries, though, Brett knows what he's doing. I'm sure they'll be just fine.'

But an hour later there was still no sign of Brett, so after a discussion with Claudio, I decided to get hold of the coastguard. The local commander arrived and we gave him the description of the boat and who was on board. He went to fetch one of the volunteers, explaining that when he got back they would go out and look for the missing boat. We stayed on the beach, watching the horizon and waiting. And of course, just as the coastguard got back, Brett came rattling into the bay.

'Sorry about that, Charley,' he said when he got to the beach, 'engine trouble again, I'm afraid. The bloody thing keeps packing up.'

'It's all right,' I told him. 'Don't worry, Brett, it's my fault: I call it the Charley Factor.'

We just about made it to Horn Island. When the engine was working we were zipping along, slapping through the whitecaps and getting thoroughly soaked by the spray. But as I was on board, it was no surprise when the outboard conked out again, and again, and again. It was the contact points on the spark plugs, they just kept failing.

'Tell you what,' Brett said when we had got it going for the fourth time. 'We'll get to Horn Island and see if we can't find another boat to take you across to Thursday. I don't want to risk it in this thing, not with the engine playing up.'

'Sounds good to me,' I told him. I was gazing across the bay now and there seemed to be quite a few small boats dotted here and there. We were bound to find something.

As it turned out there was this one large, flat-bottomed boat that looked quite official. Two young guys wearing coveralls were on board, Ben and Rob. They came alongside and we asked them if we could hitch a ride. They thought about it for a moment then Ben nodded.

'Yeah, all right, mate,' he said. 'Where do you want to go?'

'Thursday Island,' I told him. 'We're on our way to Papua New Guinea.'

The plan was to fly out the day after tomorrow, although it wasn't yet cast in stone. We had hoped to find a small boat to make the crossing but it is so cheap to fly these days that the small boats are no longer allowed to clear customs.

Perhaps it was just as well. Given my reputation.

Ben and Rob were operating what they termed a 'standby-vessel', which would attend the scene if any marine traffic ran aground, like a sort of first responder. There were reefs all over this area and we had to skirt them, crossing the strait in a zigzag to get to Thursday Island. The water was clear and blue, the sun high and the boat big enough so your bum didn't feel as though you'd been given six of the best by some Victorian schoolteacher. Ben explained that with so much 'hard stuff' under the water, the area was notorious for boats running aground.

'We hang around in case we're needed,' he said. 'In the meantime we act as a lighthouse tender.'

The area was dotted with islands, thirty or forty of them, and there were plenty of lighthouses that had to be maintained.

As we closed on the dock at Thursday Island it dawned on me that the first leg of the journey was almost over. We had left the mainland behind and in a day or so we would be landing in Papua New Guinea. I wondered what it would hold for us. We had heard all sorts of conflicting stories and I could feel the butterflies (that seem to plague me) starting up again. I really do have to stop worrying about the future. One day at a time, Charley, just deal with what's in front of you.

So I concentrated instead on the fact that we had a couple of days on this historic island. Having said goodbye to Ben and Rob, the four of us were on the dock looking up and down the road for any sign of a cab. But this was a very quiet place. There were few cars about and none of them were taxis. We had decided to transport our gear on foot when a car pulled up and a local woman wound the window down.

'Hello,' she said. 'Where are you fellas going?'

'The hotel,' I told her, pointing into town.

'Do you want me to give you a lift?'

'Could you? That would be very kind.'

'Sure,' she said. 'I'll take you two at a time.'

Her name was Louisa and she worked in local government. Her daughter Nancy was in the passenger seat and Louisa told us she was just out of hospital. Nancy had terrible taste in men apparently, and had been on one of the neighbouring islands with her latest boyfriend.

'She should've stayed in Cairns,' Louisa said.

Nancy's latest squeeze had got so drunk he'd beaten her senseless and her mother had to have her airlifted by helicopter. They drove us to the hotel and suggested we come to the Grand tonight, a local bar where Louisa's brother and uncle were playing in a band.

They played reggae music and it was quite a night. The music was good, the food was good and we had a couple of drinks. Louisa's brother was a big guy called Milton. His 'mob', as he called the tribe he belonged to, administered these islands and he played an active role in politics. The way he spoke about his culture and how much had been stolen from the indigenous people, he reminded me of Kurt at Pormpuraaw.

In a way it was fitting – we'd flown into Sydney with its high rises, the Opera House and motorbikes. And with just a couple of days to go before we left, we were chatting to a man who traced his people all the way back to the Dreamtime.

5
Of Fish Tails and Tail Fins

THERE WAS STILL no definitive plan about how we were going to get from Thursday Island to Papua New Guinea, but if all else failed we could fly down to Cairns and take a commercial airline. A much better idea was to locate someone on the island who could fly us across, and that was what Sam was working on.

The locals call Thursday Island 'TI', or sometimes Waiben, which means 'no (fresh) water'. For thousands of years this whole archipelago was the territory of the Torres Strait islanders – nomadic Melanesians who had three languages and today still speak a Torres Strait creole. During the Second World War there was fighting in this part of the world. After Japan bombed Pearl Harbor, when America entered the war, both the Americans and the Australians had bases on TI. The Japanese did not bomb the island, though they did attack mainland Australia and Horn Island. We heard a story that they left Thursday Island alone because some Japanese princess had been buried here, but whether that was true or not depended on whom you spoke to.

We were introduced to Ina Mills, one of three island sisters who had carved out a career singing traditional songs all over the world. While we were with the flying doctors, Gil had told us that her brother-in-law lived on TI and that we really ought to try to see the Mills Sisters. As it turned out, Ina's twin, Cessa, and their other sister Rita had flown to Cairns for a relative's birthday party, but we did manage to meet Ina. The three of them had been singing together since they were children and didn't stop performing until the 1980s. We found Ina at her apartment in a quiet suburb of the island township. She was a chatty and very funny eighty-one-year-old with white hair and glasses.

'Are you really eighty-one?' I asked her. 'You look so much younger.'

'I tell you what,' she laughed. 'For your programme I could be ten years younger.'

I thought about that. 'Ina, we could make you any age you want.'

Ina told me the sisters had sung in London and France as well as New Zealand, and a lot of their music had been recorded. We shared the fact that we were twins and I told her how I'd arrived just before my sister Daisy, who came feet first because she wanted to push me out. Ina 'popped out', as she put it, just before Cessa, and laughing she told me that was great because it meant she'd always have a younger sister to bully.

She had been born on an island thirty miles away. One of ten children, she didn't go to school until the age of seven, when she was brought over here to the convent. She missed her family – the only time she got to see them was at Christmas. But when the war came Thursday Island was evacuated. Most of the people went to the mainland but Ina's father came over to take her home. She was delighted – instead of being in school she was with her family, and her only real contact with the war was watching the planes go over.

We were right at the tip of the Cape here, beyond it in fact, no longer on mainland Australia, and I thought it was the perfect place to make the crossing to Papua. While I'd been talking to Ina, Sam had discovered a local guy called Greg Wright who dealt in crayfish and was always flying back and forth across the strait. His plane could accommodate us if it made two trips tomorrow, so the next leg of the journey looked as though it was fixed.

Later that afternoon and feeling more relaxed, I took a wander on the beach with Claudio. He'd been so busy, what with filming and backing up the tapes, we'd not had much opportunity to talk, so it was good to catch up.

'How are you finding it, Claudio?' I asked him. 'Are you enjoying the trip?'

He nodded. 'I love the way we're able to discover a country from the ground. Travelling the way we do, on the motorbikes particularly, we can just dive into the place, really get a feel for everything – the vegetation, the different places, the people.'

'What about the other modes of transport?' I asked him. 'I

mean, when you and I have been away before it was always motorbikes, wasn't it?'

'I like the bikes,' he said. 'But the other stuff is good as well – a Spitfire, an armoured car . . . I think my favourites so far are the electric car and the Zero bikes. I want one of those bikes, I can't believe how powerful they are.' He paused for a moment, gazing across the bay where the land climbed in a series of low hills. 'New sources of energy like that, some other type of fuel for the future, it's vital. We have to get away from our dependence on oil. Charley, for too many years I've made too many films about wars being fought where the root cause is oil.'

Waves lapped at the gradually darkening beach, the sun was sinking, and squatting down on a couple of rocks we just soaked up the atmosphere. 'It's a pity it's so difficult to cross the western half of Papua,' I said.

Claudio gave me a thoughtful look. 'You know I was there once before, don't you? I shouldn't have been, at least as far as the authorities were concerned, anyway.'

I squinted at him now. 'Yeah, I did know,' I said. 'When was that again?'

'Twenty years ago. I flew across the border to the Indonesian side to make one of the most important films I've ever made. It was called *Rebels of the Forgotten World*, about the Papuan independence movement.' He was concentrating now. 'To make it I had to fly to a clandestine airstrip they'd cleared for me on the Indonesian side of the border. They wanted me to come,' he said. 'They wanted someone to tell their story because while the international community looks away, what's happening there is the same as what happened to the Aboriginals here in Australia two hundred years ago.'

'I don't know much about it,' I admitted.

'Not many people do, or maybe it's that they just don't want to. You see, originally the western half of the island was a Dutch colony. The Germans had the north and the Australians and British the south. After the First World War, Australia took over the German region and the whole eastern side of the island was administered from Canberra. The western half had been promised independence. As far back as '62 the Dutch agreed to hand it over and the date was set for 1 December 1975. But in '63 the Indonesians invaded. They have occupied the country ever since and they are repressive, Charley. Even to raise the Papuan flag is an offence for which they throw people in prison. 1975 came and went, of course, but on 1 December, many Papuans do raise the flag and most of them are in prison because of it. Only recently one man was sentenced to ten years.

'When they invaded, the Indonesians tried to legitimise their actions by holding a referendum that they hoped would give them recognition from the UN. They hand-picked about a thousand village leaders and bribed them to back the invasion. It's been a case of repression ever since and it's ugly. People are being killed, people are being put in prison and it's one of the stories the international community just doesn't seem to care about.' He got to his feet. 'This is a travel programme and it's fun of course, but we've been talking about what happened to the stolen generation of Aboriginals. The Indonesians are not going to let us into the occupied land with a camera and I think it's important that we tell people why.'

He had a point. Claudio has always been a serious film-maker, he's even interviewed Osama Bin Laden, and while this trip was about getting from A to B by any means available, it was also about what was happening in the countries we were travelling through.

The following morning Greg picked us up in his Toyota Hilux. We shook hands and I asked him if everything was OK for the flight today.

'Sort of. We've got a couple of hitches with the plane, but nothing we can't handle.'

My heart sank. 'What does that mean?'

'A little magneto problem, it'll be all right.'

There was something about the laid-back way he was telling me, the easy drawling voice. Why did I think it wouldn't be all right? Was it just me?

I'd woken feeling nervous. We were leaving Australia and all its familiarity and heading for a country I knew nothing about. I must say my chat with Claudio last night hadn't inspired me any, although we had been talking about the Indonesian side and the chances of us getting in were remote.

On the way to his plant, Greg explained that there are two aspects to his business. One is dealing in locally caught live crayfish and lobster, the other in frozen crayfish tails that he brings from Papua New Guinea.

He runs a plane to and from Daru to pick up the frozen crayfish tails and it was from there that we were picking up a commercial flight to Port Moresby. Greg's premises were right on the water, a series of wooden buildings housing storage freezers and a packing area, as well as a large seawater tank for the live crayfish. A pair of up and over garage-style doors opened onto the sea and Greg pointed out a white buoy bobbing in the distance.

'We need really fresh seawater,' he said, 'for the big tank there.' He pointed at our feet where a pair of pipes disappeared into the sea. 'The other end of those pipes is out by that buoy,' he told me. 'We pump the water all the way from there.'

He showed me one massive crayfish, and I mean it was enormous, weighing over two kilos. He told me it was worth $100. 'Most of the fishermen use tinnies,' he told me. 'They make their catch and then we either fly out and bring it in, or they bring it to us. From there, it's Cairns mostly.'

'What about the frozen tails?' I pointed out a tray of them, grey in colour and packed solid.

'Like I said, we get them from Daru. They have to be frozen – you can't import live crayfish into Australia because of the quarantine rules. Fishing is the main industry up here in the strait. A good year will bring about twenty million dollars into the Australian economy.'

He spoke on the phone to the place where the plane was being fixed, somewhere on Horn Island. The longer the call went on, the more nervous I became. We had to catch that flight from Daru at 10 a.m. tomorrow, and missing it was not an option. Sam was concerned, we all were; there was something about how this was panning out that filled none of us with confidence. Greg came off the phone scratching his head. 'He's working on it,' he said, 'but it's not just the magneto. He reckons there's a problem with the wiring harness.'

'Can we go over there and see him?' I asked.

He shook his head. 'He said if anyone shows up with a camera he'll ground the plane and walk away.' He shrugged. 'Sorry, fellas, he's just that way.'

'We'll leave him to it then,' I suggested.

Claudio was looking at a newspaper cutting Greg had pasted on his wall. 'The Merauke Five': Australians from Horn Island who were stranded in Indonesian-occupied Papua.

Greg explained that a few months previously, five middle-aged friends had flown their light aircraft to Merauke to check out tourism possibilities. They hadn't been able to get a visa before they left, but had been told that they could get one when they landed. It was only a day trip and they had planned to be home that same evening.

'Just a day trip, and months later they're still there,' Greg went on. 'Western Papua is very sensitive; where they landed was an airport all right but it's also a military base. You see, the Indonesians are trying to dilute the population, trying to filter out the indigenous Papuans and replace them with Javanese.' He shook his head. 'It's a bloody awful situation and those people got caught up in it just by not having the right paperwork. And they're not young either – the pilot is in his sixties, his wife in her late fifties. They were held in some immigration centre and then in prison. They were told by one court that they could leave, then that decision was overturned by another court. They lost their son too; he'd been ill and since they've been gone, he's died. The authorities wouldn't let them out to come home and bury him.'

It all sounded very depressing indeed. 'You know what?' I said, glancing at Sam. 'Western Papua sounds boring anyway, there's no jungle left, all there is are open-cast mines and we've seen plenty of those already.'

'The By Any Means Four,' Claudio muttered. 'We don't want to end up as the By Any Means Four, do we?'

I thought back to the conversation we'd had last night. 'Claudio's been there before, haven't you, Clouds?' I said. 'Twenty years ago.'

He nodded. 'For six months. That wasn't the plan so much at the time, but the landing strip the rebels cleared was in the jungle and the day before we got there it rained. The plane got stuck and couldn't take off again.'

'What happened?' Greg asked him.

'Well, the pilot was worried that the plane would be reported missing and there would be helicopters out looking for it. So he went back across the border right away.'

'On foot?' I said.

'Yes, on foot.'

'And you stayed for six months?'

'Yes. You see, first I had to learn the language and then of course I had to make my film. I organised a series of couriers to smuggle my tapes across the border to Papua and I didn't want to leave until I knew they were all safely back in Europe. So in the end I was there for six months.'

We decided to take the ferry across to Horn Island and see what was going on with the plane. We were concerned. This was the Torres Strait and the place has its own timescale. No one is in a hurry and nothing is ever done in a rush, which is all well and good but we had a deadline to make tomorrow. The pilot who was going to take us to Daru, Lockie, met us at the wharf with Greg's van. We found out that he was new to the area, so new he only had five hours' flying time, and had been to Daru just once. Plenty of experience there then, I thought, but it wouldn't matter because we didn't have a plane at the moment anyway.

Seriously, though, we were really concerned about making the ten o'clock connection in the morning. To add to our problems, the wind had lifted and it was spitting with rain. Lockie reckoned the engineer was talking about it not being ready before at least 2 p.m. now, maybe even 3, and it was already eleven o'clock. I didn't have much faith that we'd be flying at all, especially as en route to the airport the van broke down on three separate occasions. It occurred to me that on an island as small as this, the mechanics who fixed the cars would probably be fixing the planes too.

The other issue was the fact that Greg's plane was a Cessna 210, which could only take two of us at a time. It was an hour's flight to Daru then another hour and a half to load the frozen crayfish tails and another still to fly back again.

'There's not enough time,' Sam stated, as we tried to bump-start the van for the third time. Or at least I did. Sam sat in the back, the fat fucker, while I was pushing the bloody thing. 'Well I can't get out,' he protested, 'the camera is in the way.'

He was right about the plane, though. If all went well there might be enough time to get two of us over to Daru before it got dark tonight, but the other two would have to wait until tomorrow. There was every chance that the plane wouldn't be fixed at all today and to cover ourselves we'd checked out the possibility of flying back to Cairns. But that was way too expensive and miles out of our way, so Sam asked Greg to phone around some of the charter companies and see what our options were. He kindly did that and a little while later he came up with a company who could get us all on the same plane in the morning. I was still keen to stick to the original plan if we could, however, so that at least Claudio and I could fly with Lockie on the crayfish run.

'So it's decided then,' Sam said, taking me to one side. 'We all go in the morning, you and Claudio on the crayfish plane and Robin and me on the charter with the gear. Failing that, we all get on the charter.'

We had some time to kill this afternoon now and decided to try and find out something about the history of Horn Island. But Greg didn't know much and neither, it seemed, did anyone else. In fact, until Vanessa arrived nobody knew very much at all. I'm talking about Vanessa Seekee, a really entertaining girl we hooked up with for a couple of hours. Since coming to the island she had become its unofficial historian. She told us that during the Second World War, the Japanese dropped five hundred pounds of bombs here, which is almost as many as they dumped on Darwin, the most bombed site on the Australian mainland.

Vanessa was great company, the perfect tour guide. She took us to an old artillery battery and a slit trench, which is a narrow hole in the ground rather like a foxhole. I had no idea that so much of the war had been fought here. I knew there were Australian pilots in the Battle of Britain and Australian soldiers at El Alamein, of course, and plenty of other places. But here on the islands off the tip of Cape York, I never would have guessed it.

Vanessa took us out to where the old airfield had been. It was jungle now, all overgrown with trees and dry grass, but in among the trees was the wreckage of a P-47 Thunderbolt. This was a beast of a plane that had been used in air combat, but was most effective when the Americans used it to attack the enemy on the ground. It was the largest, heaviest and most expensive single-engined plane in history, at least among those powered by conventional pistons anyway. During the war there had been no source of refrigeration up here and Vanessa told us that when they weren't flying missions, the aircrews would strip the ammunition banks from the wings and fill the space with beer. The pilot would take the plane up for half an hour to chill the beer off for drinking.

'People don't realise, Charley,' she said, 'that during the war Horn Island was Australia's most geographically advanced allied airbase. From here pilots could attack targets in the north and get back again the same day. That saved a hell of a lot of aircraft because it meant that no one had to stay over at Port Moresby. Any plane on the apron at night was a target for the Japanese bombers.'

She told me the airstrip had been built in 1940. The trees that surrounded us now had been cleared and two all-purpose gravel runways laid down. 'At the beginning of 1942 there were twenty men working here, and by the end of that year, five thousand.'

'But why is this plane here?' I pointed out the wreckage.

Vanessa laughed. 'I'll tell you,' she said. 'There was this one pilot who was a bit of a joker: Wing Commander Lambeth. He took off in this P-47 and decided to scare the living daylights out of the men working on planes close to the runway. Instead of climbing hard as he normally would, he stayed really low and buzzed right over the top of them. The problem was he clipped the tail fin of the first Kitty Hawk, the propeller of the next, then ploughed into a third. Finally he crashed here.' She nodded to the wreckage. 'He destroyed four planes in less than five minutes, which is more than the Japs ever managed in an entire raid. He's fine, climbs out, trips over a tree root and breaks his left thumb.'

I was gobsmacked. 'What happened to him?'

'I don't know. There doesn't seem to be any record and I can't find out whether he was court-martialled, promoted or shot.'

6
Improvise, Adapt and Overcome

THE NEXT MORNING we got up early and headed straight for the airport, where we discovered that whether we liked it or not we would have to fly with the charter company. Yesterday Lockie had told us he would monitor the situation, put our names down for the charter plane if the crayfish plane wasn't ready in time. Unfortunately that's what happened. It was a shame, but regardless of who was taking us, today we were flying to Papua New Guinea.

My God, just saying the words made me hop about like an excited schoolboy. The nerves had gone, replaced with a real adrenaline buzz. Don't you just love a bit of adventure? We seemed to have been talking about this section of the trip for ever – long before we finished the last one, in fact. Half the people we spoke to told us it was the most dangerous place in the world. The other half said we'd have the time of our lives.

The plane was a twin-engined Shrick Commander and I sat up front, co-piloting with Will from the charter company, who looked almost as young as Lockie. He had been to Daru at least twice before, so things were looking up. Actually I didn't care how many flight hours he had; nothing could dampen my enthusiasm this morning.

'The weather looks beautiful over there, Will.' I pointed towards a huge expanse of blue, cloudless sky.

'Yeah, it does . . . but we're going over there.' He pointed in the other direction, to the massed, dark grey clouds of a rain shower.

An hour later we landed, just about unscathed, on a strip of tarmac bordered by lush green grass, with smoky-looking mountains rising up on either side. The island of Daru is just a hair's breadth from the PNG mainland. The immigration and customs people were really cool – a guy took my passport and told me he'd do the necessary while Claudio and I carried on filming. Outside on the apron, we watched as the crayfish plane landed and Lockie swung open the door.

'Hey, Lockie!' I called. 'You made it.'

'She flew like a bird! No worries, Charley, no worries.'

The truck carrying the packs of frozen crayfish tails had already arrived. Lockie flattened the back seats of his Cessna and loaded the plane to the gunwales. A little while later he was airborne again, winging his way back to Horn Island having landed in Daru for the second time in his career.

This was a sweat-soaked tropical country and I loved it already. Australia had been fascinating but this was something completely new and exciting. I couldn't wait to start exploring. We took a short flight to mainland Papua and Port Moresby before boarding another plane and flying across the heel of the island. We landed at Lae, the largest city in Morobe Province and the second largest in the country. Our Papuan translator, Josh, was waiting for us as we got off the plane, and we headed straight for the centre of town on roads that were part tarmac and part dirt. This was a bustling, dynamic place with a great vibe to it. It was also very humid, and after a burst of heavy rain the potholes were brimming with muddy water.

I have a funny feeling our hotel might have doubled as a brothel. Claudio and I were sharing a room and next to my bed was a complimentary pack of twelve lubricated condoms. Twelve! We had a great time. No, I'm joking, we didn't spot them until the morning, honestly.

Seriously, though, there is an AIDS problem in Papua and it was good to see the hotels acting responsibly. I'm sure it wasn't a brothel, but it was right in the middle of town and if people were going to . . . with . . . well, you know. Anyway, we'll move on now, shall we?

Standing on the balcony outside my room I was struck by the noise, the hubbub of the place. There were so many people after the tranquillity of the islands. I was eager to get right among it all.

I took a wander along the wide and watery street where palm trees were interspersed with the tired-looking buildings. Lae was originally a gold-rush town that grew up around an airstrip in the

1920s. Food and provisions were flown in from Australia then shipped inland to the mines.

After the stillness of Thursday Island, the amount of people on the street here was amazing. It seemed to be mostly men and they thronged around me, selling all sorts of stuff – red tea and the betel nut I'd seen in India; clearly they chewed it here too. One guy in a combat jacket was flogging sunglasses. Lae is a container port, one of the main points of entry for freight coming into East Papua. It's incredibly busy – huge crowds of people out on the street, all sorts of trucks and vans, markets dotted here and there. A bit of a culture shock after Australia.

As we'd flown in I'd noticed how green and lush the country was. The hillsides were thick with trees and there was no doubt we were in the tropics. It was also very mountainous, part of the 'Pacific ring of fire' and geographically unstable. A whole bunch of tectonic plates collided in this area, and the island is susceptible to earthquakes and tsunamis as well as volcanic activity.

Despite the vibrant, positive atmosphere, there was no getting away from the fact that Papua is a very poor country. An awful lot of people live below the poverty line and they leave the countryside in their droves looking for work in the towns, despite the fact that there isn't much work available. Families become displaced, communities disrupted and people wind up in towns like Lae with no work and nowhere really to go.

We weren't staying in town for very long. The plan was to drive into the highlands as far as a place called Goroka, where we would meet up with a Dutch guy called Marcel Pool who would give us a bed for the night. He had been in Papua for a couple of years, helping disabled people try to fit more easily into the community. Tomorrow we would spend some time with a team from Voluntary Service Overseas. I had not had much to do with VSO in the past, but when it comes to fighting poverty they are the world's leading independent development organisation. People volunteer their skills to help others less fortunate than themselves: doctors, nurses, carpenters, bricklayers – you name it.

*

But before all that we had a seven-hour road trip ahead of us. Josh had organised a lift in a truck run by the Wagi Valley Transport Company. We would ride with an old fellow called Koi, a big guy with curly hair, a grey beard and a wide smile punctuated by a missing front tooth. He told me he was fifty but he looked a lot older than that. He loved his truck. No . . . he *adored* it. An eighteen-wheeler with full bonnet and bull bars, it had been shipped originally to Papua from Brisbane. It was pretty ancient now and God knows how many miles it had done, but each time it left the depot it was checked over by a mechanic in a massive open-sided inspection shed.

On this particular sticky, hot day, Koi was carrying two containers. These had been loaded by a forklift truck and placed with the doors facing each other, a tyre squashed between them. In his Pidgin English, Koi explained that when the first road was cut into the mountains there were plenty of bandits up there. There still are, in fact, but I'll come to that later. Back in the 1970s the bandits would wait until the trucks were labouring uphill at walking pace then they would hop on the back like something from *Mad Max*. Using bolt cutters they would open the container doors and steal whatever was inside, but with the doors facing each other and a massive tyre jammed in between, there was no way anyone could open them.

As soon as the inspection was over, I clambered into the cab. Koi sat behind the wheel while Josh piled in the back, ready to translate. When you first hear their Pidgin English you think you're going to be fine. It's only later that you realise you only understand about half of what anyone is saying.

Koi was a cool, laid-back guy and probably the most careful driver I've ever been with. He told me that he'd been driving trucks for as long as he can remember, but until he got behind the wheel of this baby, they had all been gnarly old things. This one had power steering and was fully upholstered, with a sleeping compartment tucked neatly behind the seats. He treated it like he would a favourite child.

We headed west, deeper into the country. Rumbling along, I realised that the cab's windows and windscreen were covered with a mesh grille. I asked Koi about it and he said it was because people liked to throw stones.

'It's like that in Ethiopia too,' I told him. 'The kids throw stones. I don't know why. It's just something they've always done, or at least that's what Ewan and I were told.'

'Not kids here. Drunk people mostly.'

Leaving town, we headed into open country where the road was bordered by trees and banks of rich grass. The cab was bloody hot. It was hot outside but in the passenger seat the heat came rippling off the engine and I couldn't put my feet on the floor without them burning. In places the mountains were burning too. We stopped at a roadside market to buy some bananas and I could see smoke billowing from folds in the land halfway up the hillside. Josh told us the villagers were burning the scrub to scare out pigs and snakes so they could hunt them. I'd seen a massive green snake on a small ridge we'd just passed and I imagined the thing slithering through the grass with half a dozen men trying to whack it to death.

I bought a coconut from a woman squatting on a grass mat, and she sliced it open for me with a machete. The juice was delicious, perfect to wash down the fresh peanuts we had picked up to go with the bananas. They were so sweet, like an explosion of sugar in your mouth every time you ate one – almost like sweet peas straight from the pod in the garden.

The higher we got the more the place seemed to change. We were climbing steadily now and at exactly the kind of walking pace where it would be easy for bandits to jump on board. Back at the truck yard I'd noticed the fuel tank had a bolt and seal over the cap, clearly there to stop anyone siphoning off the diesel. Koi said there was a good market for selling stolen fuel. He seemed a little nervous, not quite as laid-back as he had been in the low country. As we rattled through one pass in particular, his eyes were everywhere, and now and again he would point out someone with a gun. It was true, then: there were still bandits up in these mountains.

Gardens were a feature here: the higher we climbed the neater the houses were getting. Huts were made from woven grass, built on stilts perhaps five feet off the ground, clearly to keep the snakes out. The roofs were thatch and the walls beautifully patterned. The people looked fairly self-sufficient and they clearly took great pride in their homes. The lawns were mown, the vegetable patches pristine and growing everything from bananas to ginger and coffee. Koi told me that he had a little coffee plantation of his own. He planned to work there full time with his wife one day, when he finally finished with truck driving.

The hours ticked by and we climbed right into the high country. As dusk fell we arrived at the town of Goroka. Koi had been brilliant company, a great guide for our first full day in Papua, and we had covered a good few miles from the coast. We said goodbye and I watched him trundle off into the darkness while we made our way to Marcel's place and, hopefully, a bed for the night.

The next couple of days were really eye-opening. Marcel had arranged for us to stay at the VSO lodge in Goroka, a white, colonial-style building where he and his colleagues lived. I really liked Marcel, one of those people you immediately warm to. Over the past couple of years he had created a physiotherapy centre for the disabled at the General Hospital and, now it was up and running, he had branched into a programme of community-based rehabilitation (CBR).

After a good night's sleep, Claudio and I walked to the hospital, a whitewashed stucco building in the middle of town. Marcel explained that there is a huge stigma attached to disability in Papua, and in some areas disabled children are still killed by their parents at birth. I think I was more shocked by that than anything I'd heard on my travels. Marcel explained that many people believed in witchcraft and evil spirits, and disability was very much associated with that. Part of his role with VSO was to show people that someone with disabilities could not only live a fulfilling life, but be a role model to others.

Arriving at the hospital, we were greeted by a young kid who was just such an inspiration. Moloui had been born with arms that stopped at the elbows and he had narrow pads for hands with only one finger on each. Marcel explained that life for a boy like Moloui can be very difficult indeed. Many people believed that his mother must have done something she shouldn't when she was pregnant, or gone somewhere she shouldn't, and Moloui's physical impediment was the result of it.

Marcel worked tirelessly to show people that Moloui and kids like him were just the same as anyone else, and not some bad spirit or the product of any kind of behaviour. He introduced us to Cecelia Bagore, a local woman who coordinates all the work done with disabled children. She showed us around the physiotherapy department and I was struck by a couple of murals, pictures of bright-eyed, smiling children under the maxim: 'Look at my strengths, not my weaknesses'.

Now that the centre was fully functioning, Marcel had passed the day-to-day administration to a man called Bill Lyape. Bill explained how they deal with all sorts of disabilities, from things like back problems to joints, fractures, strokes and varying degrees of paralysis. When a patient is discharged they are referred to the CBR programme and Marcel continues with the therapy in their own community. That way he can not only assess their ongoing needs, but show family members and neighbours how they can get involved with the child's rehabilitation. Marcel is very keen that the villagers do not dissociate themselves from the disabled people within a given community, helping them to understand rather than stigmatise.

'It's vital,' he told me. 'Take Moloui, he's become an integral part of our team here, a role model not just for other disabled kids, but everyone.'

Moloui was a cool kid. With his two fingers he could hold a pen and write very neatly. I watched him use a calculator and a telephone. He could unscrew a bottle of water, drink from it and screw it up again. He's a normal kid, he laughs and cries and has fun.

'He's great,' Bill said with a smile. 'A real asset to what we do here. He's a young kid who is different, but he doesn't feel ashamed. He's confident and what he does is allow other disabled people to see that they can carry on with confidence as well.'

Marcel told us that the only medal ever won by PNG at the Olympics was in the Beijing Special Olympics in 2008, when Francis Kompaon, born with a deformed arm, won a silver in the men's 100 metres. He was named sportsperson of the year, which was a major boost for the department in Goroka.

The hospital is pretty well equipped considering where it is and that it's underfunded. But it's nothing like we would see in the West. They use what they can where they can and often the simplest, cheapest tools can be the most productive.

Take Kenny Ossi, for instance. He has muscular dystrophy and when he first came to the hospital his muscles were so wasted he couldn't even sit up, let alone feed himself.

'He was on his back. He was in bed all the time and that's no good,' Marcel told me. 'It's very bad for the children to just be in bed, they get bored and they can suffer from all kinds of secondary conditions – lung infection is common and that can kill them. It's important that we get them moving, not just their bodies but their brains as well. To stimulate the body you have to stimulate the mind.'

When I saw Kenny he was propped up in a sort of upright bed with a strap across his middle and one of the nurses was stimulating the movement in the upper half of his body by batting a balloon to him.

'It's simple but very effective,' Marcel told me. 'A balloon has no weight so Kenny can handle it, touch it, move his hands to get to it. And he's interacting with whoever is playing with him. When I'm out in the community I never go anywhere without a few balloons.'

Kenny was obviously enjoying it, and given that when he came in he couldn't move at all, I thought what they had achieved here was brilliant. Just like Moloui, this boy was slowly overcoming his disability. We found out that his mother had died when he was younger, he had one brother at home and another older brother who was married. His father, a really dedicated man called Bekki, looked after him. When Kenny was at home his father made sure he was stimulated by taking him to the market or into town, and when he was in the hospital Bekki was there every day to feed and wash him. I could only imagine the pressure it placed on the family, but Bekki told me he wasn't ashamed of his son. Why should he be? He was proud of what Kenny had achieved since Marcel and the physio team had started treating him.

A little later Cecelia took us out to one of the villages to see a lad called Kevin who had cerebral palsy. Claudio and I were perched in the back of a pick-up with Barama and Joseph, two guys from the CBR unit. The village – a handful of huts made from wooden planks and thatched with dried grass – was a few miles deeper into the mountains, right in the heart of the rainforest. Kevin's family brought him to meet us in a wheelchair with a little puppy perched in a basket underneath. His therapy involved lying on a mat while his limbs were massaged and stretched, a whole series of what Marcel called reflex exercises. He was attended by the CBR team, but it wasn't just them – we were able to see first hand how his situation was handled by the village community.

It soon became apparent that the CBR team are involved in a huge amount of work with the disabled. After we left Kevin, they took us to Mount Sion School for the Blind, a 'Centre for the Disabled Persons', run by Justin Wagma. It's a vibrant, colourful place and we were greeted by a group of blind men playing keyboards and guitars and singing to us about how we should look beyond their disability.

'We integrate disabled children with the other children,' Justin explained. 'That way those who have no physical impairment grow up around kids who have, so they understand that disability is a fact of life in any society. Hopefully some of those children might go on to be leaders in this country and future generations won't suffer from the stigma that others have.'

I met a man called Martin – a confident, intelligent guy – who worked at the school but spent much of his time lobbying local politicians for funding and education for the disabled. Back in 1991 he had been blinded in an accident and in 1992 he was brought to the school, where he learned how to read and type Braille. He read me a passage of Braille, skirting his fingers over the raised dots as quickly as any sighted person might read from a book, and showed me a Braille typewriter. It was quite small, and Martin bashed out the alphabet with the speed of a trained secretary. With improvisation, an amazing attitude and a huge amount of work, he had overcome a life-shattering accident and in so doing had become an inspiration to everyone he met.

Improvise, adapt and overcome: it was a motto I'd heard from soldiers I'd taught to ride off road, and it was in my mind as I took a moment to reflect on what we'd seen. Visits like these really make an expedition; they're the moments that make you pause and think, not just about your own life and how lucky you are, but about the fantastic ability people have for dealing with what life throws at them. The Aboriginal communities like Pormpuraaw, the people raising the flag in West Papua, remote, traditional communities like those we had seen here. They remind you of what can be achieved with relatively little and just how positive and adaptable people can be. It can be heartbreaking at times, but it can also be incredibly uplifting and inspiring.

Seventy years ago there had been so few white people in this region that when John Leahy's father showed up, the tribes thought he was a ghost from the lowlands below. John runs a coffee factory – the Lahamenegu – established back in the 1930s. His father, who came over from Australia, was one of the very first explorers to visit these parts and he filmed his experiences in a documentary called *First Contact*, which is now part of the Australian television archive.

John is a solid-looking guy in his fifties with a thick grey beard and a typically hospitable Australian manner. His factory is close to Goroka and local farmers bring their coffee beans here to be processed and dried. John explained that coffee production is a major component of the Papuan economy.

'Coffee is durable,' he said. 'And here in Papua with this climate and the lack of a real infrastructure, durability is very important. A dried bean has a shelf life of two to three years and a farmer can sit on his stock and sell what he wants when he wants. That's why coffee trades so well on the futures market. It's not all about this season, or this year's harvest, and here in Papua it grows year round.'

The factory was a mass of silos, sheds, conveyor belts and enormous sifting bins. You could feel the heat from the furnaces. John explained that during the war Dutch farmers had produced quinine for the allied troops in this area. His dad got involved but there wasn't a great deal of money in quinine and the Dutch had told him how they had cultivated coffee in Indonesia. The highlands around Goroka were perfect for growing coffee beans, so after the war, John's father went into arabica. Now the operation looks after all the local farmers, including people like Koi and his fifteen hectares. At the plant they put the beans through a process to shed the husks, which are stored in the silos and used later as fuel for the furnaces that dry the coffee beans. Once a bean has been reduced to 11 per cent moisture content it's classified as dry and, as John said, has an extended shelf life. What really impressed me, though, was the fact that the farmers were paid directly. There were no middle men, no government rake-off; they got the full, fair price for everything they grew.

It was strange to think that I was talking with the son of one of the very first Westerners to come to these mountains. I tried to imagine what must have gone through the tribespeople's minds when they saw a white man for the first time.

Talking of white men, I met a few the following day. These genuinely were *ghostly* white, known as 'mud men', from the village of Komunive – a tribal group who daub themselves with mud just as their ancestors used to. These days it's mostly put on as a show for the tourists. According to Andrew, who manages the displays, they get quite a few Brits, as well as Germans and Americans, travelling through here. The villagers cover their bodies in the white mud, then light great smoking fires and put on clay masks they've fired themselves, before pretending to hunt their enemies with longbows and poison-tipped arrows.

The masks were amazing – full heads shaped like gargoyles and demons, specifically designed to scare the shit out of the neighbouring tribes. Of course, they wanted me to get naked so they could plaster clay all over me. They really wanted to dress me up in a grass loincloth and put a mask on my head, as well. You can imagine how enthusiastic I was, but Claudio was adamant it would make good television.

So with the camera crew and the entire Komunive village

gathered around me, I took off all my clothes. A couple of guys fitted me with the loincloth and covered me with clay.

'People pay good money for this in England,' I told them. 'They go to health clubs and pay good money. Honestly, it's considered a luxury.'

Here the practice began by accident. Andrew told us that his great-great-grandfather fell into a swamp one day and came out covered in mud. The other villagers saw him, thought he was a ghost and dropped their bows and spears before running away. That gave him an idea.

'Hey, lads,' he said, when they realised it was him. 'We could do this, smear ourselves in mud, make some masks and raid the other tribes. We can carry off all their women and pigs.'

And according to Andrew that's pretty much what they did. It worked too: they ended up with more wives (and pigs) than they knew what to do with. Pigs are like dogs in Papua, they're really prized possessions, and wives – well, I suppose, the more the merrier.

I finished the day by beheading a live chicken for a mumu, a traditional Papuan feast organised by Marcel, Cecelia and Bill, back at the lodge in Goroka. They were preparing a real feast – in the old days it would have fed the entire village. I like to cook so I got involved not just with slaughtering the chicken, but with the guys as they heated some really big stones. When they were ready we covered them with a flat basin of palm leaves, which we filled with sweet potatoes and vegetables. We covered them with more leaves and then layered the meat on top. The next layer was peeled bananas and potatoes. Then more palm leaves, before the whole affair was soaked with water. The mound of food and stones was covered by a plastic tarp, which in turn they covered with earth. It sealed everything like an oven and an hour or so later it was uncovered. Faint with hunger, I tucked in. It may sound like an unusual collection of flavours, but God it tasted good. It was chucking it down with rain again, so we moved in from the garden and piled the food into bowls. I sat gazing about me in wonder, not quite believing I was really here. Papua is an amazing place, full of history and tradition – there was a strangeness about it I'd not come across elsewhere. I loved it, and tomorrow I would be in my element, riding a dirt bike right across the mountains.

I woke to overcast skies and a tropical chill in the air. I also woke with nerves in my stomach, a few of those old butterflies about the ride ahead. It's always good to be a little nervous before you get on a motorbike; you never know what's going to happen and it's important to keep your wits about you and not get complacent.

Claudio and I were hooking up with a dirt bike club from Lae. We would be riding to a place called Betty's Lodge on the slopes of Mount Wilhelm, which at almost 15,000 feet is the highest point in PNG. Betty's Lodge is a sort of hostel-cum-hotel, run by a lady called Betty Higgins. We were supposed to be meeting up with Emmanuel, a bloke from Madang who would guide us along the Bundi Track, a stretch of really rough road, to a place called Bundi Junction. We had been told that the road was impassable, in places completely washed out, so that even in a 4×4 there was no way anyone would get through. Sam was going ahead in a 4×4 and Emmanuel was coming from the other direction in a 4×4, and right now the chances of making it back to the coast by that route did not look particularly hopeful. Having said that, it was a bit like the cyclone warnings we had been given south of Brisbane – some people were telling us horror stories while others said the road would be fine. And some even said that no one had used the Bundi Track in years.

Anyway, we would see how it was when we got to the lodge and discovered whether Emmanuel had made it. In the meantime there was a whole bunch of guys we were riding with. The bikes were full-on enduros, and Daniel, unofficial leader of the Lae club, had arranged a couple of Yamahas for Claudio and me.

I was itching to get going. We'd had a great couple of days here, but this was fantastic bike country and I wanted to be moving again. While I was getting kitted out with boots and body armour, Daniel had a word with Claudio. 'I hope Charley's going to lead,' he said. 'Show us how it's done. He's been around the world, done a few kilometres, so we ought to let him lead the way.'

Fine by me. I had no idea what level these guys were at and I didn't know the way, but the Yamaha I was riding was so perfectly balanced the front wheel seemed to come up all by itself. I was feeling good, my stomach was healing nicely after my off in Australia, and I was really up for the ride. We were on tarmac to begin with and everywhere we went people came rushing out, yelling at us to pull wheelies. It would have been rude not to oblige, so I popped a couple of second-gear monsters that I managed to keep going for what felt like miles, but might have been seventy metres. It was brilliant fun, the most I've had on a bike for a long time. I had Claudio alongside me and a bunch of locals from Papua New Guinea following the pair of us. How cool is that?

The country was stunning – like the highlands in Ethiopia, only this was rainforest with water tumbling in runaway rivers and palm trees soaked by torrents that came down so hard whole tracts of land had been washed away. The mountain tops lay hidden in mist, and gazing across their flanks I thought about John Leahy's dad and the mud men of Komunive.

We went from tarmac to dirt and from dirt to glassy mud and potholes – great troughs of water where the back end of my bike was skipping from side to side. Up on the foot pegs I slithered around ever-tightening bends, where we had to watch for villagers wandering on the road, some of them a little the worse for drink. We were mobbed whenever we stopped, and most people seemed really friendly. There was one guy who was so enthusiastic that he was shouting at the camera. He told us we were welcome in Papua New Guinea – we should feel welcome and be free. He told us that in all the years he had lived in the village, he had never seen so many motorbikes.

There were other places, though, where it was pretty nerve-racking. The crowds swamped us and a few people were more than a little hostile. As I rode through one town, this big guy stepped from the crowd and whacked me across the arm with a long stick. It hurt like hell, knocked me off balance and I almost crashed. I remembered how cautious Koi the truck driver had been: and yesterday, on the way to visit the mud men, we'd passed a market where a couple of women were tearing lumps out of each other. Before we got here we had heard all sorts of stories, of course, so perhaps I shouldn't have been surprised.

I realised now that I didn't want to be riding at night. After dark the drink would really be flowing and I had a feeling that's when things could kick off.

As it turned out, it was pretty much dark by the time we arrived at Betty's Lodge and found Sam waiting for us. We had stopped for fuel in a town a couple of hours down the road and it wasn't obvious which way we should continue, even from Daniel's map. We were trying to figure it out when this guy on a bike showed up, a local fellow with an old open-face helmet. He said he'd just come down from Betty's Lodge and would show us the way. The road was incredibly slippery, and one or two of the local lads came off. Not me this time, thankfully. I had my confidence back and was having a great time. I was concentrating, mind you. There was the odd rank-looking barrier on the worst of the hairpins, but apart from that it was sheer and ragged cliffs, waterfalls tumbling to the valley below.

Claudio was right behind me and riding really well. Glancing back, I thought of the ground we had covered since we left Horn Island. I thought about this road and how challenging it was, and wondered what more the Bundi Track could hold in store.

7

Until the Baby Laughs

BIKERS WEREN'T REGULAR VISITORS to the Lodge. Betty, a small woman with bright, cheerful eyes, explained that most of her customers were adventurers who came up the road on foot – the lodge had become a sort of base camp for people preparing to climb Mount Wilhelm. Over a breakfast of good, hot porridge Betty told us that in all the time she had been living there, we were the first motorcyclists she'd seen. Perhaps it might be the start of a whole new line of business.

Daniel had been brilliant. He had organised this route through the mountains, an adventure as much for him and his mates as it was for us. With all our doubts about the Bundi Track, it really did feel like we were heading into the unknown. Emmanuel had not made it through, which was a problem because Sam and Robin had planned to return to Madang with him in his truck, while Claudio and I carried on with the bikes.

We'd made contact with Emmanuel through Nancy Sullivan, a woman we'd been in touch with before we left London. An artist from New York, Nancy came out to PNG after the stock market crash in 1987. She runs a private consultancy working in what she calls 'applied anthropology', which basically means she teaches New Guineans to study their own people, instead of someone coming in from England or America to do it. Nancy was a mine of information on what we might accomplish here in Papua.

Anyway, the pertinent factor right then was the road. Emmanuel had only got as far as a village on the other side of the mountains and Sam and Robin had no alternative but to go back the way we had come – all the way to Goroka – then take another route that skirted the eastern highlands to the Lae/Madang highway. It was agreed that we'd meet up again at Bundi Junction and hopefully by then we would have come across Emmanuel.

After the short ride the previous afternoon I was really up for it. This should be an amazing day. It would also be our last day on motorbikes for a while and I was determined to make the most of it. I had a feeling it would be tough, but I had faith in my ability and in Claudio's too. He was his usual phlegmatic self, of course – if he fell off, he fell off, and whatever hazards and obstacles we faced, we faced. But then this was the guy who had spent six months secretly filming across the border.

Leaving the lodge, we re-crossed the bridge over the creek and pulled wheelies all the way down an overgrown airstrip. We had to negotiate a series of steep climbs and descents. The going was slow, the track really narrow and very rocky to begin with, lots of big stones and loose shale, easy to get a puncture or even buckle a wheel rim.

Gradually, though, the terrain changed, and the big rocks were replaced by soft, sandy mud and potholes. We climbed out of the jungle briefly and rounding a sharp bend skidded to a halt. The road ahead was blocked by a pile of tree branches. Five barefoot men with machetes stood in front of it, their ringleader a little bearded guy in a cap. He scowled at us, shifting the machete from one hand to the other. According to Daniel, these were local villagers, paid by the government to keep the road clear and open. Apparently they also liked to create roadblocks, stopping cars to demand money from the occupants. Last night Betty had told us that every time she goes down to Goroka she gets hit for anything between 6 and 150 kina.

These guys wanted $50 to let us through. 'We fix the road,' the bearded guy kept saying, 'we fix the road.'

'Wait a minute,' I surprised myself by piping up right away. 'When did you fix the road . . . today?'

He nodded.

'Where? Where did you fix it?'

He gestured across the valley with his machete.

'No, you didn't.' I was shaking my head. 'You know what? I think you heard us coming and quickly blocked the road. That's not a land slip, it's a bunch of sticks. You just want to make a fast buck for doing nothing, don't you?'

Suddenly Luke, one of the guys riding with us, was right up in the bearded guy's face. With his helmet, goggles and body armour, he looked and sounded menacing. Luke was an Australian living in Lae and was fluent in the national language.

Ignoring the machete, he was gesticulating angrily and telling the guy exactly what he thought of him. He told him they had been paid to keep the road open but nobody had been able to get through in over a year, so what the hell did he think he was doing demanding money from us? He really was animated, yelling at the guy that he could whistle for his fifty bucks. If they didn't shift the roadblock, then we would.

For a moment I wondered if it would all kick off. These guys had weapons, but in our body armour and helmets we looked like a bunch of stormtroopers from *Star Wars*. The bearded guy's mates didn't seem to have much stomach for a fight, though. Two of them were no more than teenagers and seemed more interested in waving to the camera. Luke was still going for it and the bearded guy was looking more and more bewildered. In the end he muttered something to the younger guys and the road was cleared.

Engines snarling, we covered them in a cloud of dust and sped off down the road – we hadn't given them a penny. I thought about what would have happened if it had been a car coming along with one or two people in it. What choice would they have had when confronted by men with machetes? I thought about poor Betty, a woman on her own, robbed every time she tried to go down the mountain.

Oh well, we were through now and the road was gnarly enough that I had to give it all my concentration. When I say it was gnarly, of course I mean that it was delicious. It was beautiful! Everything you want on a dirt bike – steep and slippery, dusty and dry and yet damp and muddy in places too.

We climbed hill after hill and every time we stopped for a breather Daniel told me that Bundi Junction was just over the next rise. By lunchtime we had crossed plenty of 'next rises', however, and I reckoned we were only halfway. Stopping in a village, we bought some passion fruit and tried to decide what to do about one of the bikes that had broken down. It was remote up here and we knew that no trucks could get through. Then we spotted a green Toyota pick-up driven by a heavy-set guy with a braid in his beard and a beanie hat . . . Emmanuel! This village was as far as he had got. He told us we could load the bike on his truck and he would get it to Bundi Junction.

I wasn't quite sure how he was going to do that – the Toyota already had six or eight guys in the back. But Emmanuel said there was more than enough room for one little motorbike and between us we got it loaded and somehow found room for the rider too. Emmanuel told us he made the trip at least this far once a week and there was nothing to worry us between here and the junction.

By this point quite a crowd had gathered, and we'd been chatting to some of the locals. There were one or two piglets running about – cute little things, with speckled backs and delicate-looking hooves. We already knew how much people prized them – I'd seen a woman with a piglet on a lead yesterday, it squealed its heart out when I picked it up. We had also heard that if a mother pig didn't suckle for whatever reason, it wasn't uncommon for a woman to suckle the piglet instead. Mind you, we had also heard all sorts of other stuff – head hunters, cannibals, initiation ceremonies where men apparently cut elephant's ears in their foreskins . . . I was sure most of it was rubbish, so this tale about piglets and women had to be pretty tall, I reckoned. But chatting to the locals, we came across a young woman with a child on her shoulders, chewing at an ear of corn. She told us that she had suckled a pig. Daniel asked her what she meant exactly. She just smiled and shrugged.

'The mother wouldn't let the baby to her teat,' she said, 'so I give him my teat instead.'

I had never heard of anything like it, but there she was and why would anyone lie about something like that?

'Ah, what's the big deal?' Daniel slapped me on the shoulder. 'In England you guys share your organs with pigs.'

'No, I think that was South Africa,' I told him.

We rode on and on. We crossed rivers on wooden bridges and climbed steep-sided hills where the land slipped away and the drop was sheer for hundreds of feet. We came to a bridge where there were no boards, just open ironwork and a river raging below. Walking out over the metal grid, I gazed down at the rapids, wondering how we were going to make it across. But then I noticed there were two narrow iron rails that ran to the other side. The gap between them was just enough for the bike tyres to sit in and I figured that one at a time, perhaps, we could wheel them across.

That's exactly what we did, and twenty minutes later we were riding through elephant grass that drifted in great waves across the road. It was tough going, up on the pegs, down on the seat – lots of back brake and throttle. Riding off road is all about momentum: if you keep that going you're fine; slow down too much, you lose grip and you're screwed.

We climbed another mountain, slithering down the other side in a switchback of savage twists and turns. We forded shallow rivers and passed beneath a wild waterfall. Whenever I could I popped the front wheel. Emmanuel was still right behind us in the truck and so far he had negotiated the road with no real drama. There had been the odd land slip, and we met three guys with an axe and shovel between them, who really had been mending the road.

But not far from Bundi Junction, we had to stop at another bridge where there were no boards. We walked the bikes across as we had before. Then the truck tried to make it. Emmanuel eased the Toyota onto the rails in first gear, his head bobbing at the open window. It all seemed to be going fine, until all of a sudden the wheels slipped and the back end slumped, shifting so hard it dislodged a crosswise section completely. Claudio and I were already on the other side. I saw Emmanuel blanch as, for a nanosecond, the truck just seemed to hang there. Then he floored it, stamped on the throttle and the wheels span, caught the crosspiece and somehow he got enough purchase to make it the rest of the way.

'No problem,' he said breezily as he got out and inspected the damage to the bridge. 'No problem at all . . . truck's all right, bike in the back is all right. No problem.'

I could tell by the look in his eye, though, that for a moment there he thought he was going down.

By the time we finally crested the last hill I was pretty weary. It had been a great ride, with loads of memorable moments. One gully in particular was surreal and beautiful, with massive swarms of butterflies flying against my goggles as I rode. But still, it was a relief finally to see Sam and Robin waiting for us, delighted that we had met up with Emmanuel and made it unscathed. Sam took me to one side and told me that he and Robin had had their own little drama as well.

'We were in this village,' he said, 'somewhere on the Rumu Pass, and we got a flat tyre. It was all right, we had a spare and I changed the wheel while Robin filmed it.'

'What happened?'

'Well, nothing to begin with. We had a few people watching but then from down the hill this guy starts yelling about the camera. He came up the hill, shouting and screaming about the bloody camera. He was a little drunk I think, and he was swinging this big iron bar. He told us to turn off the camera, to stop filming or he'd smash up the truck and us along with it.'

'So what did you do?' I was remembering Luke getting in the machete man's face.

'The only thing we could do,' Sam said. 'Stopped filming, got in the truck and high-tailed it out of there.'

We said our goodbyes to Daniel and the other guys in the rain. In the true spirit of *By Any Means*, it had followed us right across the mountains and was really hosing down. I was soaking and there was no chance of getting dry because the only space in Emmanuel's truck was the bit of flatbed the broken-down bike had occupied.

A couple of hours later, wet but happy, we rolled into Madang and pulled up outside a large house next to a construction site. We were greeted by Nancy Sullivan, an energetic-looking blonde woman wearing a print dress and carrying her young son on her hip. He was around five years old – an adopted Papuan boy – and wearing sunglasses with Elvis sideburns attached to them.

'Hey, boys,' Nancy said, 'great to see you.' She was all smiles. 'Come on in and make yourselves at home. There's food, and beer in the fridge. There's even a gin and tonic if you fancy one.'

Nancy, who had been such a help to us when we'd been preparing for this leg of the trip, was putting us up for a couple of nights. The house was spacious, with the living area on the upper floors and the balcony enclosed with mosquito netting so we could get some air without being bitten to death. Gratefully I accepted a G&T and slumped down in a chair. Nancy told us that tomorrow was the Queen's birthday and although that was taken seriously here in PNG, she didn't think much would be happening in Madang. But the day after that, she had arranged a river trip – we were heading up the Sepik River from Bogia to Gapun, a tiny community of thirty houses where a linguistic anthropologist called Don Kulick was conducting a study.

There was, however, a potential fly in the ointment. Earlier that evening Nancy had received a text from the guy who owned the boat we would travel in, Milson. He told her he had been shot at by bandits and was no longer sure he was coming. My thoughts immediately turned to head hunters and cannibals, but Nancy assured us that Milson would show up at some point and all would be fine.

'The guy was shot at, Nancy!' I said. 'I'm not sure *I* would turn up if someone shot at me.'

'Don't worry about it.' She flapped a hand at me. 'It happens all the time. He wasn't hurt and he'll be here, so there is no need to worry.'

Security is a major issue in Papua New Guinea, particularly in the towns. Nancy told us that there were lots of 'settlers' in Madang – people from the highlands who had come down to look for work. But there was no work. There *were* lots of properties to break into, though. The police were pretty ineffective, so people paid private security firms to patrol the streets. It was big business.

We spent the next day just mooching about and buying gifts for the villagers we would be visiting. Keen to find out a little more about the private security, Claudio and I went on a brief tour of the rain-soaked streets with a guy called Norbert Belele, who worked for Bitamu Security Services. He took us to meet one of the guys on foot patrol and explained that his men carried only a radio and a baton. They were not allowed to carry firearms, although many of the burglars did. I asked Norbert what happened if they came across someone with a gun and he told me his men would not confront them. Often just the fact that the would-be burglar had been spotted was enough – even an armed man would scuttle away and the security guys would call the police. I wasn't sure how that worked, given he'd already told me the police only work in the daytime. Anyway, we had someone outside our house all night and, according to Nancy, the private firms were the only way to guarantee any kind of security.

Nancy had suggested we should buy machetes or files as presents for the villagers. They used machetes to cut back the grass from around their homes and needed files to keep them sharp, so we bought a stack of both as well as balloons for the kids.

'What are they like, the people in – what did you call the village – Gapun, was it?' Nancy nodded. 'Are they head hunters . . . cannibals? I mean, I didn't think any of those stories were true, but then I didn't think that women breastfed piglets either so . . .'

'Charley,' she said. 'There are no cannibals, not any more.'

'Were there ever?'

'Oh yes, of course there were. Back in the 1970s there was a tribe in the eastern highlands that ate human brains.'

'You're joking!'

'No, no, the women ate them during mortuary ceremonies.'

I was staring at her.

'You see, the women in particular didn't get a lot of protein and the men allowed them to eat the brains of their relatives when they were laying out the bodies. They'd chip off the back of the skull and take the brains out anyway, so it was just another step to cook and eat them. There is plenty of protein in the brain and it was one way of getting what they needed.'

I wasn't sure if she was pulling my leg, and I shot a glance at Claudio. He nodded.

'The interesting thing was the kids,' Nancy went on. 'Most of the women performing the ceremony would have a two-year-old on their knee and to keep them quiet they'd be fed some of the brains. Now thirty years later, some of those grown-up children have developed a kind of human mad cow disease.'

That night over dinner Nancy gave us the full anthropological tour. From the women who ate brains we moved on to discussing various tribes and tribal customs – grisly-sounding initiations where the men tried to distance themselves from their mother's blood and horrendous rites of passage including circumcision for boys in their late teens (with details of the various ways of cutting a foreskin that made us squirm in our seats). Then there was something altogether different, where the men rammed canes down their throats and scraped the inside till it bled. She told how the men in some tribes had a fear of the menstrual cycle, and once a month the women were banished to a separate house.

The next day there had been no more word from Milson the boatman. Nancy's assurances that he would show were beginning to look a little optimistic and even she was getting concerned that he hadn't turned up. The problem was that he was not just the boatman; he was supposed to bring down a van for us to travel up to Bogia.

None of us were overly worried, mind you. This was Papua New Guinea, after all, and what we were told one minute generally changed the next. We were confident that not only would we get a bus, but a boat as well – whether it was Milson's or not.

'Charley,' Nancy said, 'I think this will be quite a day. You're going to need the resourcefulness of the Papua New Guinean. I've arranged for Arthur and Dixon to go with you, they're friends of mine – local boys who travel between here and Bogia all the time. And Emmanuel is coming too, so you couldn't have better security.'

That was fine by me, the more local knowledge we had the better, and I already knew how valuable security was. We had the team all right . . . we just didn't have a means of getting where we wanted to go.

Nancy took us into town to try to find a PMV – or Public Motor Vehicle – a little bus, a bit like the dolmus I'd driven in Turkey. They're privately owned and the operator waits until the last seat is taken before he goes anywhere. We had been told various different stories about how long it would take to get up the coast to Bogia – some people said two hours, others three, others still said four. There were plenty of PMVs in the market area, a vast and dusty space between rows of ramshackle buildings, but most of them wouldn't be leaving until that afternoon. People came into town in the morning, did their shopping, and left again after lunch. So that was the timetable the PMV drivers liked to keep to.

Not to be deterred, Sam set about trying to locate a bus that would get us to Bogia in time to get on a boat. Meanwhile, Nancy pointed out a young man in the crowd that had, as usual, gathered around us. His name was Herbert and he was Tari, a tribe from the most remote region of the central highlands. It was one of the areas where the men were afraid of women's blood, and Nancy being Nancy, she slipped her arm around his shoulders and quietly told him she was menstruating. I have never seen anyone's face fall quite so far quite so quickly! He looked terrified, backing away from under her arm until she told him she was joking.

After that he and his mates could not stop talking. They were holding court for the camera, jabbering away nineteen to the dozen while the local men from Madang just looked on in a kind of laid-back silence. I asked Herbert about initiation rites and he told me that all the boys in his tribe did was grow their hair. It sounded pretty tame. He assured me it was meaningful, though, and when a man was deemed a man, women were no longer allowed to touch it.

'Not touch your hair? But, Herbert,' I said, 'what about when you make love? You know . . .'

He stared at me for a moment then proceeded to assure me that when he was making love the women did not need to touch his hair – the rest of him was all the man they could want.

According to Nancy, the Madang men had no such hang-ups or initiation rites. The lowlanders were beach guys, and like beach guys the world over, they just liked to hang out and make love under the stars.

After much negotiation on Sam's part, we finally found what we thought was our way of getting to Bogia. Given that most of the regular PMVs weren't going anywhere until later, he arranged to hire one. The driver struck a deal, then jumped behind the wheel to go and tell the owner. We never saw him again.

It was getting later and later, and in the end Emmanuel suggested that he go and get his truck and we'd all pile into that. I liked and trusted Emmanuel. He did what he said he would do, and he'd survived the bridge crossing yesterday. Given that the road to Bogia was where Milson had been shot at, being driven by a guy like Emmanuel made perfect sense to me.

We finally had a plan of action in place. Then, lo and behold, Arthur got a call from Milson. Our boat guy. He was on his way after all, and he would be with us in twenty minutes.

'What happened, Arthur?' I asked. 'Why is he coming now, all of a sudden?'

Arthur shrugged. 'He was always coming.'

'You mean we got our wires crossed, we made a mistake?'

He nodded. 'It's not his van,' he explained. 'He's in a PMV bringing stuff from Bogia and they made a lot of stops on the way.'

Ah well. All that mattered now was that we got moving soon because we still had a full day of travelling ahead of us. Don, the linguistic anthropologist, was expecting us tonight and there was no way of contacting him – the village was a good distance up the Sepik and even if he had a mobile phone there would be no signal.

We had hoped to be on the road by 8 a.m. but it was almost noon by the time Milson arrived. He was a taciturn, capable-looking guy. Loading our gear into the PMV, we quickly said our goodbyes to Nancy.

'Do you think Charley will be OK?' Claudio asked her. 'I mean, the coast road is where the shooting took place, and even if we make it to the river, he's useless in a boat.'

'Actually, I think it will be an absolute disaster,' she told him. 'That's it, Claudio, the end of the programme, we're sending him off into the abyss . . .'

Joking or not (and I hoped she was joking), I had that little gem ringing in my ears as we set off towards Bogia and the bridge where Milson and his mates had been ambushed. The coast road alternated between spectacular views of the sea and thick, soaking jungle. To begin with the road was pretty good, albeit single lane with no markings, but a couple of hours from Madang it narrowed into a thick grove of palms at a river crossing. The bridge was solid enough, but there was room for only one vehicle. Asking the driver to stop, Milson and I got out. This was where the shooting had happened.

'We were in a car,' he said, pointing towards the bridge. 'We come up here and two men are in front of the bridge.' Gesturing now, he pointed beyond the bus. 'Two more back there behind the car. They just stepped out of the trees.' He went on to tell me how the guys in front fired two shots to make them stop and the guys behind fired a couple more. Then they took all their money.

It was incredible. Highway robbery right where I was standing. I walked across the bridge, the river swirling in mud-coloured eddies under my feet. I could see betel-nut stains where the bandits had spat the juice.

Back in the bus we motored on and the road remained reasonable until we got close to Bogia. There it fell apart – the forest was really dense and the tarmac became dirt and stones. We slowed to a snail's pace at a series of brimming potholes. They spread the width of the road and were deep enough to beach the front of the van if we weren't very careful.

We made it, though, the only misadventure when I asked the driver to stop so I could take a pee and they took off without me.

It turned out that Milson ran a pretty slick operation. His boat was docked at a little place called Boroi, deep in the jungle and accessed from a pitted track blocked by a bamboo pole that we had to lift to get the van through. Beyond it the track snaked through the trees before opening on to the inlet and the sea. There were two large houses made of grass and built on stilts at the edge of the inlet, and just beyond them I could see Milson's boat, an open dinghy with a pretty new-looking 60 hp outboard. I began to think that this might actually work.

It was the middle of the afternoon and I doubted we would make Gapun before it got dark, but the river was before us and I was seized by a sudden sense of adventure. We could do this, we could make it unscathed, if only the Boorman boat curse didn't strike again.

I couldn't quite believe that we'd be that lucky. But as it turned out we were. The trip up the inlet to the mouth of the Sepik was uneventful, if you can call being in an open boat with your mates in the middle of absolutely nowhere uneventful. It was wonderful. We zipped along, the water calm and the breeze keeping us fairly cool. As the sun set gradually behind the trees, the sky became a haze of purple and blue, one of the most spectacular sunsets I think I've ever seen. All along the banks people came out of grass huts to wave at us.

At the mouth of the Sepik we had to stop – the tide was low and we had to wait for it to rise again so we could make it up the section of river where we would disembark for Gapun. Milson knew the area but he didn't know every individual waterway and the Sepik is littered with forks and tributaries. The village was not right on the water either so we wouldn't be able to spot any lights from the boat. We needed a local guide to take us to not only the right tributary, but the landing point.

It was quite dark now, the canopies of trees lit up by millions of fireflies. I wondered how we would negotiate the rest of the journey in the pitch dark. Milson seemed pretty relaxed, though, and his sense of calm inspired confidence. Of course, the local villagers had come out and were trying to persuade us to stay the night with them instead of pressing on in the darkness, but we were eager to reach our destination.

The tide came in, our guide arrived and we were back in the boat for the final leg. It was hot now and humid, the surface of the water buzzing with insects and a cacophony of cicadas lifting from the trees. We entered the narrow inlet with palms close to the water on either side. This was crocodile country. Keeping our hands out of harm's way, we scanned the darkness for points of light glinting in the deep.

Milson was steering and the engine was on really low revs now. The guide was in the bow using a pole to make sure we were avoiding the shallow stretches. Clearly he knew what he was doing and half an hour later we came to the jetty and unloaded. I was feeling pretty exhausted now, but we still had to hike through swamp and jungle to the village. It was pitch black, the only light what we could muster from head torches. I set off across the forest floor with my pack strapped on my back and another bag hung around my neck. We seemed to walk for hours, through thick bush and damp palms, over log bridges and into the swamp. Much of the way I was knee deep in black and muddy water. 'How deep does it have to be for a crocodile?' I asked nobody in particular.

No one answered.

We made it. No crocs, no snakes and nobody drowning in the swamp. I had no idea where we were or what anything looked like. I had no idea how far we had come or where the river was, but suddenly a torch was shining in my face and a slim guy with sandy hair and glasses was peering at me.

'Charley?'

'Don?'

'We thought you weren't coming.'

'I know it's late but we got held up in Madang. Look, I'm sorry, but we thought we'd try and make it rather than wait till tomorrow.' I looked him up and down: neat shorts, clean shirt and immaculate hair. 'I must say, Don, you look very chic for a man who just stepped out of the jungle.'

Don showed us to the house where he was staying. He had been to Gapun on four occasions since his first trip back in the 1980s, but this time he was staying for 'an extended visit'. He described the village as an 'isolate', one of hundreds in Papua New Guinea. The Gapun people, roughly two hundred of them, have their own language, which is different from anything else that's spoken anywhere in the country. In the old days the Gapuns learned the languages of some of the other villages, but nobody learned theirs – apparently it was too difficult – and because of that it was dying. It was what Don called an 'undescribed' language, and his task was to attempt to describe it.

There are some three million people in Papua New Guinea and over a thousand different languages; not dialects but actual languages. They are as different as Basque is from Russian. Don told us that if you walk an hour or so in any direction you'll come to a village where the people speak a completely different language from the people you just left. His mission was to document the Gapun language, to write it down before it was lost. Even the young children were no longer learning it; they spoke the national language. Samson, the leader of the village, was conscious that they lived in the modern world and had to become part of it.

Gapun was an idyllic place, a strip of land cut out of the rainforest in the middle of a swamp, where palms grew along with betel-nut trees and the spiky sago that gave them most of their food. We spent the night in Don's hut – Claudio finding a place for his hammock, and me on the floor in my sleeping bag. I was pretty knackered and fell asleep straight away. By seven the following morning I was up and about, taking a stroll along the thoroughfare that separated the houses.

It was amazing. I've never seen anywhere quite like it. There were some thirty houses, all the same, all on stilts and lining each side of this grassy road that the villagers called 'the highway'. When Don first came here the houses were individual and snuggled in among betel-nut and palm trees, and it remained that way until 2007. Then they decided they wanted the place to look more like a town so they cleared the highway of trees and built new houses, all of which were the same.

The thatched houses had walls made from dried and woven palm leaves. Inside each there was a single wooden floor divided into sections for dining, cooking and sleeping. The way the village was laid out – with each house the same, the gardens immaculate, saplings in the middle of the highway with fencing around their trunks – it looked like a slice of suburbia in the middle of the rainforest.

'They want to be modern,' Don explained. He broke off to point out where a woman with a shovel was picking up pig shit from the square of grass around her house, muttering irritably as she did so. I saw her toss it into the bush.

'The women have to do that every morning,' Don said. 'Their first job, and they hate it, especially if they don't have any pigs or dogs, because that means it was someone else's animal that shat on their property. It can cause all sorts of arguments – you know, the neighbour-to-neighbour altercations that occur over the world.

Just yesterday I woke to one woman yelling about the people in the house next to mine.'

'So it's normal life here then,' I said. 'Just like anywhere else.'

'Oh yes.'

'But how come there are so many languages?'

'It's a good question,' he said. 'Originally anthropologists thought it was because the people were isolated, nobody coming into contact with anyone else. I suppose you could argue that that might have been the case in the highlands, but down here on the Sepik people moved about in canoes and have always come into contact with other villages.'

'So why then?'

'We think it's basically because Papua New Guineans like to be different. They're pragmatic, practical people and they like to be perceived as different. One very demonstrative way of being different, of course, is to speak another language.'

He explained that these days the people saw a common language as progress. The white people speak a different language altogether and villagers believe that if they can speak the white people's language, then the wealth of the Western world might be opened to them.

'It's not just the language, though; it's religion,' Don went on. 'The New Guineans believe that the whites have a better god than them, which is why they are richer. And some of the missionaries are not at all bashful about stoking that fire. They will lie openly to the people and promise them that if they become Christian they will get the cargo that goes with it.' He smiled then. 'Like I said, New Guineans are pragmatic. If they think something new will be beneficial to them, they'll try it. That goes for religion along with anything else. They might become Catholics for a while and when that doesn't work they become Seventh Day Adventists or one of the fundamentalist groups that have a foothold here.'

We ate a massive breakfast of sago, vegetables and pork. Sago, made from a particular kind of palm, is a staple of the Papuan diet. The men spend all day in the bush cutting and transporting the stuff back to the village. They cross swampy inlets on log bridges then walk barefoot to get to it. The plant looks like a giant, skinny cactus – the outer skin covered with razor-sharp spines. They cut it down, skin it, cut out the flesh then load it into cylindrical hods they cut from the trunks. At the end of the day the men will bring back eighty kilos of sago slung over their shoulder.

Then it's down to the women to take the flesh and pulverise it for hours and hours until the starch separates. It congeals into what looks like a log stripped of its bark. The gloopy stuff that we ate is produced by crumbling a chunk and mixing it with boiling water. They serve it in great basins and I have to say it looks and tastes like wallpaper paste. If you swallow without chewing you can just about avoid gagging on it.

All the time he is in Gapun, Don is 100 per cent dependent on the villagers. They feed and house him and in return he records their language. He loves what he does and sees the anthropologist as someone who's there to listen and observe. Unlike a missionary or journalist, he has no agenda. He's fascinated by what these people do and how they live, but mostly by what they talk about. He is determined to keep the language alive. He asked the people to bring him plants and animals so he can describe them in the vernacular. While I was there one man brought him a bat, but he's had all sorts of insects, a baby crocodile, a massive spider, snakes, rats, everything.

We had met Samson the moment we arrived – as the village leader that was customary. His vision is to bring cars here. Back in 2007 he had wanted a town for his people rather than the old village. He wants a water supply and a power supply and vehicles to take them to the landing point where we had left the boat. It was an example of what Don had been saying about pragmatism. These people wanted what other New Guineans had, and Samson was an enthusiastic leader determined to get it. Historically they had sold sago, but that brought in paltry sums. Now they were producing and selling small amounts of cocoa, which after only three months was worth triple the annual return they got for the sago.

They sought to be modern and yet they had their own very particular customs. Don showed us a couple of what he termed 'maternity huts' on the periphery of the village. He explained that women go into the bush to give birth; indeed, one woman had done so last night. When the baby is born they take them to the maternity huts where other women bring them food and the men are not permitted to see them. They consider blood to be 'hot', or powerful, and a woman who has just given birth is too 'powerful' to come home right away. She stays in the maternity hut, unseen by her husband or the rest of her family, because she could hurt or even kill a man just by being in his presence.

'How long do they have to stay in the maternity huts?' I asked him.

'They stay until their baby can laugh, Charley.'

'Laugh?'

'That's right . . . a couple of months generally. They say that when a baby is strong enough to survive it will laugh, and that's when its mother brings it home.'

Don likes to give something back to the villagers in return for their hospitality. He brings medicine to treat a contagious disease that affects the children's skin. There is a particular fungus that grows on some of the palms here, which creates a skin condition a bit like ringworm. The children's bodies become covered in a scaly irritation that is really inhibiting. It's easily treatable but the medicine is expensive, so whenever he comes to the village, Don makes sure he brings enough to treat them.

'They're a tactile people,' he explained. 'If you watch they're always touching one another; children are hugged and caressed all the time. They're never kissed, mind you, they don't kiss here – it's considered disgusting. But they hold the children all the time and a child with the "alligator" disease, as they call it, never gets any physical affection. Nobody wants to hold a child with scaly skin.'

With that he grabbed a bongo drum from a shelf, and outside on the steps he summoned the children to his surgery by beating it.

8
Grandma's Hair

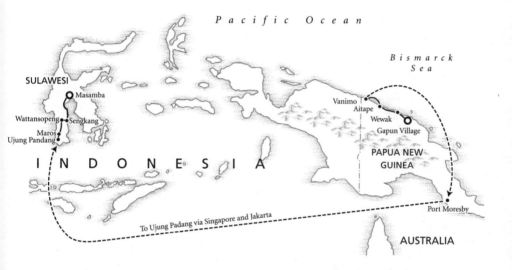

WE ONLY HAD a couple of days left in Papua New Guinea, and I was determined to make the most of them. Today – our twenty-fifth day out of Sydney – we were aiming for Vanimo, a town on the border with West Papua. It was here that we would learn whether we would be able to cross into the Indonesian-occupied territory. It didn't look promising, but it was sure to be an interesting journey anyway – travelling by canoe then a couple of PMVs and finally an open dinghy.

We rose early, eager to get going. The walk back to the river was much easier in daylight, of course. On our way in we had been dead tired, knee deep in the swamp in the pitch black with no idea where we were going. This time we could see the walkways and log bridges and we had half the village accompanying us. Kids were running around and everyone was singing. It only took twenty minutes through the forest and it was a beautiful walk – a highlight of the journey so far and one I'll never forget.

A local man called Melchio and his wife Margaret were waiting with a couple of canoes, one a long and narrow dugout canoe, another fitted with an outboard motor. We loaded our bags into the boats and said goodbye to Don and Samson. I wished the village leader all the best with his plans for the future. It had been a fantastic couple of days but I was looking forward to the next three days of travelling.

It was turning into a beautiful day – the water calm and flat, the sun shining. Melchio took us back down the narrow tributary to the inlet, the canoe zipping along merrily with its big motor. We were heading for the town of Angoram, where we hoped to take another PMV to a coastal town called Wewak. I'd heard it had the most amazing beach, but I was most looking forward to the fact that, after a week of being on people's floors, I would be sleeping in a bed tonight.

Crossing the width of the inlet, Melchio guided the canoe through a tiny gap in the trees and cut through the swamp back to the main body of the Sepik. No wonder this part of the world is still so remote. I could have sailed up and down that inlet and never found my way through.

At Angoram we had to wait for the PMV. The guy in charge told me they left in the morning and returned at around one, maybe two o'clock. This was Papua New Guinea time, of course. But it did eventually arrive, after a couple of hours, and we had our ride to Wewak.

The truck was flat-fronted with a canvas tarpaulin and was not only carrying lots of people, but tinned food, corn, potatoes and rice. Once everything had been taken off, fresh goods from Angoram were loaded before we could find a place to sit. It was smoked fish mostly, a local delicacy that tasted of very little but smelled to high heaven. It was packed in large wicker baskets that took up lots of room.

I'll be completely honest – it was not a great journey. We were sitting against the back of the cab and as time went on more and more people got aboard until we were squashed up and bounced around to the point where my bum was red raw.

The beach at Wewak more than made up for it, though. As the sun went down Claudio and I took a walk along the sand and stopped for a beer at a beach house belonging to an English guy and his wife. They had been with VSO for a couple of years but stayed on when their stint was over. Twelve years on and they wake to the sound of the waves every morning and fall asleep to them every night.

I woke to the sound of birds screeching, my head filled with thoughts of West Papua. The five Australians were still being held, and given Claudio's background with the rebels, the chances of us being allowed in were looking rather less than slim. The Indonesians are very sensitive and the politics extends far beyond their government. American mining companies have a significant foothold in the country, logging companies too. There is a lot of foreign influence. In fact, you could say the place is one great open-cast mine – the land is rich in minerals and there is a lot of interest from many different places. Not a straightforward place to visit.

With kids from the VSO lodge in Goroka, Papua New Guinea.

Workers at the coffee factory in Lahamenegu.

Terrifying! (Especially the underpants).

On the way to Betty's Lodge on a road they said didn't exist any more . . .

On the bridge that nearly defeated us.

In Gapun village with
anthropologist Don Kulick.

Harvesting sago in Gapun. Not the tastiest thing I've ever eaten.

Canoes were the best way to get around here, if you knew where you were going . . .

Riding a *becak* in Makassar, Indonesia. I know where I'm going – honest!

We stumbled across this wedding ceremony as it entered its third day. No wonder the bride and groom aren't smiling.

Arriving at the UNICEF project in the remote village of Cendana Putih.

Sumarna with her son Adrianto.

Fitting the water filter that would transform Adrianto's life.

One of the dramatic saddle-shaped roofs in Rantepao, Torojoa.

The eerie burial grounds in Kete Kusu.

Me and the crew. Just kidding . . . Or am I?

On the way to Makale.

Now *this* is the way to ride! Heading for Parepare and the 'Erotic Mountain' on a 1994 Road King Harley.

I've learned on my journeys that you can't worry about these things. You certainly can't plan for them. We would just have to see what happened when we got there. It was still a two-day jaunt to the border and the plan tonight was to make it as far as Aitape in the company of Ben Keri, the owner of a flatbed 1975 Toyota lorry. We were getting the lift for free, but Ben explained we would have to share the back of the lorry with the goods he was taking north.

Our bags loaded, we drove to the local hardware store where Ben bought everything from lengths of corrugated tin to tools and nails, planks of wood, all sorts of building materials. Sitting on the loo, contemplating my still-tender arse, a thought occurred to me. Maybe the hardware store sold some sort of foam? On a mission now, I hunted down four cushions, including a particularly garish pink one, and when I presented them to the boys, the back of the truck no longer seemed so unwelcoming.

Ben had a crew with him so he was able to alternate between the passenger seat and hanging out with us. It was hot today and the four of us had floppy hats to protect us from the sun. The bed of the truck was open, the sides protected by metal rails that extended behind the cab. I spent many hours standing there with the wind in my face, watching the road unfold ahead.

There was good tarmac to begin with, but it didn't last long. Crossing a wooden bridge above a disturbingly swollen river, we hit dirt and that was as good as it got all the way to Aitape. We were in deep jungle again – surrounded by thick foliage, tall mountains and fast-flowing rivers. The truck was rolling along at thirty-five, sometimes forty. Thank God for the cushions – the suspension needed oiling and the four of us were bouncing around like crazy in the back. We forded maybe a dozen rivers before coming to one place where the road actually *was* the river. Turning downstream, we drove the shallows for a few miles before picking up the dirt again.

We had left Wewak much later than we had hoped, but then that had been the case all throughout our time in Papua New Guinea. The journey would take as long as it took and there was nothing we could do about it. Luckily Ben was good company and very knowledgeable. At one point we came across a sea of elephant grass and, rapping a fist on the roof of the cab, he got the driver to stop and we jumped down.

The elephant grass had overgrown what once had been an American airstrip, much like the one we had seen on Horn Island. We found a rusting engine from a P-47 and Ben explained that this spot was quite close to where the Japanese had surrendered to the Australian army.

Our thirteenth river crossing almost proved unlucky for us. A river too far. Back in the truck we drove until the dirt road descended into a gully of shale and sand with a fast-flowing river cutting across it. And I mean *really* fast flowing. There was a jeep on the bank, waiting to cross, the driver wandering barefoot up and down, ankle deep in the water. A couple of locals standing close by told us that three cars had tried to get across earlier only to be swept downstream. The drivers had been forced to swim for their lives.

I stared down at the wide, wild water. 'So what do we do, Ben?'

'We wait. There's nothing else we can do.'

He was right, and the level of the river wasn't going down any. In fact, it was getting higher and the current was incredibly strong. The water was riotous, brown and grey and swirling with mud and stones, bloated with rainfall from the mountains. Ben reckoned it would be a few hours at least before it started to drop. The last time I was stuck at a river crossing, in Siberia, Ewan and I had no choice but to wait all night.

So we spent the next few hours in the back of the truck or sitting on our cushions on the bank just watching the river flow by.

Whenever I got up to take a walk the water was lapping at my feet, and I began to wonder how long Ben's 'few hours' might actually turn out to be. We were due in Aitape tonight and tomorrow we were supposed to be on another boat, only this one was at sea and that worried me. There was a road from Aitape to Vanimo but it was meant to be pretty rough. An open boat hugging the coast would be a lot safer than trying to go by road.

Ben had made this trip more times than he could remember, but it had been a while since he had seen the water this high. He pointed out a smooth, black boulder that was all but submerged by the current.

'Charley,' he said, 'when the water is about halfway up that stone, it is safe to cross.'

Still the time ticked by and, glad of the cushions, we lay down on the bank to wait.

We waited and we waited. We waited a little longer. It got dark, and at 7 p.m. we were still waiting.

With the darkness came the locals, and with the locals came the beer. On both sides of the river now there were groups of drunken men. It was suddenly a little tense down there and even Ben seemed wary.

This one guy and his mate came lurching over to us. Bottles in hand they started slurring on about a bridge that had gone down on their land; they wanted compensation. Ben told me the bridge had collapsed thirty years previously and these two barely looked old enough to remember. It was the drink talking, the drink and the compensation culture that I was beginning to realise exists here. People build their homes right up against the road so if a truck swerves and hits a pig, or takes down a wall or something, they claim off the government.

A couple of hours later the river looked as though it was finally beginning to go down, although now I was wondering if we would get across before these drunks lost it completely and things really kicked off. The gangs of men were hurling insults from one side of the river to the other. They were beginning to hurl them at us too and for safety we retreated to the back of the truck. Then they started to fight among themselves – two guys were right in each other's faces, shouting and shoving. Another was circling them and when I saw him pull a flick-knife I thought things were going to get nasty. It calmed down in the end, though, and there was a lull in the yelling from both sides.

Finally, Ben could see enough of the rock he had been talking about and said we could go. Only now he wasn't sure we *should*, because the drunks on the other side had started shouting again. He thought they might attack the first vehicle that tried to cross, so he suggested we go downriver, camp out the rest of the night and come back in the morning. It was so late now and we were so tired that we were resigned to doing whatever he told us. But then the jeep started and with a couple of guys in the back it lurched into the water. The driver pointed the nose upstream a little way then came down at an angle to keep from being broadside to the current. We watched through the darkness as, with the water rushing over his wheel arches, he inched his way across.

No sooner was he on the far side than our driver fired up the engine. Ben told us to grab a few handfuls of stones in case we had to defend ourselves. We did that and, taking the route the jeep had followed, we finally got across. Fortunately no one attacked us. Indeed, one kind soul used a torch to guide us in. It was after 11 p.m. now, though, and it was another five hours before we lurched into Aitape.

At four in the morning a small motel was the only place we could find. It was a bit of a dive, the beds as hard as the back of the truck and the showers so foul smelling I gagged. But who needed a shower? The downpour the following morning was torrential, hammering against the tin roofs so loudly I could barely hear myself think. From the veranda I could see the ocean where waves were rolling in great foaming whitecaps and I imagined spending four or five hours in an open boat without any life jackets.

I hate bloody boats. So far we had been lucky with the Boorman boat curse, but surely this was tempting fate.

Not according to Joyce Rainbubus. She came over in the boat we were supposed to be taking, a large open dinghy crewed by our translator Josh's brother and piloted by his uncle John. They were from Sissano, a village on the coast between Aitape and Vanimo that had been hit by a tsunami in 1998.

Joyce assured us the crossing would be fine. The sea might look choppy, but once we got beyond the breakers there was nothing that would bother Uncle John. Joyce was a young, attractive woman with the air of a philosopher about her. It was obvious she had lived through a major disaster; anything less was merely one of life's little irritations and barely mattered.

As it turned out the crossing was just as she said it would be, a bit of a swell but nothing to worry about, though I am never very comfortable at sea. Clouds filmed as nonchalantly as he always does. I sat there gripping the gunwales until we came to the beach.

I chilled out completely later, though. After what the locals told me they had been through, I realised that this little trip was nothing.

The earthquake had struck early evening on 17 July 1998, about twenty-five miles from shore. Nobody realised at the time, but the quake caused a landslide under the sea that in turn created a tsunami that decimated the coast.

Joyce's father, Shubert, told me he had been on the far side of the lagoon when the waves struck, but he heard the noise even from over there. Joyce remembered it vividly; she said that it was too early to get dark but as the earth shook, the sun seemed to die in the sky. Nobody understood quite what was happening. It was during the school holidays and there were lots of children playing on the beach. They watched in awe as first the sea seemed to be sucked from the sand, and then there was only silence. Moments later the wave came. It was the first of three and over fifteen metres high. Shubert said the kids came rushing inland, screaming for their lives. The wave tore up trees and homes, every scrap of bush and scrub. I could only imagine what it must have felt like to be picked up and tumbled around, drowning in sand and stones and debris.

In all more than 2200 people lost their lives that day. Entire villages were washed away. Almost ten thousand people were made homeless and the Rainbubus family said that even now life was not completely back to normal. Only one building in Sissano had survived the tsunami, and sadly that was due to be torn down soon because of termite damage. Walking around that village, I was conscious of the silence that seemed to remain. Shubert's son showed me a buckled aluminium dinghy, flattened now and upturned: he and his father had found it wrapped around the trunk of a palm tree and they kept it as a memorial to the people whose lives were lost.

Back in the boat we were all a little subdued. I was no longer concerned about the remainder of the trip, this open boat or the Boorman curse. I could understand Joyce's demeanour completely. Somehow her family had survived that day when the sun went dark. She was right: a trip around the coast to Vanimo was nothing.

We didn't get into Western Papua. I suppose in reality we never were going to. After a day in Vanimo we rocked up at the border to be told that we were not being given entry visas. We didn't bother to argue. Mindful that those five Australians were still being held, we just bit the bullet and set about trying to find a flight out. We had planned to make our way across the Spice Islands but now that was out of the question. It was a pain in the arse, but then I suppose there had always been a sense of inevitability about it. The really irritating part was we had to take a flight back to Port Moresby in order to continue our journey. After two days we finally reached the Indonesian island of Sulawesi, by way of Singapore and Jakarta. I'd picked up a cold in Papua and spent the flights coughing and sneezing, and getting the hairy eye from other passengers convinced I was carrying swine flu.

We'd originally planned to arrive in the far north of the island, but landed instead in Padang in the province of South Sulawesi. We travelled on swiftly to Makassar, a city that had once been the most important trading port in the region. Both the Portuguese and the Dutch came here and the Dutch tried to colonise it, but the Makassarese kings kept a policy of free trade, allowing anyone to do business in their city. Because of that neither the Dutch nor the Portuguese could get a proper foothold.

I'd been to Indonesia before of course, on the last trip, but not this part of it. That's the beauty of the place – there are so many islands, there is always somewhere new to explore. When Ewan and I crossed borders in Africa it always took a couple of days to acclimatise to a new country and to figure out how things worked. It was the same here – it was only on leaving Papua that I realised how tough it had been to get around there. You can't just get a bus or rent a car, and the roads are awful, with no real infrastructure to speak of. Food is also quite hard to get hold of. Now we were here, with a million and one restaurants on the same street, it struck me that we had been hungry much of the time in PNG.

*

I could feel a real vibrancy about this place – an Islamic country in the middle of the Indian Ocean with all the trappings of the West. Historically, Makassar was a centre for shipbuilding, where pinisi – the traditional Indonesian two-masted ships – were built in their thousands before being sailed all over the world.

Because the route had changed, our plans were thrown up in the air. The day after tomorrow I was due in a tiny village called Cendana Putih to help UNICEF install a water filter. I just had to work out a way to get there . . . We had hooked up with a local guy called Berthy Joris who had agreed to travel part of the way and act as translator, but that was as far as we'd got.

Berthy had Dutch and Portuguese in his bloodline and also some Japanese on his mother's side. He was a knowledgeable man and suggested we could make it as far as Sengkang tonight, via the towns of Maros and Watansoppeng. The best way to travel was by bus and we ought to head for the terminal.

I had seen hundreds of little blue buses when I came outside this morning, but of course now we were off and running there didn't seem to be one anywhere. I flagged down a rickshaw instead; they're called becaks here. I hadn't been on one in a while. I did pedal one in Varanasi on the last *By Any Means* trip, mind you. I remember the delight it gave the onlookers and how confused the owner had been.

The owner of this becak was much younger than that guy, and less anxious-looking. His name was Nanharman and he said he could take us to the bus station in the heart of this bustling, noisy city. Of course, I wanted to have another go at pedalling and when I asked Nanharman he was only too happy to take a load off. When I ended up making a wrong turn, instead of yelling at me, Nanharman jumped out of the rickshaw, grabbed the bars and physically pulled the machine around so we were facing the right way.

We made our way along the front for a while before Nanharman directed me inland. We cut through narrow streets, passing a mixture of rickety old shops, bungalows and high-rise office blocks. It was a hot day and I thought of the miles ahead in a bus with some trepidation – I was glad to be in the open air for now at least.

*

The buses are very small and privately run. While they are all pale blue in colour, some of them are customised with go-faster stripes and racing-style steering wheels. But of course the only ones we could find were going in the wrong direction. Finally Berthy spotted one heading towards Maros and we flagged it down. The driver took us out of town to another stop and we changed to a second bus and finally a third that would take us all the way to Maros, about an hour's drive north. The driver was a cheerful guy with large gaps between his four front teeth, and we chatted away with Berthy translating. He told us his name was Idris Dewa, which I thought was a pretty cool name, and he assured me it was after an Indonesian pop band.

I'm not sure where Makassar ended and the other towns began but as we headed north the city just seemed to sprawl along with us. Finally, though, we did leave the buildings, the dusty streets and tin roofs, and for a while at least we were in the country. Here the road was lined with trees, thickly forested hills climbing left and right. I sat back and enjoyed the view.

Half an hour later we got held up in a procession of cars playing loud music and hooting their horns. They stopped outside a tiny, tin-roofed house where smoke lifted from an open cooking yard and a stream of people in brightly coloured silks carried trays of delicious-looking food inside. Breakfast had been barely a snack and I was still suffering from the hunger pangs of New Guinea. We went to take a closer look and maybe hunt out some food. A young woman in a silk headscarf spotted me and came over to introduce herself. Her name was Opi Supiyari and she explained this was the final part of a three-day wedding celebration for a man called Sida and his bride Rasyid. She told us we were welcome to join in. It was fantastic! So much colour and music, a great chattering crowd all crammed into this tin box of a house. But I felt a little sorry for the bride and groom, who looked pretty flummoxed by the whole thing. They were very young, dressed in matching pink silk and perched in what looked like a grotto while their guests had a party around them. Opi explained that on the first day of celebration a cow is killed and the bride and groom each have separate parties with their family. On the second day they hold the marriage ceremony and on the third they get together for this party. At the end of today they would go off and begin their married life.

The family could not have been more hospitable. They invited us to eat with them, and I tucked in to a plate of curry. After that someone gave me a banana that had been baked for eight hours in a leaf. It was gorgeous. Finally, Claudio reminded me that we still had to get to Sengkang and the bus driver was waiting. We said our goodbyes and I wished the not-so-happy-looking couple all the very best. I'm sure that after three days they just wanted to get away by themselves.

Finally we got to Maros, where Idris dropped us at a dusty crossroads surrounded by ancient colonial bungalows with stone steps leading up to wide verandas. The next place on our route was Watansoppeng and of course there was no bus to be seen. There were a couple of guys in yellow jackets, though, standing next to a line of mopeds. I'd seen these before, they were ojeks, motorbike taxis, so we asked the drivers if they could take us. Claudio was given a rock-climbing helmet to strap under his chin, while I had this plastic thing you could bend any which way you wanted. I forced it onto my head, and soon we were on the back of the bikes and off down potholed streets, with every vehicle imaginable overtaking us.

I didn't care. With the kind of protection I was wearing, speed was not the issue. I was enjoying myself. The air was hot and sticky and I could smell all kinds of spices. The noise was constant – horns blaring, people shouting, the streets reverberating with the guttural growl of diesel. It was all wonderfully manic.

Leaving the ojeks in the middle of Watansoppeng we set off to try and find another bus. Berthy pointed out a tree full of fruit bats hanging upside down and screeching at one another. He said they were not native to these parts and there was a legend telling how they came to be here. When their old land ran out of food, the god of the animals told them to find a new place to live. They flew for many miles until they found fruit here in Watansoppeng and they had been here ever since. It's claimed that if one shits on you, you'll be married inside a year. So bear that in mind if you're single and ever in Watansoppeng.

Again there didn't seem to be a bus anywhere. It was late afternoon now and we thought we would try to find someone who was driving to Sengkang and ask them to give us a lift. We tried a few people but either no one was going or they didn't want to take us, so we thought we'd ask at one of the many business premises instead. It might be that some freight was going north and we could hitch a ride that way. Cutting down a side street we found a computer shop and a kid called Eddy. Eddy liked the camera. Arms folded and trying to look cool, he told us he had a truck and for a fee he would take us.

That settled, we went outside to wait for him.

Eddy took off upstairs and about ten minutes later he came down again, but now he was complaining of stomach problems. He didn't think he would be able to take us after all. He had made a phone call, though, and his friend Joyle would drive us to Sengkang instead. Great, fine, brilliant . . . we didn't care who the driver was just as long as we got there. Eddy took us across town in his truck to meet Joyle. He was older and somehow looked more reliable. Swapping places with Eddy, he climbed into the driver's seat.

'So, Joyle,' I said. 'Thanks for doing this, man. Eddy wasn't feeling well, apparently.'

Pulling away from the kerb, Joyle looked sideways at me. 'Eddy doesn't have a driving licence,' he said. 'Eddy got caught by the cops, in a car after taking drugs.' He glanced at Claudio's camera. 'We think it best I take you.'

Fair enough.

Sengkang was a small town with palm trees lining the streets. The houses were built closely together, most of them three storeys including a basement. When we arrived we met one of Berthy's friends, a guy called Dedy, and were introduced to his family. He told us the area was renowned for silk and suggested we pay a quick visit to the Amina Akil silk factory. The following morning Dedy led us down a side street where all I could hear was the clack-clack of weaving machines coming from the basements.

The factory was run by a lady called Ida Sulawati, who sells the silk to Java, Sumatra and Makassar, as well as the local area. I had no idea how much work went into making silk, how many processes there were from the silkworm to a finished piece of material. Downstairs in the basement, the walls were slatted to let in light and air. Four girls were working at traditional wooden weaving machines, each one fitted with thousands of single lines of thread and operated with a hand bar and long foot pedal. Each worker could produce between seven and nine metres of silk per day. Upstairs the walls were lined with cabinets of finished material, some of it very expensive indeed. Ida told us that she wonders sometimes at the silk people buy – often they fall in love with stuff that's hardly the best quality, yet ignore the really good stuff. She put it down to her weavers. She told us they had magic in their fingers and were able to create wonderful material from the poorest-quality strands.

The factory spanned a number of buildings up and down the street. One balcony was devoted to spools of silk, the threads spun across the interior like a spider's web before being rolled onto a massive drum. In another room a handful of people were painstakingly inserting each strand of silk onto the rack that fitted onto the weaving machine; a process that took a minimum of two days. The raw silk came in thick, off-white braids ready for washing, and looked and felt like hair – 'grandma's hair' was how Dedy referred to it.

I could have stayed for hours, but it was already late morning and we were due in Masamba tonight to meet Coco from UNICEF. Dedy led us to the main street, lined with small, open-fronted shops with tin roofs. There was no recognisable bus stop and talking to the shopkeepers we discovered there was nothing scheduled to leave today either. I was beginning to get a little worried. But then a red bus pulled in, the driver hopping out to get something from a nearby shop. The bus was crammed full, not just with people but baskets of washing, tyres and parts for motorbikes. The roof was stacked high with luggage and there was even a motorbike strapped to the back. As far as I could see there was no room for any more passengers, but Berthy said we should talk to the driver anyway. Following him into the shop, Dedy asked if he could take us to Masamba.

'No,' he said, looking warily at Claudio with the camera.

'How far could you take us?' Dedy asked him.

He didn't look as though he wanted to take us anywhere, but he said maybe Palopo. According to the map, that was on our route, so we decided to pile aboard and go that far at least.

The passengers were mostly families and we gleaned that many of them had already been on the road for a day and a night. I couldn't quite grasp where the starting point of their journey had been, but I did work out that by the time they made it to their destination, they would have been travelling for four days. There were two drivers and an assistant; one of the drivers had been doing the same route for fifteen years. He said he'd all but grown up on the bus.

We stopped at a place called Suli and ate some lunch. This was high country, the road twisty and the shops shoulder to shoulder. It was not unlike Papua actually, though there was more stuff on sale, more to eat, and it felt far wealthier. Taking a stroll across the road I was stunned by the sudden view. Below I could see a fish farm in a glistening valley – great banks of water where the sun sparkled, separated by wooden walkways.

'It's one of those views, Claudio,' I said. 'One of those moments when you stop and stare and remember how lucky you are to be here.'

Leaving the bus in Palopo, we located a pete-pete, a little yellow car/minibus that operates more like a taxi. After a brief discussion the driver said he would take us the rest of the way to Masamba.

When we arrived Coco was waiting for us. I've known her for years and she greeted me with letters from my wife and children. I tucked them away to read later. I love receiving them but they always make me homesick and a bit tearful. I was pretty knackered now. We'd been on the road most of the day again and the pink hotel where Coco was waiting looked more than a little inviting.

'You're not staying here, Charley,' she told me.

'No?'

'You're in the village with the head man's family. You're on a floor in a hut.'

'Am I? Right. OK then, that's fine.' Desperately I tried to sound enthusiastic.

It wasn't a hut actually. A hut was what we'd stayed in at Gapun. This was a house in Cendana Putih. I had a room to myself with a basin and squat-down toilet and the family could not have been more welcoming. Very humbly the head of the village apologised for the accommodation. He was a small man with narrow shoulders and a thin face and he shook my hand warmly.

'It's a village house,' he said. 'My apologies if it's not up to the standard of the city, but I hope you will be comfortable. We greet you as one of our own, Charley. You are part of the village.'

'Thank you,' I said. 'Thank you for making me welcome.' I shook hands with him again and with his wife and their young children. Then they left me alone and I opened the letters from home.

9
Squeal Like a Pig

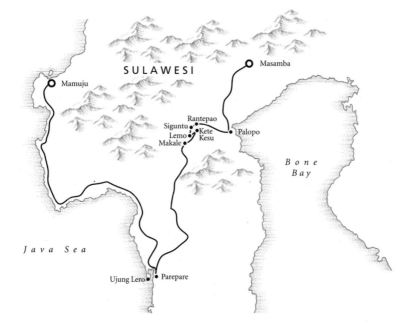

EVERY CHILD IN THE WORLD has the right to drink clean water. That's not some idealistic statement, it's a fact. Every country has signed up to it and UNICEF is at the forefront of the efforts to make it a reality. Ewan has been a UNICEF ambassador for a number of years now, but prior to *Long Way Round* I had not had much to do with them. Since then, however, I've been privileged to visit nine or ten of their projects around the world.

The Cendana Putih project focused on providing safe drinking water. The village was established in the 1960s by Javanese migrants, who sank the original wells. When UNICEF came to inspect them, most were found to be contaminated. The plan was to dispose of all the existing pumps and install new ones, together with an adequate water-filtration system.

We were working at the home of Waniasri and Sumarna, whose four-year-old son, Adrianto, suffered from what they called a rigid stomach, a debilitating ailment caused by bacterial infection from drinking contaminated water. He was prone to severe and very regular tummy upsets and was clearly in distress when we met him, clinging to Sumarna the whole time we were there. The family had no way of cleansing their water other than a laborious tablet-based system whereby each pot had to be left for at least two days. This new system should have a huge impact, and stop poor Adrianto from falling ill in the future.

It was a fairly straightforward process. We built two shelves onto the back wall of the house, one above the other, and then placed three plastic barrels on each shelf. These were linked by a series of plastic pipes that culminated in a single pipe with a tap fitted to it. The filtration was gravity-based and completely natural; there were no chemicals and no tablets, just a layer of scrubbed stones and a layer of sand separated by a sheet of mesh.

The first job was to wash the stones in a wheelbarrow. It was hard work in the heat, hosing the stones down and scrubbing them. We did the same with a barrow-load of sand. It was painstaking work – before I'd done half of it the sweat was pouring off me. But this was a vital part of the process: the cleaner the stones, the better the water was filtered.

Once everything was clean we heaped a few shovelfuls of stones in the bottom of each barrel and covered them with mesh netting before spreading the sand. When the sand was settled we fixed a short section of pipe in the barrel, one end floating while the other passed through an outlet cut in the side.

This done, we connected each barrel to a series of T-bends and further pipes that fed the lower shelf of drums. These were connected to the single pipe and tap. Finally a much wider-gauge pipe had to be connected inside the well. The only way to accomplish this was to hang over the side while two guys held my legs. I just about managed it without falling headlong into the muddy water.

A few minutes later I went into the house, switched on the pump, and watched as muddy brown water pumped into the upper barrels. Gradually the water seeped through the first layers of filtration, leaving behind little bits of dirt and stone, before flowing into the barrels on the second set of shelves. There it was filtered a second time, before ending up in the single pipe.

It was simple and effective. By the time we'd run the system through, all we had to do was turn on the tap and clear water flowed out. The pump kicked in automatically and the barrels on the upper shelf were refilled. Turn off the tap, the barrels settled and the clean water backed up. Taking a glass I scooped some water from the upper barrels then filled another from the tap. One glass was dirty brown and the other completely clear. I showed them to Claudio. 'Tell me if that is not fantastic,' I said.

Waniasri and Sumarna were delighted. Now all they had to do was step outside their back door, turn on a tap and they had clean water. Their neighbours were pretty pleased too, because until each house had the system installed, every ten would share.

I was thrilled. The first person we had met that morning had been a four-year-old boy with a fever caused by drinking contaminated water, and just a few hours later we had installed a filtration system that fulfilled the global pledge. Physically it was the toughest UNICEF task I'd undertaken – hard work under the hot sun. But it was also one of the most satisfying, with immediately visible results. The difference it would make to this family was immeasurable.

Sumarna told me about her other son. At fourteen he had to have a white shirt as part of his school uniform, and trying to keep a shirt clean in the old well water was impossible. Now they had clean water to drink, and they would have clean clothes as well.

More than five thousand children a day die from diseases contracted from poor sanitation and contaminated drinking water. A few hours of labour, a pump, six barrels, some pipes and some gravel and this family no longer had to worry.

We were not far from Rantepao, a town in the Toraja region famed for its extravagant funerals. So with the filter system in place we said goodbye to Adrianto's family, and the UNICEF crew gave us a lift back down to the coastal town of Palopo. From the mountain road we could see the dome of a mosque dominating hundreds of red roofs, while beyond it the quay drifted as a thin, black line into the sea where a single container ship lay alongside.

Almost immediately after the UNICEF people left we hitched a lift with the owner of a pick-up truck, who took us on to the village of Siguntu. We arrived just after dark. There were no streetlights, of course, and unless we put on head torches we couldn't really see anything. We could hear the shriek of night birds, though, and the squealing of hundreds of pigs. It was hard to make out where we were exactly and it was a little eerie, the houses nothing more than shadows.

A local man called Luther showed us to a house with steep steps leading up to the front door and even steeper ones leading to our bedroom. One of the roof supports was a mass of buffalo horns, which at first glance looked a little intimidating. But there was a comfortable-looking mattress on the floor and, according to Claudio, within minutes I was snoring.

Waking at sunrise, I pushed open a wooden shutter and saw a grassy thoroughfare bordered by the most amazing houses. The living area of our house was spread over a couple of floors, but the building was dominated by the roof. A sort of heavy thatch, it climbed sharply at either end. It was really bizarre, I'd never seen anything like it. It looked almost saddle-shaped, with the tall gables and the dip in the middle.

I took a wander through the village with Luther. All we could hear were pigs, screeching and squealing – there were pigs in individual pens attached to each of the houses. Luther explained that they are revered here almost as much as the buffalo. Animals form a large part of the local currency; buffalo (particularly males) can be worth a lot of money. They don't look like the Cape buffalo I saw in Africa; they're smaller and less muscular, more like oxen maybe, with their massive sweeping horns.

Both pigs and buffalo are reared with tender loving care. The pigs get a hot mash twice a day and the buffalo only the best grass. They're a family's most prized possession because they are bred for the most important time for any Torajan – their funeral. Every morning the women cut and cook vegetables for the pigs, and the buffalo are even more mollycoddled. The male sleeps in what Luther called a 'cottage', a large shed at the far end of the village. They get the best stall and bedding and a man's primary job is to cut enough grass to keep his buffalo fed. The females are taken onto the hillside to graze, but the male stays in his cottage until about 10 a.m., while his master prepares his food.

Using a hand sickle he cuts what he needs then goes to collect the bull. He leads him down the valley and then feeds him the grass by hand. When the buffalo has had enough he's free just to hang out or wallow in the mud. If he gets too dirty his master will wash him, then feed him again before taking him home.

Neither the pigs nor the buffalo are slaughtered for meat, except for a funeral. Sometimes a buffalo might be traded for a car, though – a spotted buffalo can be worth upwards of £8000.

Their primary purpose, however, is to be given as funeral gifts. Most families attend five or six funerals a year. These are lavish affairs lasting three days, and the more important you are the more guests you have. Luther took me to one in a neighbouring village, where the houses were built around a dusty square. The home of the deceased was open, the walls of the ground floor folded back and the whole building painted a vivid red. The floors were spread with mats for the guests to sit on and the square between the houses looked like a livestock market. Honestly, it was bedlam. People kept arriving with pigs in the back of their trucks; you couldn't hear anything above the squealing. There were about a dozen buffalo in the square already, together with a bunch of pigs either loose or trussed to bamboo poles.

The funeral was for a lady called Augustina Posi Thumaman, who had passed away six months before, aged seventy. Her family had kept her body in the house until they could afford the funeral. Luther told me that some people spend their entire lives saving for their funerals, and some parents didn't send their children to school because they wanted the money they could earn in the fields to buy the best buffalo. We had no pigs or buffalo to offer, so we took a couple of cartons of cigarettes, which Luther said was the right thing to do because everyone in Sulawesi smokes.

I could see Augustina's casket from the square. Beautifully carved and decorated with old Indonesian coins, it was displayed on the upper floor of the house and accessed by a bamboo ladder. Buffalo horns hung on the walls and the floor was laid with rugs. Augustina had been mother to five children and there were lots of grandchildren. They were all there and all had invited their own guests. What really amazed me was that each invited guest subsequently invited guests of their own. They would bring gifts of pigs or buffalo and check them in with the master of ceremonies before taking them to show to the family. Once the gift had been presented, the family would note down who gave what and how big it was, so when the time came they could reciprocate without any embarrassment.

It was all very serious, and it seemed to be much more about the guests' social standing than a ceremony to remember the deceased. Luther explained that if an invited guest did not show up with a whole bunch of guests of their own, they were clearly neither popular nor important. The number of people who 'followed' an invited guest would determine how many pigs or buffalo he brought. If he brought two beasts, one would be given to the family of the dead person and one kept back to feed the guests he'd invited. I watched women arriving with great baskets of rice strapped to their foreheads; I saw men carrying bamboo cups and others with jerry cans of palm wine. The family of the deceased would designate a room for each invited guest and their guests, and it would be the invited guest's responsibility to feed them.

It was quite extraordinary and extremely chaotic, what with trucks arriving and the incessant squealing of pigs. The pigs were carried in on sacrificial scaffolds and when it was time to eat them they were stabbed behind the shoulder with a sharp knife. It was not something I liked to watch, but I suppose if you're going to enjoy your bacon sandwich you'd better be prepared to see how that sandwich is made.

There were no bacon sandwiches here, of course. I was treated to palm wine and a plate of chillied pig's liver. God it was hot! Just one bite and I thought my tongue was going to swell up and suffocate me.

I spent some time with a lady called Veronica, a guest who lived in Australia. She was from Sulawesi originally; her birth home rather than her life home, as she put it. She told me that the deceased's younger sister had been her neighbour and years ago the old woman used to visit them. I asked her what she thought about keeping the body in the house for six months.

'It's normal. We inject the body with formaldehyde and it can stay with us for more than a year. You see, when the person dies their spirit leaves the body, but if we keep it then the spirit remains around us until we let it go.'

'At the funeral.'

'That's right.'

Luther and I hopped in a motorised becak to visit the burial grounds in the cliffs above the neighbouring village of Lemo. The coffins are placed in holes in the walls and the narrow path up is laced with piles of bones and human skulls. Macabre, to say the least. A little further we came upon the village of Kete Kesu, a living museum to the Torajan culture. High above the village is a large burial cave that is still in use. We could tell one of the coffins was relatively fresh because the stench was so foul as I entered the cave that I almost gagged. I couldn't move without my T-shirt covering my nose, but taking a good look around I was amazed to find not only numerous coffins, but bottles of water, bags and cups. There was even an electric fan and a copy of the phone book. Initially I thought that this must be a burial ground and a dumping ground, but all this stuff had been placed here deliberately – the creature comforts you might need for the next stage of your journey.

The smell was getting to me: I had seen enough of the dead and their funerals. Down in the valley again, I grabbed the map and spread it on my knees. We were making for a place called Makale and it would be nice to arrive in the daylight if we could.

'We should try,' Claudio said. 'We're always getting to places after dark.'

'I know we should. But how are we going to get there?'

As we started looking for a bus a truck drove up with a bunch of lads in the back – teenagers in jeans and baseball caps. I recognised them as guests from the funeral. They told us they would take us to Makale. Job done then. Things were looking up – this was the second quick lift we had found in as many days. A couple of the guys appeared to have been supping plenty of palm wine and it wasn't long before the bamboo cups came out. Someone opened a package of palm leaves and, drink in hand, we tucked into some pig meat I'd seen cooking on the open fires.

We spent the night in a small boarding house close to the lake in the centre of town. Makale is a picturesque place, the buildings quite modern and none more than a couple of storeys high. The lake is dominated by an enormous statue of a hero from the days when the Dutch were trying to colonise Indonesia, a muscle-bound warrior with his fist in the air. We were told he was meant to symbolise the collective history of the country. It's funny, there are so many islands and each is so different, they all seem to have separate identities. It was easy to forget they are all part of one country.

This morning we were heading south-west to the sea, after

which we would make our way around the western coast. Actually I didn't care where we went today, because wherever it was it would be on a motorbike. We were joining a group of Harley riders, who were big fans of the show. A guy called Onny had been in touch with us before we left London and suggested we meet up. Now here he was in a white T-shirt and open-face helmet, grinning from ear to ear. He was riding a 750 Harley built for the army in 1951. Painted khaki green, it came complete with a foot clutch and stick shift on the left side of the fuel tank. The rest of the group rode big cruisers. One even had fake police lights.

I checked out Onny's bike. 'It looks like it might be quite difficult to ride,' I said, 'what with the stick shift and everything.'

'Not for Charley Boorman! You can ride anything.'

I appreciated Onny's confidence in me, but I wasn't so sure. I mean, I'm not bad, but I'm no Valentino Rossi. I wanted to have a go, however, so I swung a leg over, Onny showed me how to work the clutch and gears and I pulled away. It was lumpy, of course, a bit of a bone cruncher, but then the engine was mounted on the frame. I rode down to the crossroads, turned right, then did a little circuit to see what it felt like.

'You went the wrong way,' Onny said when I got back.

'What?'

The other guys were laughing their heads off.

'You went the wrong way,' Onny repeated. He was pointing now. 'It's one way, Charley. You went the wrong way.'

There is something about me, motorbikes and relaxation. When I'm worried or wound up about anything, I'll jump on a bike and whatever it is that's bothering me just fades away. Today I was riding a 1994 Road King, one of the first of Harley's evolution engines, and as soon as we left town any worries I might have had disappeared. It's a physical thing, especially on a big comfortable bike like this. I had a full screen, an open-face helmet and a pair of sunglasses. The last couple of days had been hectic, noisy – so much to see and take in. To be on a bike again was just what I needed.

After an hour or two on the road we stopped at a spa overlooking a mountain shaped like a . . . actually, I'm not sure how to put it exactly. If I tell you the place was called the Erotic Mountain, it might give you a clue. It wasn't phallic and it was a natural formation. I mean very natural, a sort of shallow cleft in the hills, perfectly formed and . . . Anyway, the place had become a beauty spot and tourist attraction. There was a spa, hotel and bar, all so you could gaze on the wonders of what looked like . . .

The valley below was covered with what Onny called rain trees, not unlike acacias to look at, only the canopy was much thicker. Onny explained that he was involved in forest conservation, a government plan to plant five million trees all across Sulawesi. I didn't quite understand it, but he said he had access to the seeds and the army helped him to distribute them. Anyone wanting to plant a nursery could come to him.

He was a special guy; they all were. At a filling station I topped up the Road King and was about to pay when Onny told me my money wasn't valid in Sulawesi. They reminded me of the guys we had met in Daly Waters – a great laugh and there for each other. It's the same with bikers everywhere; we share a common bond, a brotherhood that is borne of people with the same passion.

We made it to the coast and Parepare in time to grab a late lunch, and as we pulled up I spotted an old Toyota Land Cruiser parked up the road. It was the 40 series, the jeep version I really love. They haven't made them since 1984, but I remembered that Diane Cilento had owned one when I was helping her clear the land for her theatre. You don't see them in England very often, and the ones you do see are really expensive. I love them because they are just so functional. A bit like a Willys jeep from the front, they're hard top and have a short wheelbase. I suppose they're more like a Land Rover. This one was silver and I wanted it. God, I thought, if we could find one of those on this trip I'd be in my element.

I was sad to see the guys leave. Harley riders in Indonesia, you touched my heart, boys, you really did. But they had to go and we were supposed to be making our way around the peninsula to Ujung Lero, a shanty town where we hoped to find a boat builder.

To get our bearings we walked to the docks where we found a group of kids loading blocks of ice onto a little white boat. The ice was for the residents of Ujung Lero, which we could just about make out on the far side of the natural harbour. Thinking that a short boat trip was a much better idea than a long road trip, I helped the lads with the ice while Sam asked the skipper if he would take us.

He was more than happy, though there were four of us plus the gear and the boat was tiny. The skipper sat in an open hatch steering with his feet, his upper body above deck and his legs below. It was mad, the engine clattering away so loudly it sounded bone dry and completely bereft of oil. The driver didn't seem worried, however, and with him only half visible, we made our way across the water.

I had things on my mind now. No sooner had I got off the bike than we took a call from London. Apparently the border between Indonesia and the Philippines had been closed. We were due to take a ferry across the Celebes Sea but as far as we could gather that was no longer an option. No one seemed certain about what was going on, but it was something to do with drugs and people traffickers. It was a real problem, in any case.

When the ice boat docked we made our way along a rickety old wharf to Ujung Lero. This really was a shanty town: shacks made from poles and planks of wood, doors cut from curtains and roofs of rusting tin.

We were here to find Guntur, the boat builder, and we knew his house was somewhere around . . . we just didn't know where. So we spent the next hour or so wandering the streets. It was a labyrinth, a mass of ramshackle buildings permeated by the smell of cooking, and a maze of alleys and little roads.

It was also filthy, a real slum. But there wasn't the air of menace I'd felt in other places. On the contrary, it was very friendly. People smiled and nodded greetings, kids followed us wherever we went and we found the kind of hospitality I'm not sure we would get in Western Europe.

Finally we found Guntur, his place only a stone's throw from where we had originally landed. His boatshed backed on to a beach covered with rubbish – paper and bottles, rotting vegetables, rice and God knows what else. A herd of goats was scavenging on it. If this had been in Brazil we wouldn't have come, because there would be little chance of ever getting out. Here, though, it was chilled. For the most part I'd found the Indonesian people we'd met very welcoming and hospitable, and for all the poverty and filth, I never felt even slightly threatened.

I watched Guntur making a fishing boat. It looked like a shallow-bottomed canoe, only it was thirty feet in length. He used no pattern, no plan or blueprint – he had been making them for fourteen years and the plans were in his head. He didn't use screws or rivets, everything was held together by wooden pegs that he dipped in paint before hammering them into place. He told me he made five or six boats a year and each one took thirty-five days to complete.

That night his wife cooked us a lovely meal and then she showed me to a bedroom beyond a sliding door off the kitchen. There were no windows and, given the heat, I thought it might be a little stuffy. So with Guntur's permission I unrolled my sleeping bag on the balcony. Claudio strung his hammock.

I half slept, I suppose. It was cool enough on the balcony but the sounds of the little town never really subsided. I heard music from radios and people talking, ships on the water and one skinny cockerel that had no idea when dawn would break so he crowed every fifteen minutes just to make sure he didn't miss it.

The following day – the thirty-sixth since we left Sydney – we were taking a bus up the coast to Mamuju. I still had things on my mind, not just the border problems, but the idea of being on a bus for seven or eight hours. The day after that we were picking up an army truck and I imagined it would be yet another flatbed, which would be nice. I'd briefly thought about trying to find some more cushions. I say briefly, because I kept seeing this image of some Indonesian soldier telling me not to be such a wuss and to give him twenty press-ups.

Sitting on Guntur's balcony in the hot sun, I could feel my face burning from being on the bike yesterday. I could also see the bloody cockerel who had kept me awake all night. He was across the street, tethered by one foot, and if he'd been any closer he would have crowed his last, believe me.

'Hey, Charley!' Sam calling from below caught my attention. 'Guess what?'

I looked down at him. 'What?'

'You can forget about the bus today.'

'What do you mean?'

'I mean the bloke we stayed with last night knows someone with a Toyota Land Cruiser. A jeep, Charley! He reckons we can borrow it.'

'You're joking.'

'No. I mean it. We were talking to him last night and I mentioned you'd seen one and he said he knows someone who'll lend us his. We're driving it to Mamuju.'

I couldn't believe it. The best car in the world and we were going to borrow it.

An hour later it arrived. A 40 series, it was dark green with a white roof and all-terrain tyres. With the gear stowed, Sam and Robin in the back and Claudio alongside, I got behind the wheel. It was diesel of course and there was no power steering. The gears were something else – first was where second should be, and third ... well, there were only three. The steering was a bit unpredictable – when you hit the brakes it pulled to the right and there was plenty of play in the wheel. Being so short at the back there was plenty of under-steer as well, but hey, I'd wanted one of these for ever and we could have been spending the next seven hours on a bus. This ought to be quicker and it was a hell of a lot more fun.

We could only drive in daylight, however. Sam had been told that further up the road some people had been hijacked – gunmen were stopping cars and robbing people. Some tourists had been pulled off a bus and now the buses weren't driving the road at night. No one was, and that included us. So, we would get as far as we could and find somewhere to spend the night.

Today Regina, Claudio's long-suffering wife, was celebrating her birthday. He phoned home, got the answer-machine and we all sang 'Happy Birthday'. After seven hours on the road we reached Mamuju just before dark. We'd taken every twist and turn, been through forests of rain trees and driven high in the mountains before descending to the beach then climbing all over again. I loved the jeep and more than ever I was determined to find one for myself.

Designed in 1951, it had been called the BJ originally. To test its durability, the designer took it up Mount Fuji, where it surpassed the height any vehicle had climbed before. As soon as word got out, everyone wanted one. I suppose someone must've realised the implications of its name mind you, because the BJ suddenly became the Land Cruiser. Anyway, whatever the name, it's the preferred choice of off-road users from the forest service in Indonesia to UNICEF. And, of course, the Taliban.

10
Batman and Robin

THE NEXT COUPLE OF DAYS were a bit of a disaster. We already knew that planning anything in this country was far from easy, but now things took a turn for the worse. The drive up to Mamuju in the Toyota had been an unexpected bonus, but somehow I'd got confused about when we would be in the army truck – it turned out it wasn't today, but tomorrow. I don't know why I'd thought otherwise, but we still had to get further up the coast and that meant twelve hours on a bus.

I was less than enthusiastic at the prospect, my bum red raw from bus seats already. But at 5.30 a.m. and in total darkness, Claudio and I picked our way across a building site to get to the bus terminal. Of course it was deserted; in this part of the world, bus terminals always are.

One did come by eventually, but it was full and didn't stop. A couple of locals told us there would be another at some point, so we found a place for breakfast and settled down to wait. Finally, at around seven-thirty, a second bus arrived. This one had sharks painted on the side and what looked like a rusty water tower strapped on the roof, not to mention the sheets of plywood tied on behind. Inside it was bulging with mothers and their children, old men, young men, every inch of floor space taken up with tyres and barrels and bags. The seats next to the driver were going spare, however, so Claudio and I squeezed on.

There were other things on my mind this morning, apart from the bus journey. Because the border had been closed, the ferry across the Celebes Sea was now only going as far as another island. From there all we'd been able to find was a privately owned boat that was just twenty-four feet long, and if the border *was* closed, we would have to see if even that was possible. I'd been at sea in a small boat before, and this crossing would be at least two days. We've already discussed the Boorman boat curse, so you can imagine how I was feeling. And I've not even mentioned the pirates . . .

This bus was interminably slow. I've grown used to transport that moves at all speeds – from very fast to barely walking pace – but this was unbelievable. It took eight minutes just to crawl out of this tiny town and no sooner had we hit tarmac than a traffic cop stopped us. He spoke to the driver then crossed the road to his motorbike and rode away. We just sat there. Nobody seemed to know what was going on, but clearly the driver wasn't going anywhere. Five minutes later the policeman returned with a girl on the back of his bike. Nonchalantly he helped her aboard, gave her a peck on the cheek and we were finally on our way. It turned out that she was both his girlfriend and a fellow police officer. I asked her what sort of crimes she had to deal with.

'Adultery mostly,' she said, 'that and domestic violence.'

'Is there a lot of domestic violence?'

'Yes,' she said, 'a lot.'

'Why is that?'

'Cell phones,' she said, matter-of-factly.

'Cell phones?'

'More men have cell phones now, so it's easier for them to talk to other women.'

Later that day we heard about another shocking crime, one that touched us personally this time.

Around midday we stopped for something to eat and Sam, who had been following in the support vehicle, laid his cell phone on the table.

'Have you been talking to your girlfriend?' I asked him.

'What?'

'Oh, just something someone said on the bus . . .' He didn't smile, and I asked him if something was wrong.

He took a moment before he answered. 'Do you remember Bogia village back in Papua New Guinea, the place where we started the journey up the Sepik?'

'You mean where that guy had the sixty-horsepower outboard?'

He nodded.

'What about it?'

'Just after we left a little girl was murdered. Three years old . . . she was abducted and decapitated.

'Decapitated?'

He nodded. 'A group of men carried her into the bush and cut her head off. It was something to do with a dispute over land rights.'

'But she was only three?' I was numb with shock. 'My God.'

Apparently there had been tensions in the area since 2004, when a series of volcanic eruptions had forced fifteen thousand Manam islanders to the mainland at Bogia. Earlier this year four islanders had been killed. This time a young Manam mother had been attacked by seven men. She had two children with her and managed to get away with one of them. But the toddler had been carried off and her head was discovered later by the police.

This terrible news brought everyone down, and we all felt very subdued. The journey went on and on, and though people had suggested it was not advisable to travel after dark, it was pitch black when we finally got to our destination, the town of Palu.

The army truck didn't show up. We had been assured that everything had been set up, but when we got to the rendezvous the following morning, the only thing we found was a man in uniform, waiting for us. Although he looked like a soldier, he was actually a member of the tourist board, and as the day wore on he was joined by eleven of his colleagues. It wasn't our first encounter with officialdom. We didn't realise it at the time, but Berthy's friend Dedy worked for the government, and it turned out he was there to make sure we were not filming anything they weren't happy with. Now here was the tourist board trying to dictate our day. They gave us no explanation as to why there was no truck, but they told us all would be well because they were sending a Toyota Hilux instead.

We waited outside a little kiosk where they sold petrol in bottles to passing motorcyclists. Various people came and went, and I chatted to one fellow who had been a tour guide until he got married. The time ticked by.

There was no sign of the Toyota, but after a while a car containing more uniformed officials pulled up. Before we knew what was happening, we were being treated to some traditional music and dancing, which was a bit of a surprise.

The officials said they would accompany us to Palasa, the village where we had hoped to visit the Lauje tribe. They were going to take charge of that element of our trip, which hadn't been part of the plan. We thought we would be able to spend the night in a traditional mountain hideaway, much as we had done at Siguntu. Now we discovered that the Lauje village was a day's walk from Palasa, when we'd been told it was at Palasa itself. The officials said we could see the Lauje on Friday when they came down on their bamboo rafts to sell fruit at the market. That had some potential, I suppose, except that today was only Wednesday.

I'd had enough. The story about the little girl had disturbed me, I was sick of buses, and the last we'd heard of our man with the boat, he was still at sea. It was supposed to be thirty hours from his island to where he would meet us at the ferry port, but he had left two and a half days ago. He had not been that keen to take us anyway – the last time we spoke to him he was worried that, with us filming, every pirate in the area would be coming after his boat.

'So what do we do?' Sam asked me. 'I can't see the point in going to Palasa. Can you?'

'No.' I was eyeing the support van. 'I've had it with this entourage, I hate this.' Claudio had the map spread across the windscreen. 'We're here, right?' I said, tapping the page at Palasa.

'Almost, yes.'

'And we've got to get to Guantanamo Bay?'

The others burst out laughing.

'We've got to get to Gorontalo Bay,' I corrected.

Sam was killing himself. 'It's just Gorontalo, Charley: there is no bay.'

'Like I said, we've got to get to Gorontalo.' I glanced over my shoulder towards the twelve government officials. 'Let's just get in the van and get out of here. We'll forget this village thing, it was never going to happen anyway. Let's get to "Guantanamo" and pick up some motorbikes.'

So far we'd managed to avoid using the support vehicle, but now it was the only option. There was no bus and the truck the officials had brought wasn't going to take us any further. 'The van,' I said. 'We'll just take the van.'

Claudio clearly agreed. 'If you'd asked me, I would have suggested that hours ago,' he muttered.

Sam nodded. 'It makes sense. It'll give us time to work out what we're going to do. If this boat guy doesn't show up, we may have to fly. And that means getting hold of some tickets.'

'Fly where exactly?'

'Singapore,' Claudio stated. 'If the border's closed, that's the only way.'

You know the old saying about how things can only get better? Well, finally, they did. First, in the form of a Suzuki, which was loaned to me by some guys from the Thunder Community bike club. And second, by a night on a beach.

We had driven through the afternoon and much of the night, despite the threat of hijackers, and arrived – in one piece – in Gorontalo in the early hours. Maybe they had heard about the kind of mood we were in. I don't know. Anyway, we made it and this morning we decided we had no choice but to reserve some flights via Singapore; with our man still somewhere at sea, and given the situation with the border, it was doubtful there would be enough time to try negotiating with immigration.

It was pissing me off. Given what had happened with West Papua and now this, we just couldn't seem to cross any borders.

Oh well, we just had to suck it up. And at least these last two days would be on motorbikes. The bikers were all local guys and three of them were riding with us to Manadao, the capital of North Sulawesi, right on the northernmost tip of the island. Two days in the open air, and we would arrive tomorrow night.

The Suzuki was all right. Not the best – the steering was fucked and the front brake all but non-existent. But I didn't care. I was on a bike, dossing about, standing on the seat and weaving between the vans and buses. Gorontalo was a humming, busy town, and the road was narrow and noisy, choked with becaks and tuk-tuks and hordes of people.

Claudio and I were accompanied by Minto, Dal and Ivan, together with about twenty of their mates. Their mates rode with us as far as a massive pagoda-style monument that straddled the road out of Gorontalo. The guys got off their bikes and said a little prayer before clasping hands in a circle. It was a ritual, a word to the god of the roads to keep us bikers safe. The prayers offered, we parted company and headed across country to the village of Minauna.

There was a lot of traffic on the road and plenty of villages along the way. We were on motorbikes though, not in some stuffy bus with someone else driving. We forged our own path, made it up as we went along – that's the beauty of riding. We could avoid all the bumps and potholes; we could go where a bus or car couldn't.

Even a puncture couldn't bring me down. When Claudio's back tyre started losing air, we just loaded his bike onto the van and Claudio hopped on the back of mine until we reached the next village.

One of the great things about Indonesia is how you can find what you need in the smallest of villages, like bottles of petrol, or a workshop in a tiny shack with a tyre hanging off a hook to identify its business. The mechanic had the wheel off and the puncture fixed in no time.

Once we hit the northern coast the landscape changed. It was truly awesome country here – stunning hills and forests with white beaches and crystal waters far off in the distance. I longed for those beaches. I thought we should forget about finding a homestay for the night and camp on the beach instead. We had the gear, waterproof hammocks, ropes, and nylon sheets that we could hook up as a makeshift tent.

I knew Claudio would be up for it, Robin and Sam too, probably. I wasn't sure about our Indonesian friends, but by the time we got to Minauna, my mind was made up.

'So what do you think, Claudio?' I said as we inspected a sandy clearing. 'This would be a good spot to hang the hammocks.' The clearing was ringed by palms, the only downside being that they were laden with coconuts. If one of those dropped on your head in the night it would give you more than a headache.

We had to ask the village elders for permission to sleep on the beach, but they said it wasn't a problem. Minto, Dal and Ivan weren't so sure, however, and as darkness fell they slunk away to negotiate a floor in one of the houses.

A little further down the beach Claudio organised the rest of us. He asked me to tie a piece of rope between two trees so we could string up a tarp in case it rained. Right now the sky was clear and the wind light, but we knew it could rain at any time. It had been piddling down when we rode out this morning.

'Claudio,' I said, 'I don't think this is the right place.' I indicated a big hole in the ground. 'We should move it a little, that hole will only get in the way.'

'It will be fine,' he assured me.

He was stubborn. He was on a mission. Having travelled the world with the guy, I knew there was no point arguing.

With the shelter more or less set up I went back to the clearing to put up my hammock. Satisfied that it was secure, I blew air into my mattress before arranging my sleeping bag. I was having a great time. After the past couple of days I had no intention of being in a stuffy room anywhere. With my bedding ready, I tested the strength of the knots, and of course the hammock collapsed.

'You didn't tie it properly,' said Claudio, stating the obvious. 'I saw it right away.'

Retying the knot, I tested the hammock a second time and it was fine. We finished off the shelter by tying a large sheet of nylon to the rope and then stretching and pegging it to the ground. I could feel rain in the air now and I was still worried about coconuts.

Sam went up into the village to buy some food and it seemed like the entire population decided to follow him back to the beach to check out the new arrivals. I asked one taciturn bloke about the coconuts.

'Has anybody ever been hit by one falling from a tree?'

He shook his head. 'A kid broke his legs falling out of a tree once, but nobody ever got hit by a coconut. No.'

'Good,' I said. 'Good.'

He indicated the hammocks. 'But then we don't sleep under them, do we?'

'It'll be all right,' Sam assured me. He had some wonderful-smelling rice and fish wrapped in paper and fastened with elastic bands. He also had some local kids with him and as the rain started we all took shelter under our makeshift tent. Claudio had been modifying it, of course – we had two sheets of nylon now, clipped together to give us more room and supported from the ground by a huge piece of driftwood and the camera tripod.

I patted Claudio on the back. 'Ray Mears would be proud,' I told him.

Claudio considered his handiwork for a moment. 'Yes,' he said. 'I think he probably would.'

It was actually pretty cosy there, eating rice and fish, with rain rattling on the nylon roof and half a dozen locals sitting with us. The rain didn't last long and, checking to make sure my hammock had stayed dry, I thought about a fire. I wandered down the beach looking for driftwood to burn. One of the kids must've seen me because he scuttled off and came back with a fisherman who was carrying a bundle of wood and some dried palm leaves. He didn't say anything; he just arranged the sticks, laid the kindling and got the fire going. It was all very mellow, and with Berthy interpreting we managed to chat to some of the villagers.

I was pretty tired though, and with the fire beginning to die I knocked the sand off my clothes and clambered into my hammock. 'Sam,' I said, 'just so you understand . . . if you snore tonight, I'm going to batter you with coconuts.'

It took me an age to get to sleep. I'm not sure why exactly, but after a great day on the bike I lay in my hammock with all sorts of thoughts swirling around in my head. We only had one full day left in Indonesia and much as I had enjoyed the country, and the people in particular, I had been frustrated by its officials. Things are actually very tightly controlled here beneath the friendly surface. On top of that there seemed no way to sail to the Philippines now, which meant we had to fly.

At first light I took a walk along the beach and found our

fisherman friend surrounded by bottles, curled up by the embers of the camp fire. He was sound asleep, wearing just a T-shirt and shorts; I'd been so cold in the night I'd had to put my clothes on. It had been great to camp though, being in the open air with the sound of waves crashing on the beach. Definitely the right call.

Minto, a policeman in his 'real life', had to ride back so he could go to work, but Dal and Ivan were coming with us all the way to Manadao. We saddled up and left early, while it was still cool. I was back on the Suzuki, dossing about as I always do and waving at villagers laying out half shells of coconuts to dry.

The roads were pretty rough for the first part of the day – lots of dirt and mud and very little tarmac. But at least it wasn't raining, not yet anyway. It did look like it might, though. All morning the skies were plagued by an ever-thickening blanket of cloud. It was still beautiful, though – the sea was blue green and mottled with hundreds of the canoe-style fishing boats we had seen Guntur building back in Ujung Lero.

Manadao Province looked a bit wealthier than most places we had seen. Crossing a river on a temporary bridge, we left the last of the dirt and hit smooth, black tarmac. Just as well, because finally those clouds began to dribble. A few raindrops would patter on the visor of my helmet for a while and then stop. It would start again and then stop. The tarmac looked polished and quickly it became very slick. Any road racer will tell you that you want it either wet or dry. What you do not want is that undecided in-between, because then the surface is just greasy and you can be down without ever knowing why.

It didn't stay undecided for very long. The last few hours into Manadao it absolutely bucketed down. The closer we got to town, the worse it got. It was torrential, the road almost flooded and I was wearing just jeans and a jacket and a pair of canvas shoes. I was soaked to the bone. I don't think there was any part of me that wasn't wet through and I was amazed when a couple of guys from the bike club came out to meet us. The Thunder Community has chapters all over Indonesia and these new guys were from the Manadao brigade. I couldn't believe they had braved the weather.

But they had and they rode with us through the waterlogged streets. The final half hour . . . I remember Dare telling me in Sydney that the last half hour of any bike ride is always a half hour too long.

We found somewhere to stay and I took a shower, though I hardly needed it. The rain was warm, the temperature still right up there and every time a truck went past I had been soaked in hot spray. Meeting Claudio and the others in the early evening, we went off to find something to eat. Not far from where we were staying, we came across a traditional Indonesian café that was serving paniki. Fruit bat.

We'll have some of that then. I mean, here we were, and along with dog, paniki was a local delicacy. I've never eaten dog. I've never wanted to eat dog. Just the thought of it brings to mind my spaniel Ziggy, curled up at home. And as for fruit bat . . . when I was a kid my friend Jason used to keep one as a pet.

Armed with plenty of bottles of Coke, we sat down, and already I could feel my stomach beginning to tighten. First off, this was a buffet and any traveller worth his salt knows that you never eat from the buffet. Secondly, I was not only eating from a buffet, I was eating bat and dog.

The bat looked like bat. I mean, it was minced up with spices and everything, but the meat was black and the wings were in there – claws, the whole thing.

Claudio dived in first. Stoic as ever, he plucked a wing and gnawed on the leathery-looking thing like a veteran.

'It's all right,' he said. 'Too many bones perhaps.' Sitting back, he reached for a bottle of Coke. 'It's spicy,' he said. 'Very, very spicy.'

I had a little nibble. It tasted OK actually but I had the Coke handy just in case I gagged. The dog, though – could I eat a bit of dog?

The owner told me that people buy puppies, rear them in cages, then, when they're ready to eat, they knock them on the back of the head. The dog meat was black, like the bat. I tried it, a nibble, not even a mouthful. Next to me Robin had a plate of rice and spooned on the bat and dog without batting an eyelid. I was still eyeing my tiny piece of dog meat.

'Daddy.' Robin's voice lifted in a high-pitched mewl from beside me. 'Daddy, why did you kill me?'

That was it. I dumped the dog, drank the Coke and headed for KFC.

11
More than a Handful

Samar

Panay

Leyte

Cebu

Cebu

Bohol

Negros

*Bohol
Sea*

Camiguin

White
Island

PHILIPPINES

Manolo Fortich

Cagayan
del Oro

Malaybalay

M i n d a n a o

Mintal

Davao
City

C e l e b e s   S e a

BEFORE WE SAID GOODBYE to Indonesia, there was, inevitably, one final complication. The boat we'd hoped might take us across the Celebes Sea turned out to be an illegal fishing vessel. That was it. We had taken the precaution of booking flights and now it was decided. We flew via Manila, landing in the Filipino island of Mindanao on 28 June.

The Philippines – made up of 7100 islands – was under Spanish occupation for 360 years and the cuisine still has a Spanish influence. More recently it had been colonised by the Americans, who helped establish a nationwide education system, so many Filipinos speak English, but we had a translator with us just in case – a guy called Inkee.

After a night in Davao City we hit the road. We were on our way to a Benedictine monastery high up in the mountains in northern Mindanao that produces Monk's Blend coffee. I was really looking forward to the trip – I love coffee, and after a hectic few days the idea of spending the night in a remote, tranquil monastery was particularly appealing.

But first we had to get there. I wanted to find a jeepney, the most traditional and recognised form of travel in this country. These are vehicles derived from the old Willys, jeeps that were left behind when the Americans went home. The basic jeep was given a longer body and painted all the colours of the rainbow. The inside was decorated and the canvas sides could be rolled up to let in the air. Fifty years later you still see customised versions all over the country.

Claudio and I walked to the market where a local translator offered to help. He knew a guy called Ray who delivered fruit and vegetables from the mountain villages in Bukidnon Province, which was where the monastery was. He generally made the return journey with an empty truck so it made sense for us to try to get a lift with him at least part of the way.

I love markets. In Ethiopia I visited one with Ewan where they had every kind of spice imaginable, along with camels and donkeys and great flocks of vultures watching from the trees. This was purely a food market though – a cluster of huts and stalls with brightly coloured parasols to keep off the sun. Everywhere you looked there were piles of mangoes, pineapples, bananas and the sweet peanuts we had eaten in Papua New Guinea.

We found the dusty red jeepney parked at the side of the road. Ray was unloading tomatoes stacked on the roof, so I clambered up and gave him a hand. I asked if Claudio and I could hitch a lift and, after thinking about it for a moment, he said it would be fine.

'Can I drive some of the way?' I went on. 'I really like your truck, Ray. I'd love to have a go at driving it.'

It was the most bizarre vehicle. The front end was just like the old jeeps, with twin headlamps and a squared-off nose. But it was much taller and longer and the rear axle was fitted with two wheels on each side, which was very unusual. The side panels were pretty beaten up and there was no glass in the front doors. But there was a home-made air-conditioning fan built into the driver's side.

'Do you think it might be possible to let me drive then?' I asked again. So far Ray hadn't responded. To be honest, he looked less than enthusiastic. 'What do you think, Ray? I'd really like to drive.'

Still he looked doubtful. He squinted at me, then at the jeepney, then at the amount of traffic on the road. I still had the last crate of tomatoes in my hands, and finally he shrugged, showing me three white teeth. 'You work for me,' he said. 'OK, you can drive.'

He insisted on taking us out of town before he let me take the wheel. I didn't mind that, the market was very busy and the roads choked with vans, mopeds and loads of little motorbike taxis. It was baking hot too. Glad to be out of the sun, Claudio and I settled in the back.

This place really was humming, all we could hear was the clatter of diesel engines and people banging their horns – the kind of bedlam we had not seen for a while. Indonesia had been nowhere near as busy. There was a buzz to Mindanao – a real feeling of industry.

I asked Ray how often he delivered the fruit and vegetables.

'Every Monday and Friday.'

'What do you do the rest of the week?'

'I drive a habal-habal.'

'Oh right, the motorbike taxi.' As I spoke one passed us, the driver hunching under a grimy parasol.

Once we were out of town Ray finally let me drive, though he was still a little reluctant. Actually his eyes were bulging with anxiety.

He took my seat in the back and I took his. Claudio tried to tell him it would be all right because I was a good driver, but nothing seemed to placate him. Especially when I couldn't find first gear. I tried and tried. I tried until the gear knob came off in my hand, but all I could hear was the horrible grinding sound of a gear not engaging. Finally I worked out that first was where second would normally be; second where third was, and so on. Even so, I still missed the odd change and the gearbox would howl in protest at my ineptitude.

Around noon I pulled over and Ray looked more than a little relieved. We were on the edge of a little town called Mintal, and this was where he turned off. He shook my hand, the sweat still beading on his face, and then jumped behind the wheel, heading for home where he could lie down in a dark room to recover.

We had heard about a restaurant in the next village famous for catfish, and as it was getting close to lunchtime I flagged down a habal-habal. The driver informed us that if I had been a girl he would not charge me, he'd try to chat me up instead. He was a young guy wearing a bandanna round his head and he drove a habal-habal for the sole purpose of meeting young women. Anyway, he took us down the road between flat fields and palm-fringed bungalows as far as the restaurant. It was a cool-looking place, built on stilts above a rice paddy, the roof part wood and part foliage from the rain forest. The owner, Wilfredo, greeted us with handshakes. In excellent English he told us he was very happy for us to be there and explained that he not only served but farmed the catfish himself, along with the rice and vegetables.

The place was totally organic. He only had two hectares but what he did with them was quite amazing. Wilfredo asked if I would like to cook my own catfish. I love cooking, so grabbing a fishing rod he took me out to the pond. He told me how he hatched his own fish in a pair of metal basins under the roof of a small lean-to.

'People told me I couldn't hatch fish like this,' he said, indicating the basins. 'But so long as the temperature of the water and the pH balance is right, it is fine.'

To get to the pond we had to cross a series of dykes built between the paddies where carp swam among the rice plants. 'They eat the snails,' Wilfredo explained. 'So I don't have to use pesticides. Their waste acts like a fertiliser so I don't have to worry about that either. When I harvest the rice I put the carp into the pond with the catfish.'

We reached the pond, which was surrounded by palm trees. The surface was covered in a layer of water hyacinths that kept the fish free of fungal disease. When the hyacinths died and started to decompose they became a natural fertiliser too.

Wilfredo was totally committed to the organic way of life, so much so that in English his granddaughter's name means 'organic farmer'. He said he had a responsibility to future generations and his children shared his vision.

Using a couple of shelled snails as bait, we hooked two catfish and took them inside. Wilfredo showed me how to hold the fish without getting stabbed by their spines. Once they were gutted and cleaned we stuffed them with lemon grass and cooked them in boiling oil. I ate mine with a ginger and pepper sauce, together with a cup of rice. It was delicious – there's nothing like eating something that you've caught and cooked yourself.

Claudio wasn't filming, or eating either. This was unusual, to say the least. Instead he was drinking beer and carefully inspecting infected mosquito bites on his legs.

'Are you all right?' I asked him.

He made a face. 'You get one little mosquito bite and you scratch it in the night. Then it gets infected and it just goes on and on . . .'

'But beer before lunch, Clouds?'

'It's medicinal.' He waggled the bottle at Robin. 'He has a saw on his Leatherman, we're going to amputate later.'

Stuffed full of rice and catfish, I was back on the road, looking for a bus to take us to a place called Malaybalay City, before the last stretch up the mountain to the monastery.

As usual there was no bus to be seen and no jeepney either. Standing outside Wilfredo's restaurant I began to feel like Steve Martin in *The Jerk* – the part where he leaves home then has to wait for days outside his parents' house, hoping to hitch a lift.

At last a bus came along. It was a Fiera, a more modern version of the jeepney we'd been on this morning. It looked pretty crowded but there was room for a couple more and we were only going as far as Los Amigos anyway.

I took a seat and started to think of the journey ahead, how many islands we had to cross and how much of this part of the journey would be by water. It would be ferries, mainly. I don't mind ferries so much . . .

After changing buses at Los Amigos we arrived in Malaybalay City late that afternoon. We were only half an hour away from the monastery now, so we hailed a couple of tricycles – motorbike taxis with a sidecar – and left the main road for the mountains.

It was an interesting journey. The drivers weren't exactly sure where they were going and the road was bumpy and pitted, twisting through the palms that covered the hillside. There were no signs anywhere so we just kept climbing. Eventually I spotted a clutch of white buildings in the distance and decided that must be the place.

It was dark by the time we reached the Monastery of the Transfiguration, and I was exhausted. Father Adag, a gentle but enthusiastic man with an infectious smile, came down to meet us. He showed us to the guest quarters – simple, comfortable rooms with just a bed and a basin. And it was peaceful too, just as I'd hoped it would be. Father Adag promised to show us around properly in the morning. He suggested we meet up some time after seven, because he would be at prayers between three-thirty and six-thirty.

*

The Benedictines came to the area in 1982, taking over what had been an old American ranch. They not only built the monastery but planted all the trees. Father Adag told me that originally the whole area was clear – the ranch ran cattle and there were no trees. Now all you could see were trees, and to think that the monks had planted every one of them was mind-boggling. He also said that in those first days there was no dirt road up from the highway either, so they had to walk.

Back in the 1980s the Filipino government encouraged people to grow coffee. Seed plants were given out and while most of the villagers did not have enough land, the monks took full advantage of the scheme. This was prime coffee country with the perfect tropical climate, much like the mountains in Papua New Guinea, and the coffee bushes grew in abundance.

The Benedictines not only grew the beans but harvested, roasted and ground them. The blend was then shipped all over the world. They did the same with peanut brittle. I love the stuff – they make it from boiling water and sugar, peanuts, salt, sesame seeds, vanilla essence, yoghurt and lots of butter. The whole place is a hive of activity employing a lot of people from the surrounding area. The revenue goes into a collective fund and everything the monks need comes from that. Not that they need very much. Theirs is a simple life and, according to Father Adag, a very happy one.

Father Adag kindly provided us with our means of getting down the mountain again – a little red bus called a multi-cab. It was only 1000 cc and so slow even the petrol tankers were overtaking us. We were doing about 20 kmph and there were at least fifty between us and the Del Monte pineapple plantation where we would pick up a truck to take us to the town of Manolo Fortich.

Oh well. The only thing to do was sit back and ignore the sight of buses and bicycles meandering by. We trundled through tiny towns of multicoloured buildings, market stalls, little shops selling cold drinks and take-away food. In one town I noticed a barber's shop and, stroking my goatee, I suggested that later we should find somewhere I could get it trimmed. I'd heard that barbers in the Philippines are popular because of their prowess as storytellers, rather than their ability with scissors. Apparently the better the story, the more custom the barber is going to get. A local idiosyncrasy; it would be interesting to find out if it were true.

We stopped briefly at the Del Monte plantation, just because I'd grown up with the man from Del Monte saying yes. The plantation was colossal – 25,000 hectares covering five municipalities. Every year they harvest 750,000 tonnes of pineapples and the operation goes on 24/7. Pineapples are native to the Philippines, but not the kind used for canning. These pineapples had been brought over by the Americans from Hawaii. According to our guide, the canning variety was grown here because back in the early 1900s Hawaiian pineapple farmers suffered a pestilence disaster. Their land was ruined so they had to look for another economical place to grow them. The soil here was perfect apparently, so the company moved its operation. Now Del Monte employs four thousand workers in the fields and another two thousand at the cannery. The fruit is cut by hand from thorny-looking ground plants that cover entire hillsides. I pitched in and had a go. It was pouring with rain now, the landscape coated in mist, and I was wearing shorts. By the time I'd been working for half an hour my legs were not only covered in mud but cut to ribbons. The mud got into the cuts and from knee to ankle I felt as if I were on fire.

After being sorted on a conveyor the pineapples were transferred to a lorry, then driven to the cannery, forty miles away. We weren't allowed into the cannery because the owners were terrified we might be carrying swine flu, but we did get a lift in one of the lorries, and the driver dropped us in Manolo Fortich.

En route we stopped so I could wash the mud off my legs and I spotted a barber's shop across the street. A sign in the window indicated they were advertising for an expert barber. I needed a beard trim and Claudio had been looking to have his hair cut for a while now.

'A number one,' he told me. 'Someone with a pair of clippers will be just fine. It's too hot to have my hair this long.'

'I'll do it for you.' I nodded to the sign. 'I'll get my beard trimmed then see if they'll take me on. If they do, I'll tell you a story while I cut your hair.'

Inside, I told the barber what I wanted and with a hot towel over my face I waited eagerly for his stories. He didn't seem up for telling any though. In fact, none of the guys were. It's not that they were unpleasant and the place seemed popular enough. It's just that it's difficult to tell a really good story when your face is covered by a dust mask. The subtleties are lost, the little nuances that make a good story. It seemed everyone here was terrified of swine flu.

Anyway, I let him shave me with a cut-throat razor. I had my beard trimmed and my head massaged. Then, persuading the owner I was an expert barber, I sat Claudio down and picked up a pair of clippers. I must say I was slightly hurt by the anxious expression on his face . . .

The next morning, with Claudio successfully shorn of his locks, we set off for the island of Camiguin, or 'Come Again', as I dubbed it. It was two hours by ferry and after we got our tickets, we made our way to Cagayan de Oro and the docks. Three army trucks were lined up next to a naval vessel and a troop of soldiers was unloading boxes of ammunition. We wandered over to have a look and instead of the security guard demanding to know what we were doing, he told us to make sure we didn't leave without seeing the General MacArthur memorial. The soldiers didn't seem worried by us either, they were all waves and smiles, even the skin-headed guy in charge of loading. He just waved to us and asked us how we were doing.

Taking the security guard's advice we climbed some steps and there was MacArthur's hat . . . literally a gigantic sculpture of his military cap, facing out to sea and supported by five gold stars.

The ferry was a large catamaran. I'd been on something similar when we crossed from Iran to Dubai during the last trip. They're made in Australia, very comfortable and very fast. The sea was calm and the two hours it took to get to the island flew by. Once ashore we quickly found a jeepney. It was another of the 1000 cc multi-cab things we'd been on yesterday, so I knew it wouldn't be very fast. No matter – I was getting used to the different pace.

Heading up the coast, we met up with Benjamin, an anchovy fisherman, who was waiting with his crew beside a slender outrigger canoe. Benjamin was forty years old and had been fishing all his life, though these days his income was supplemented by what he could make from coconut oil. The Philippines is a poor country with 80 per cent of the people living below the poverty line, and although much of this island looked like paradise, there were lines of little shanties dotted along the shore.

Benjamin explained that the fishing is not what it once was. He could remember when the whole area was teeming with anchovies, but like so many other places it's been overfished and now much of the coral is dead. The only section that is still alive surrounds a sandbar he called White Island, a few hundred yards off the beach.

Clambering aboard the canoe, we chugged out to where a dozen or so other boats were already fishing.

'The sea is too calm,' Benjamin muttered. 'Not enough waves, there won't be many fish today.'

It is a very hard life. These guys get 10 pesos per can of anchovies and when you think there are about 70 pesos to the pound, that's not a lot of money. A kilo of fish brings in £1.05 and there are at least three men per boat, all of whom have families to feed.

At White Island we paddled out on a second boat Benjamin had prepared with the nets. The waters here were so still and clear you could almost see the bottom. Paying out the folds of narrow mesh, we formed a semicircular barrier while one of the crew put on a dive mask and slipped over the side. His job was to try to spot the shoals and scare them into the net, but Benjamin said that when the sea was as calm as this, it was much easier to scare them away instead. A few waves made things a lot easier.

We didn't catch anything – it was just one of those days I suppose, and we spent most of the afternoon fixing the engine. Benjamin had left it in the other boat and it got soaked, the coil was wet and it wouldn't start. It was only after much banter and exchanging of spark plugs with other fishermen that we finally got it going.

Nevertheless the sandbar had been a pleasant place to while away the afternoon – the island a dramatic backdrop, very green and dark against the sky. The mountains looked like a sleeping giant, the head at one end and a big stomach in the middle, his feet lost in cloud at the far end. I just felt bad for Benjamin – it really was a tough way to make a living.

Back on the beach we had a couple of beers and one guy picked up a guitar and sang us a song about how happy he was with his simple life as a fisherman. But it's a way of life whose days are numbered, a reality that was brought home to me when another boat came in and we helped unload the catch. By the time the anchovies had been bagged and weighed the three-man crew had made a profit of just £3.50 between them. It was seven o'clock in the evening and the boat had been fishing since four that morning. Benjamin told me that he doubted there would be much fishing for the next generation and that didn't bode well. Apart from a little farming and a few jobs in tourism, fishing was the mainstay of the economy. Every day some two hundred boats fished the area around White Island and that just wasn't sustainable.

Benjamin and his family were the perfect hosts. They cooked us a beautiful dinner of fish-eye soup and rice, then I strung my hammock between two palms and spent another perfect night on the beach.

In the morning I woke to the sound of a cock crowing, although thankfully this one hadn't spent the entire night trying to bring in the dawn. Cockerels are prized here in the Philippines; cock-fighting is big business and on Sundays, while the women and children are singing hymns in church, the men are taking their birds out to fight.

There were a number of large birds wandering around the little encampment there on the beach. Benjamin wasn't into it, not being a gambler, but lots of the other fishermen were and they kept a number of prize birds. I watched two red cocks having a go at each other – wings spread, neck feathers puffed, pecking and tearing and generally trying to claw one another to death. One of the men told me that in the actual fights a sharp knife is strapped to each bird's left leg and it can be very bloody. They always fight to the death. The winning owner takes not only the money but the vanquished cock to eat.

We thanked our hosts and flagged down another tricycle to take us back to the docks. This was different from the one we had hired before. The driver was enclosed in a cab with the trailer behind him, rather than fitted as a sidecar. It was a sort of tuk-tuk I suppose, designed to carry six people although we'd seen them carry many more. It was called the *Mariner* and had been painted yellow and blue with a mural of a container ship on one panel. The driver sat on the Kawasaki it was built around. As far as I could see, the only difference between it and any other motorbike was the front tyre. Normally they're rounded so you can grip when you lean the bike into a corner, but this was squared like a car tyre because you don't lean, of course, you turn the handlebars. He told me his children had bought the tricycle for him – they all worked at sea, hence the name and the picture of the ship.

Back at the docks we boarded a ferry going to the island of Bohol. The ferry was carrying two cars and a truck loaded with watermelons. The crew were all young men, a couple of them stripped to their shorts and hosing themselves down right there on the cargo deck. They told us it was typical to spend a year working on the ferry before going on to crew for the bigger ships. On my last trip I travelled from Dubai to India on a container ship with a Filipino crew. They'd had a great time, and these guys were cheerful souls too, despite the basic living conditions. There seemed to be just one cabin where three of them would take it in turns to sleep – a metal door, metal walls, no porthole and a bed with a sheet of cardboard for a mattress. The others slept upstairs on the vinyl benches occupied by the passengers during the day.

It was a pretty monotonous life, but the skipper told us it was a way of moving to bigger and better things in other parts of the world. There is so little opportunity in the Philippines that many people work abroad for at least part of their lives.

It was all very laid-back and I spent much of the four-hour crossing flaked out on a bench, but when we finally docked in Bohol I jumped up, itching to get going. We were making the next island hop, from Bohol to Cebu, with the navy. Their gunship left at 5 p.m. from the north side of the island.

At the dockside we said our goodbyes to Inkee our translator, who was leaving for another job. We were supposed to be meeting another translator here, called Justine, but there was no sign of her. Standing on the concrete wharf with the sun burning my scalp, the only vehicle I could see was a police car and it was making a beeline for me.

'Oh shit, Claudio,' I muttered. 'Here we go. They probably think we're drug traffickers or something.'

There were two uniformed cops in the front and a woman in plain clothes in the back, all of them Filipino. They jumped out and the younger cop placed his cap squarely on his head, then adjusted the automatic on his hip. I waited, wondering what this could be about, while through the windscreen the older, more solidly built cop just stared at me.

The woman came over. 'Hello, Charley. I'm Justine and this is Ramon. He's come to take you across the island.'

Once my heartbeat was back to normal we drove through town and along the coast road into the mountains. This was a normal patrol for the two policemen, who went back and forth across the island, only today they stopped at the Chocolate Hills so that we could see them. There are 1268 hills in total and I'd been told they looked like breasts, which seemed fair enough. I mean, back in Indonesia we'd seen a mountain in the shape of . . . Well, anyway.

It was a bit touristy, with a million and one steps leading up to a viewing point where the world and his wife were gathered with their children. But it was worth it. The hills *did* look like breasts, and there were hundreds of them, stretching as far as the eye could see – all different shapes and sizes, not too big, but then they say that more than a handful is wasted, don't they? Ramon told me that in the hot, dry season, when the grass turned brown, they really did look as though they were made of chocolate. Legend has it that thousands of years ago a giant fell in love with a mortal woman, who died. He spent eternity mourning her. He cried and cried; he cried so much that his tears washed away most of the land and left just these hills behind. It was a good story and they were spectacular hills, with paddy fields and little plantations carved in between them.

Back in the police car Ramon took us to the port on the north shore. By the time we got there it was close to 5 p.m. but I could see no sign of the navy boat. My heart sank; I thought we might have missed it. Luckily it turned out that the boat was tied up a little further along the coast. It was a patrol boat, a gunship, and it looked pretty ropy, to be honest. But the crew seemed pleased to see us. All save for one wary-looking guy carrying an M16 that was so old it might have seen action in Vietnam. He really liked that gun; in fact, he didn't put it down all the way to Cebu. But then I suppose he wasn't meant to, this was a military vessel after all, and just as Ramon and his driver had been on a routine patrol, so was the navy. The boat, built in 1971, was Korean and very rusty; I imagine that no sooner did they get to grips with one patch than another broke out. It's in the sea all the time and with the heat here, it must be a nightmare trying to maintain it. We chatted to the captain – a cool, affable guy called Peter wearing a baseball cap emblazoned with the words 'Team Navy' – and he confirmed my hunch.

We cast off and were soon under way, smoke billowing in great black clouds from the exhaust. A little later I took a look in the engine room, which was unbelievably hot and noisy. The motor was a V16 that at 10 knots used 350 litres of diesel every hour. They carried 18,800 litres of diesel, mind you – enough to get us all the way to Manila if we wanted. Peter showed me the full extent of their armaments – 22 mm guns at the back and an old 30 mm in the bows that had never been in use. What were in use were two pairs of 50-calibres that could take out an oil drum at a distance of a nautical mile.

'Who are you after when you're out here, Peter?' I asked. 'Drug traffickers, people traffickers; that kind of stuff?'

'Sometimes,' he said. 'But mostly we're looking for illegal fishermen.'

Glancing over my shoulder to where the guy with the M16 was patrolling, my thoughts returned to the boat we had planned to take from Sulawesi.

'Illegal fishermen,' I said. 'Where from? Indonesia?'

Peter shook his head. 'No, in these waters it's local people mostly. Each island has a ten-kilometre zone where you're not allowed to fish, and beyond that there are restrictions that we have to enforce. We rescue people from ships in distress as well, of course, answer mayday calls, that kind of thing.'

'I suppose you must be out in some pretty rough seas?' It was calm now but I could imagine these waters when the wind was up.

He smiled. 'I remember one call. The weather was so bad that by the time we got to the boat half my crew were seasick.'

They carried out a couple of exercises – what they called general orders – which involved manning the big guns, swivelling them round to mark various targets to port and starboard. Then later they threw a lifebelt overboard and rescued it, with much shouting and pointing. Crewmen were leaning over the side with boat hooks, while another threw a lifebelt to the one already in the water; I was just glad no one had volunteered me to play 'man overboard'.

By the time we landed on Cebu it was dark. I stepped ashore, taking a final glance at my friend with the M16. He really did love that gun. All the time they'd been hauling the stricken lifebelt aboard he'd had the rifle trained on it.

'Just in case he's an illegal alien, I suppose,' I said. 'Or a drug trafficker maybe.'

He didn't say anything. Just gripped the gun tighter.

12
Field of Dreams

TODAY – ONE WAY OR ANOTHER – we would cross from Cebu to the island of Leyte. The more exciting possibility was to go by army helicopter, which would be fantastic. If not, well, there was always the ferry. Not quite as glamorous, but never mind.

In the meantime – breakfast. Cebu is famous for its high-quality pork and I'd heard there was a great restaurant near the market that served a roast at any time of day. A couple of furniture-makers agreed to take us over there. Sixty-seven-year-old Manny and his nephew Andi had created two incredible tricycles using recycled polyethylene – plastic, in other words, but they had designed it to look like woven bamboo. They had taken two Yamaha motorbikes and converted them to shaft drive, before attaching the back of a multi-cab just like the ones we had been in before, with the passenger section shaped to look like a traditional Filipino house on wheels. They were perfect, and a novel way of going to breakfast. Which gave me an idea.

'Let's have a race to the restaurant.'

'OK,' Sam said. 'Two teams, then?'

I nodded, indicating the motorbikes. 'We'll have Andi, Claudio and me in one; and you, Robin and Manny in the other. How about a side bet, Sam? The loser has to eat or drink anything the winner says.'

I didn't realise it then but before we even got going we were at a disadvantage, because Andi didn't know where the restaurant was. It didn't matter, though, because I was behind the wheel and I had a cunning plan – we'd stick close to Manny, right in his wheel tracks in fact, and as soon as I spotted the place, we'd slipstream him to the line.

So off we went through the busy streets. Every now and then I'd practise the slipstream manoeuvre and move up alongside Manny, only to drop back again when he thought I was going to overtake.

But then I stalled the bloody thing. I missed a gear and it conked out, and as I tried to kick-start it they just steamed ahead.

I did my best to catch up, weaving in and out of the traffic, but I couldn't get close and they made it to the restaurant before us. Gutted, I slowed for the entrance only to see that Sam was still in the back of Manny's vehicle. Seizing my opportunity, I pulled right up to the door and we piled into the restaurant ahead of them.

'We won!' I declared as Sam followed us in.

'What do you mean? *We* won. We totally won. We were here first, Charley!'

'No, no.' I wagged a finger at him. 'You might have technically got here before us, but we were parked and in the restaurant before you.'

It was tenuous, I know, and in the end I had to accept defeat, which meant Sam would decide my culinary fate. I could tell from his expression he was already dreaming up something suitably unpleasant.

The restaurant was buzzing and clearly very popular. Behind a glass partition a group of young women were taking meat cleavers to entire pigs. They were really going for it – with one chop they were through the bone. How they missed their fingers I will never know. I wanted to have a go, so they gave me a plastic glove to wear on my non-chopping hand and introduced me to a pig that had spent four hours on a spit roast. I got the head off fairly cleanly, but the rest . . . well, I was worried about losing my fingers so I made a bit of mess. To tell the truth, I destroyed it – sawing instead of chopping – but regardless of the presentation, we each ended up with a plate of meat and crackling.

Just before I sat down to enjoy it, however, Sam handed me a bowl brimming with a thick, brown liquid.

I raised one eyebrow. 'What is it?'

'Soup.'

'What kind of soup?'

'Sort of oxtail.'

'Oxtail? Sam, this is a pork restaurant. How can it be oxtail? OK, come on, what's really in it?'

He had a gleam in his eye now. 'Kidney,' he said, 'and liver . . .'

'And . . .?'

'Pig's blood.'

Actually it wasn't too bad. I had a couple of spoonfuls, but there was no way I was going to neck the bowl in one as Sam was demanding. It tasted salty, like liquefied black pudding. The pork was amazing though, very moist and succulent, and the crackling was perfect. If you're ever in Cebu you have to try some; people come from all over the Philippines to eat here.

The army weren't able to provide the helicopter after all. It had been a long shot and given we'd had help from the police and the navy already, we thought we had done pretty well. Instead, Andi and his uncle took us to the port where we bought tickets for the ferry to Leyte.

The ferries – a couple of old container ships – were moored along the wharf. I went up to the bridge to talk to Jasper Nacita, one of the captains. A quiet, assured kind of guy, Jasper had spent ten years sailing the world on ships just like these. I took the opportunity to ask him about the next major leg in my journey – the proposed crossing from Manila to Taiwan.

'What do you think?' I said. 'The only boat we can find is a thirty-metre fishing boat.'

He glanced at me, the lines of his face just a little rumpled. 'When are you leaving Manila?'

'In a week maybe? That's the plan, anyway.'

Twisting his mouth at the corners he said: 'You'll be at the peak of the southwest monsoon.'

That didn't sound very promising. 'Will we?'

He nodded. 'The current is very strong and it comes at you on the port side. You'll feel it as soon as you leave Manila. Then it's four or five days and you don't know if it will create a typhoon, but if it does . . .'

'It would be slow then,' I said, 'that kind of crossing?'

'Slow and very rough. Lots of big waves.'

I swallowed. 'How big exactly?'

'Six metres maybe. But it's a really long swell and with the current, the wind . . .' He was shaking his head. 'No,' he said, 'I don't think that's a good idea at all.'

It was clear we would have to think about it. The terrible

crossing I'd made from Timor to Darwin the year before was still fresh in my mind and I wasn't keen on repeating that kind of experience.

Landing on Leyte, we found a couple of kids delivering batteries who agreed to take us to Carigara, which was halfway to Tacloban, where we planned to spend the night. Before that I spent some time in the local market – an old building with dark, narrow lanes and stalls piled high with fruit and vegetables, children's toys, live pigs, a coconut grinder and a massive tub of minced pork that I helped knead into sausage. I even saw a couple of old boys steaming the skin off goats' heads.

I took a moment to look at the map, reminding myself just how far we'd come in the past few days – all the way from Mindanao, travelling almost due north to the coast and across to Camiguin, then northwest to Bohol, before making our way around the coast with the navy. Now we were heading east across Leyte. I loved this place. The people were so friendly and welcoming, so interested in us and what we were doing. Our translator Justine told us that something like 42 per cent of the Filipino population are children. I don't know if that's partly because this is such a strongly Catholic country, but families certainly seem to have a lot of kids.

Talking of kids, an hour or so later Jon-Jon and Bernard, the two lads driving us to Carigara, showed up with their Isuzu truck. Bernard's girlfriend was pregnant and he told me he would marry her if he could, but right now he didn't have enough money. They let me out in Carigara, a tiny little town with narrow streets that were part cobble and part dirt. The houses were hunched up to the kerbs – tiny, single-storey places with tin roofs and darkened interiors. On one side of the main street were a couple of run-down colonial places. A few of the local kids sat watching us on the ancient steps. On the other side was an open-fronted shack with hundreds of decoratively carved knives on display. Crossing for a closer look, we met the stall-holder, a woman called Gloria, who seemed to radiate an aura of serenity. She was in her late forties, wore her hair in a single plait and was wearing a pair of John Lennon-style glasses. There was something about her; just being around her left an impression on me. I can't describe it exactly, but it was almost spiritual. I told her she was wonderful to talk to, and the fact that she sold knives somehow seemed incongruous.

She just smiled and explained that the knives were ornaments not weapons. She and her five sons ran the business and she enjoyed the fact that they had visitors from all over the world.

'I like to think of the world as a small place,' she told me, 'a positive place where everyone gets along. It's lovely to spend some time talking to a man all the way from faraway London.'

She was wonderful. One of the special people you hope to meet on journeys like this. Someone whose presence seems to linger long after you've left them behind.

I spent the last leg of a very long day with a girl called Rochelle, in a vehicle her father had designed. Dr Rusty Balderian was the mayor of Tabon Tabon, a small, very poor town, where it seemed the only form of transportation was a regular motorbike. Rochelle told us that people would ride four or five up all the time. It was dangerous and there were lots of accidents, and because it was the only way of getting around, there were very few visitors to the town. The economy was suffering badly, and conscious of his responsibility to the people who had elected him, Dr Balderian decided to come up with an alternative.

His creation was the most bizarre vehicle I've ever driven, something between a tuk-tuk and a van, but made from woven strands of bamboo. There were bamboo benches in the back for passengers, a bamboo chair for the driver and, under the bamboo bonnet, an engine that ran on coco-bio-diesel, which is made from used cooking oil.

Rochelle and her three brothers had grown up in LA, but they came home to Leyte to try to help their father do something about the poverty in Tabon Tabon. They created opportunities by employing rice farmers (who have little to do between planting and harvest) to make these vans. Three had been completed so far. I drove this one all the way to Tacloban. The gears were the wrong way round and the brakes a little unpredictable and by the time it was dark the whole thing was becoming quite dangerous. Having said that, it was still far safer than four or five people balanced on top of a motorbike.

Rochelle was another inspiring person. She could have stayed a California girl, yet here she was on Leyte, trying her best to raise the standard of public transportation in an eco-friendly way. She seemed to exemplify the sense of purpose and ingenuity I could feel here. Thinking back, although we'd had a good time in Sulawesi, we'd also struggled a bit. It had been hard to get around, and the travelling hadn't been as enjoyable. There were more smiles here – more laughter – and there wasn't the sense of government interference that we'd experienced in Indonesia.

We spent the night in Tacloban, a big and noisy city that has been the capital of Leyte Province since 1830. Before that the capital had moved from one town to another, but eventually they settled on Tacloban, largely because it has such a sheltered port. Centuries before the Spanish showed up it was known as Kankabatok, in reference to the nomadic people who settled here. For years after it was a favourite spot for fishermen, who used a particular piece of gear called a taklub – they called the place Tarakluban, and eventually that became Tacloban.

The city is perched on the edge of the Leyte Gulf, which in 1944 was the setting for the largest naval battle in modern history. When the Japanese invaded the Philippines, General MacArthur made a promise to the people that he would return. He did, with the biggest modern fleet ever assembled. For three brutal days, over two hundred American ships locked horns with sixty Japanese vessels, before finally landing on the island on 26 October.

I'd been told about a local historian called Alex Montejo, who ran an elegant hotel in the middle of the city. Alex had been fifteen when the Japanese invaded. The hotel – a beautiful, colonial-style wood building with pillars either side of the entrance and a balcony above – had been Alex's family home. A number of Japanese officers had been stationed in the house during the war, while Alex, his parents and eight brothers and sisters were confined to one room, which was now the hotel office.

'What was it like?' I asked him. 'It must have been terrifying when the Japanese invaded.'

'It was to begin with. The Japanese expected the people to bow before them and if they didn't, they were slapped in the face.'

Alex was eighty-two yet he could remember everything in minute detail. I asked him whether the Japanese committed the kinds of atrocities you heard about in other parts of Asia.

'Not really,' he said. 'The lower ranks could be a bit rough, but the officers were educated and they were courteous. One of the ones who stayed here played the piano beautifully. There were only three beheadings and two of those were thieves. The Japanese invited the whole town to come and watch and after that you could leave your door open all night and nobody would steal anything. The big problem was food. There was just no way of getting any to the island. There was nothing in the markets, so we planted vegetables in every vacant lot across the city.'

He showed me some photos from the days of the liberation in October 1944. There was one with a young Imelda Marcos on a float and I could see that even then she had a thing for smart shoes.

When MacArthur upheld his promise to return the first the local people knew about it were the massive explosions coming from the airport. They rushed out to see what was going on and, instead of Japanese planes, there were planes with American stars on the wings. For three days the locals stayed in the air-raid shelter while the Americans dropped bombs and sent up shells from the big ships. Then, at the end of the third day, 26 October, the Japanese fled and MacArthur landed at a place called Red Beach.

That moment has been captured in the most amazing memorial of the general, walking through water as if he's just stepped out of a landing craft, surrounded by five men, two of whom are Filipino. Alex said that after the liberation, the Japanese carried out air raids at night, and unlike the Americans they targeted civilian areas. His abiding memory, though, is the food – for two years they had been half starved and suddenly here were the Americans again, with more food than any of them could remember.

I wanted to see Red Beach for myself, so outside the hotel I hunted down a tricycle, one of the motorbike and sidecar outfits that are all over the place here.

'Is this yours?' I asked a young guy wearing a pair of black wraparound shades, who was standing beside one.

'Yes.'

'Could you take me to Red Beach?'

'Yes.'

'Do you think I could drive maybe?'

'Yes.'

A few moments later my monosyllabic companion and I were driving past the Price Mansion where MacArthur had stayed, heading out of the commercial district into the suburbs, where the houses were more like the shacks we had seen further south. The beach isn't actually a beach any more. The shoreline has been reinforced with concrete and the memorial is a massive square with a flagpole in the middle. A series of steps climb to where MacArthur and the others appear as if they're walking from the sea. I stood there trying to imagine how it must have been – lines of jeeps, tanks and landing craft and the water thick with every kind of US warship imaginable. It was very moving; another piece of Second World War history but very different from what we had seen on Thursday Island.

It was time to move on – northeast to Samar. I jumped in a Spider. Not the eight-legged variety but a yellow taxi with no windows. The driver took me across the longest bridge in the Philippines – the San Juanico Bridge – two kilometres of ironwork and concrete that connects the islands of Leyte and Samar. He let me out at a place called Basey – literally at the side of the road, where a path cut a passage between the palms. It was baking hot and I was sweating like a pig. Even the trees seemed to be suffering; the tops were moist and heavy, drooping wearily over the road.

The patterns meshed into Rochelle's bamboo van in Tabon Tabon mimicked the banig, the hand-woven mat used everywhere for sleeping and sitting on. From here I was going to visit some banig-weavers – all women – who work together under a rocky overhang, almost like a cave. To get there I had to follow the path through the palm trees. After about fifty yards it broadened into a clearing. The weavers were sitting on banig mats under the overhanging rock, a dozen or so of them working individual strands of dried leaf into the most amazing mats. Squatting down, I spoke to one woman with a big smile and not so many teeth.

'Wow,' I said, pointing at her work. 'That is incredible.'

'Yes, sir,' she said. 'Thank you.'

I asked her what it was made from and she showed me some sea grass growing beside the path. 'We pluck the strands one at a time,' she explained, 'then dry the leaves in the sun.'

'Then they're dyed?'

'Yes, sir.'

'And do you come here every day?'

'Yes, sir.'

'Why here? Why the caves?'

'Because the temperature is cold, sir,' she said.

'And you make the mats to sell?'

'Yes, sir.'

'How long does it take?'

'For this family-sized one,' she indicated a large multicoloured mat, 'three days, sir.' Then she gestured to another that was two-tone and patterned like tweed. 'This one is just for you and your wife, sir,' she told me. 'It's smaller, for two people, not the whole family.'

My wife. I hadn't seen Olly for such a long time and suddenly I really missed her. The woman unrolled the mat. 'Just for the two of you, sir,' she repeated with a smile.

'How long did it take to make?' I asked her.

'One day. Do you want to buy it for you and your wife, sir?'

'Sure, why not. I haven't seen her for a long time and when I get home we can lie down together and . . .'

With the mat rolled up under my arm, I managed to hitch a lift with a delivery man called Rommel, who drove a van for a company called 2GO, delivering parcels and packages all over Samar and Leyte. I helped him make his rounds and it was well after dark by the time he dropped me in a small town called Calbayog. It was only as I found somewhere to crash for the night that I realised what day it was today. Much of the morning had been devoted to General MacArthur and the American liberation of these islands. Fitting, somehow, given it was the Fourth of July.

Sunday 5 July turned out to be an amazing day, ending at the eight-thousand-foot Mayon Volcano, where I watched the smoking summit through a telescope. It began, though, with Ronnie the scrap metal guy, a likeable rogue who operated a yard in Calbayog. The entrance to his place was marked by two trucks set ten feet above the ground on a metal scaffold. In the yard there was an open-sided workshop and line upon line of scrap metal. Ronnie – a big man with a real sense of fun – had three young lads working for him and carried a pistol in his pocket.

I greeted him with a handshake. 'So this is your kingdom then.'

'No,' he said, 'it's my empire.'

'Ah, even better then.'

Ronnie bought scrap metal from ex-fishermen, who had exhausted the supplies of fish by blowing them up with home-made sticks of dynamite, and were now using explosives to tear great chunks off wrecked ships in the bay, including a US warship that had been sunk by the Japanese. Part of this warship was awaiting collection at Ronnie's brother-in-law's place in Allen, where we were due to catch the ferry. Ronnie offered to take us with him.

I took an instant liking to Ronnie, a bright and inventive guy with an infectious good humour. Not only did he work in scrap metal, he also crushed plastic containers in a home-made press, then transported them to the port where they were shipped for recycling.

As we drove along I asked Ronnie about the gun in his pocket. He explained that it was for personal protection. He came across a few tough characters in his line of work and it was not unknown for people to 'disappear'. I knew there was a lot of political instability here, with at least two rebel factions fighting the government. In the south it was Abu Sayyaf, an organisation trying to create a separate Islamic state. Up here it was the New People's Army, the armed wing of the Communist Party. More about that later . . .

Ronnie was great company. He had a degree in engineering and architecture, which meant he could design a plan and see it through to completion. He'd built his own salvage truck, a massive flatbed with a crane on the back, from three different vehicles. After he obtained his degree he went to Saudi Arabia and was working in construction during the first Gulf War. Back here he dealt first in ice, then fish and now he was buying scrap. His wife runs the shop where the scrap is initially purchased; what is rubbish to some people is cash to her and Ronnie. The shop building itself is made entirely from reclaimed materials, including the windows from a bus.

Ronnie was also into all things mechanical, including motorbikes. I told him that we seemed to have a lot in common.

'Yeah, Charley, we sure do. What's that old English saying? Birds of a feather fuck together, is that it?'

'Flock together,' I told him. 'Birds of a feather flock together, Ronnie.'

He laughed. 'I always thought that was a weird expression!'

At his brother-in-law's place I helped Ronnie and the three lads load up scrap metal from the rusted American warship. You could still see the rivets that once held it together. It weighed a ton and in the midday heat I was sweating buckets. We finally got it all on to the salvage truck and he drove us to the ferry terminal, where we said our goodbyes.

One more ferry. Old and rusty, it looked about ready for Ronnie's scrap yard itself. Ah well – once we had crossed the short stretch of water to Matnog it would be overland all the way to Manila.

Another ancient hulk was tied up alongside our ferry. I watched a group of kids climb a rope to the top deck before leaping into the sea and thought about our journey so far. This country really was fascinating – so many different people doing so many different things. And the most enjoyable part was being allowed a glimpse into the lives of a few special people. People like Ronnie, Gloria from Carigara and Alex Montejo yesterday; people who left a lasting impression. Leaning on the rail as we steamed across the bay, I took a moment to consider the low hills of the island ahead and let the whole experience just work through me.

When we landed at Matnog we were met by volunteers from the Kabalikat–Bicol Province Rescue Ambulance Service, together with a whole bunch of people on scooters. They must have heard there was a film crew in the area and come out to see us. The ambulance reminded me of the volunteer service I saw in Mumbai. This organisation had been started in much the same way by concerned citizens and was funded entirely by donations. There are sixty-two chapters spread across the country and each chapter has a number denoting the area they cover. There are over three thousand members in total, and their achievements have just been recognised by the Regional Disaster Coordinating Council for this part of Asia. Each member is also given a number – their individual call sign – and that's how they address one another. The Kabalikat chapter is number 30 and the guy I was talking to was the founder member, so he'd been given the number 01 by his colleagues. He told me it was an honour to wear it on his sweatshirt.

The ambulances were kitted out with stretchers, first-aid equipment and oxygen. Some of the volunteers were doctors and every item had been paid for either by individuals or by local companies. These guys were part of the emergency services, on call whenever a disaster struck.

01 was in his fifties, his hair cut very close. He proudly told me that his team attended every disaster that hit the region. 'We know what to do and how to do it no matter the situation.' Back in 2006 Mayon Volcano had erupted and at the same time a typhoon hit, setting off flash floods and mudslides. More than a thousand people were killed, entire towns destroyed and apparently hundreds of people were still listed as missing.

'You have to have a strong stomach,' he said. 'Last year when the ferry went down our members were asked to help with the bodies.' He was referring to the *Princess of the Stars*, a passenger ferry that sank in another typhoon. As the divers brought up the bodies, the volunteers helped get them ready for identification.

These are incredibly dedicated people who refuse to let the lack of government funds stop them providing a decent ambulance service. They were not only caring and dedicated but extremely hospitable, and they drove us all the way to the army base where we had been invited to watch a demonstration given by the Scout Rangers. The 3rd Battalion are the crack troops, guys whose job it is to deal with insurgents like the NPA and Abu Sayyaf. I had read in the paper that just a few weeks ago Abu Sayyaf claimed to have beheaded an American hostage, and two more Americans were still being held.

The rangers are led by Lieutenant Colonel Cirilito Sobejana, a forty-year-old guy who received the Medal of Valor from the government in 1995 – the country's highest honour. He was awarded it after leading fourteen rangers in an attack on an NPA camp. He and his men were vastly outnumbered, and Sobejana was shot five times. He had that look about him: the killer instinct, I suppose you'd call it. I've seen it in a few soldiers I've worked with. Having been shot in the arm, his right hand was curled in a permanent fist. He had also taken rounds in the side and the back and spent two years in hospital as a result.

The rangers are a superb fighting force. They are jungle troops, their camp half hidden by palm trees. With billets made from bamboo with thatched roofs, it looked tranquil, almost sleepy . . . except for the armoured cars and guys walking around in military green. The sign on the gate read: 'At your service across the land . . . any time . . . anywhere. The NPA's worst nightmare.'

Sobejana wore jungle fatigues and a black beret with a red battalion badge above his left eye; he exuded confidence, as did the six hundred men he led. They work in teams of seven – including a sniper, a man trained to kill with a knife, another with his bare hands and another with a rocket launcher. They all carried M16s. Sobejana told me that only three weeks ago they had been in a fire fight with a faction of the NPA. They killed the rebels and recovered all sorts of weapons, including home-made landmines. The recovered weaponry was on display in the mess, including the machine-gun the leader had been firing when he was killed. It was pock-marked with bullet holes and his automatic pistol was shredded too. The bullet had torn through the grips and smashed his hip – it was apparently this shot that killed him. On the table were magazines, an assortment of other guns, the defused landmines and personal items, like the watches worn by some of the rebels.

We watched the seven-man teams put on a display, armed to the teeth, with camouflage painted in stripes across their faces. Sobejana told me they had one principle. It was brutally simple – life for the ranger and death to their enemy. As far as the rangers are concerned, the rebels will never succeed. They are in action all the time and the spirit of camaraderie was evident. Watching them, listening to them talk as we sat down to a 'boodle fight', I was struck by their collective sense of mission. A boodle fight is a meal without cutlery or plates – the rice and crayfish, fruit and coconut juice are served on banana leaves on a long trestle table. It's a traditional way of eating and among the soldiers it's a symbol of unity.

I had heard that the NPA had a lot of support among the poorer sections of the population, but the situation is complex and I'm not familiar enough with the politics to make any kind of judgements on the rights and wrongs of it all. Anyway, politics aside, you couldn't help but be impressed by the commitment of Sobejana and his men.

The rangers knew we were travelling on to Legazpi City and offered to take us in one of their trucks because that stretch of road was dangerous for foreign travellers. Fine by me: with all this talk of gun fights and rebel armies, I was happy to be escorted by the most elite troops in the whole of Asia.

After the boodle fight we climbed into an army truck for the drive north and found the Kabalikat–Bicol chapter waiting outside. I thought they had gone ages ago but we were all heading in the same direction, so they had decided to hang around. Forming an unofficial convoy, we followed them, and half an hour up the road we were able to see them in action.

I had been talking to 01 earlier about the high number of motorbike accidents here. On the road to Legazpi City we came across a man who had ridden his motorbike into the back of a van. He was in a bad way, lying beside his mangled machine with a crowd of shouting, chattering people gathered around him. The ambulance crew leapt into action.

His right leg was a mess. Below the knee he was missing a

huge chunk of flesh. Looking at the back of the van, I could see the indentation where his bike had hit – the exhaust pipe bent at ninety degrees.

It was an ugly wound and provided a physical reminder of how vital the volunteer service here is. In no time they had the poor guy stabilised, and with a pressure bandage applied to his wound they lifted him onto a stretcher. Moments later he was in the back of the ambulance and they were on their way with lights flashing and siren blaring. I take my hat off to them, I really do.

It seemed fitting that we ended the day with Ed Laguerta, a local vulcanologist. His observatory was at the foot of Mount Mayon, just outside Legazpi City, and we'd just spent the earlier part of the day with the people who responded the last time it erupted. There it was, rising above the valley with clouds swirling about its flanks and smoke billowing from the summit. I could smell the sulphur and Ed told me that right now the volcano was particularly active. It was at what he called Level 1, which was the first stage towards an eruption. Inside the observatory he had a stack of computers monitoring various sensors. It was getting dark, but he had his telescope permanently trained on the summit. Taking a peek at the smoke, I watched it spitting bolts of boiling magma.

That night I stared at the mountain from my hotel bedroom. It was incredible to be so close to such an active volcano. It was even more incredible to think that tomorrow I would get even closer. I had been promised a visit right up to the lava field.

Outside in the morning sunshine, the view was even more spectacular. The mountain climbed from an ocean of green, where palms grew tall and the water sparkled in the sun. Gradually, though, the green became grey and the grey black, as the lower slopes gathered at the base of the lava. I tried to imagine what it must be like living so close to nature at her most malevolent. The volcano could blow at any time, although the activity is monitored day and night and Ed assured me that in general it erupts only every five or ten years. The last eruption had been three years ago so despite the level of activity being at Defcon 1, as I called it, we were . . . apparently . . . pretty safe.

It was a blisteringly hot day; so humid that after ten minutes of walking, my clothes were sticking to me. A local councillor called Mr Chan was waiting for us on the other side of the river, wearing a white floppy hat and a warm smile. Hoisting my shorts to my thighs, I waded across and shook his hand. He had brought us some quad bikes, which was brilliant. Mine was green, 250 cc with non-existent brakes, but it was perfect to get me along the dry river bed to the foot of the volcano. I couldn't quite believe we were actually going to a lava field; it was really exciting. Ahead of us the mountain was swathed in cloud. I could see the blackened field where the lava had cascaded down to nudge the valley below.

Following Chan, I criss-crossed various streams, where a group of guys were shovelling small stones to be collected by truck for the construction industry. It was back-breaking work for which they were paid the miserly equivalent of £2 per day. We came across teams of them all through the valley.

Initially we were riding on black sand, but that gradually gave way to rocky banks and larger boulders interspersed by patches of tall grass. You would think that a place like this would be fairly devoid of human inhabitants, but I saw kids washing where fresh water was gushing from pipes set into banks of stones; farmers watering buffalo, or carabao as they're called in the Philippines; and more teams of men shovelling stones. Waving to them as we passed, we eventually came to a small encampment where Chan usually kept his ATVs. There was a line of bamboo huts set in the trees on a little rise, to the right of the dry river bed. Here even more people were gathered, Chan's friends, his family – lots of children. Keeping a discreet distance were three heavily armed soldiers. Yesterday we had heard that there had been a series of bomb blasts in the southern part of the country, and with two missionaries still being held by Abu Sayyaf, the government was taking no chances. Whether we liked it or not, we had been assigned this army patrol and they had been following us since we left the rangers yesterday. We liked it, believe me. There is so much uncertainty in the world these days that it's not worth taking chances. If this area was dangerous and kidnapping a possibility, I'd rather have armed guards than not. They were really on their mettle – one guy in particular was as tough as I'd ever seen: shaven-headed, sleeves rolled up and eagle-eyed. Nothing moved in the bush without him spotting it.

On foot now, Chan led me the rest of the way up the valley. I could feel the atmosphere beginning to thicken; so humid that my breath seemed to catch in my throat. Together we walked to where a wall of bulging, black rock rose above my head. I had never seen anything like it – this was as far as the lava had travelled, where it had solidified. I was face to face with a three-year-old eruption and I could feel heat still in the rock.

Climbing up it was like being in a dream. This was a lunar landscape and all I could see was a field of black boulders. Three years previously they had been red hot, molten and moving. It was truly awe-inspiring. Looking back the way we had come, I could see the town lying quietly against the backdrop of the bay and I tried to imagine being there when the volcano had erupted.

Studying the lava more closely now I could see where the earth had been pushed up, brown patches that looked moist in the sea of black. I picked up a piece of rock and was surprised to find how light it was. Further on wisps of smoke drifted from between the stones; they were damp underfoot and there was a strong smell of sulphur. It was like being in some gigantic open-air sauna.

Chan had set up a wire zip line which ran from the lava field all the way back to his camp. Only two people had tested it so far, so I volunteered to be the third. It was easier and much quicker than climbing down again and walking. As I whizzed down I had visions of the line breaking and me plummeting into the rocks. But it was secure enough and I made it unscathed to the braking point back at the camp.

We took a moment to refresh ourselves with some coconut juice. Chan gave me a machete and I was about as useful with that as I had been with the meat cleaver back in Cebu. But I got the coconut open somehow and drank the sweet juice gratefully. After that we were back on the ATVs and Chan led me around the foot of the mountain, pausing first at a church that had been swamped by mud from a typhoon and then at the Cagsawa ruins. This was a town that had been built by the Spanish and all that remained was the tower of a once-beautiful church. In 1814 the volcano erupted and in a bid to escape the lava the townspeople of Cagsawa fled to the church. But there was no escape and the church was engulfed; everything burned and every one of them died.

My trip to the lava fields had been incredible – seeing the volcano up close was a truly spectacular experience. But this was a reminder – as if I needed one – of its terrible capacity for destruction. I took heart from the knowledge that these days there were people like Ed, dedicated to monitoring the volcano day in, day out, and 01, ready to serve in any calamity. While Sobejana and his soldiers were fighting one kind of war out in the jungle, Ed and 01 faced their own battle against a very different force – nature herself.

Helping Ray with his fruit delivery at the start of our travels through the Philippines.

Walking through the grounds of the Monastery of the Transfiguration with Father Adag and Claudio.

The man from Del Monte . . .

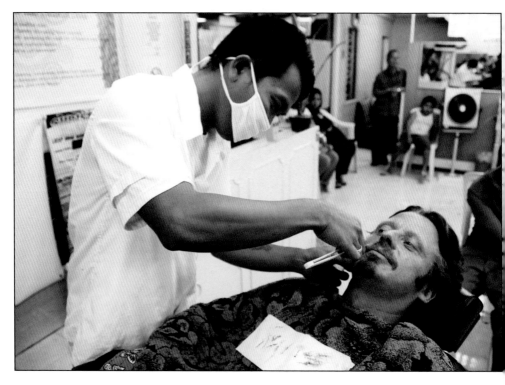

Something for the weekend? The barber took one look at me and put on a swine-flu mask.

Fishing with Benjamin on White Island.

On Camiguin island, riding to the docks on an elaborate home-made tricycle.

It was only a matter of time . . .

About to race through Cebu
and eat something
unspeakable.

Another day, another tricycle.
Off to the MacArthur memorial.

These *banig* weavers create the most beautiful, highly-prized rugs.

Quad biking to the lava fields of Mount Mayon with Mr Chan.

With the Kabalikat-Bical Province Rescue Ambulance Service – real heroes making a real difference.

Riding a 'skate' to Lopez. An amazing way to travel.

Boodle fight!

Mucking around with the X3M scooter club.

Meeting street kids in Manila. Their stories were at once harrowing and inspiring.

With the Mad Dogs Harley Club of Manila.

13
Free Range

WE HAD TRAVELLED a long way and the days were passing surprisingly fast. I remembered how nervous I'd felt that first morning back in May before I saw all those motorbikes waiting for us, and now here I was in the Philippines what felt like a lifetime later. I was looking forward to Taiwan and Japan but the days were slipping by . . . I thought about how much we had accomplished already – travelling up the east coast of Australia before crossing the Torres Strait to Papua New Guinea, witnessing VSO's work with the disabled, and helping UNICEF with the water-purification system. I remembered that river crossing when things had almost got out of hand and I thought about the poor little girl who had been beheaded in Bogia. I'd ridden through a lava field and heard frightening stories about bombs and kidnappings. Until this morning we'd had the army with us, but they left last night, saying that the road was pretty safe from here to Manila.

What an experience. It's only when you stop for breath that you really appreciate it. Over the last few years I've been privileged enough to see a hell of a lot of the world and my overriding impression is always of the people. No matter who is fighting whom, or what any particular political group or faction is trying to do, the vast majority of people just want to get on with their lives. They want a home and a job; they want normal, everyday things like friends and family around them. Of course there are differences in terms of lifestyle, but people are people wherever you go. And the bikers I'd met on this trip were like bikers anywhere: fun-loving with a shared appreciation of the freedom you feel on two wheels. Yesterday, for example, after we left the volcano, we rode with some guys from the X3M scooter club in Naga City. We dossed about a bit holding drag races, most of which I lost, and this morning we parted company at the market town of Calauag. I loved the fact that so much of this trip had been on motorbikes.

But that was yesterday. This morning my thoughts were on cock-fighting, of all things. We had had our first glimpse of the birds when we were on Camiguin, and since then I'd caught glimpses of the fights on TV. I'm no gambler and I'm not into any form of blood sport, but this was very much part of the culture here and a part of me wanted to witness it before we left. We were passing through Lopez today, where I knew they were holding some fights. To get there we needed to take a train . . . only there weren't any trains, only train tracks.

Our translator Justine was from this part of Quezon Province and she introduced us to her husband Webster, who explained that nobody used the train any more. Over the last few years the trains, now rusty, lumbering hulks, had become pretty much obsolete. The government was in the process of rebuilding the railways, but in the meantime the people had taken them over.

They used the tracks as a road, moving up and down on what Webster called skates. These were basically platforms with some bench seats and a canopy – most were about eight feet long and could be lifted on and off the rails. They were used as taxis and delivery trucks and carried passengers or livestock. In some areas there were still trains running, so if you were on a skate when a train was coming you had to keep one ear open. Thankfully, there were no trains running here (or we'd be on one!). There was only one line of tracks, however, so when two skates were coming from opposite directions, the lighter one had to give way. Whatever was being carried was unloaded and the driver would hoist the thing on his shoulders and move it off the line. When the heavier skate had passed he would put it back again.

I had seen something similar in Cambodia, although then there had only been one. Here there were hundreds of them and entire shanty towns had grown up along the track. We hopped onto a skate powered by a five-horsepower engine that the owner started with a fan belt. Not all of them had motors, though – some had bicycle-type assemblies and others still were pushed along by hand. It was ingenious, typical of the industriousness of the Filipino people.

We left Calauag and headed into the countryside, where in some places palms overhung the rails and in others the tracks rode the ridge of high banks and we could see paddy fields stretching to the horizon. It was certainly a unique way of getting to a cock fight, although it was very slow and we had to keep stopping to lift the skate off the track so others could pass.

For all the fun, I have to admit I wasn't in a very good mood. I don't know what was causing it – possibly the thought of the cock fights – but this was the first time my mood had threatened to get the better of me on this trip. So far none of us had fallen out, and as yet I hadn't let my mood affect the group. It didn't help when I got tipped off the skate. We had just crossed a muddy river and I was hanging my legs out the back – thinking that perhaps that wasn't a good idea – when the skate jerked to a halt and I was sent flying. We had hit an old set of points, the wheel jammed and off I went. The driver seemed unconcerned – it must happen a lot – and just lifted the skate off the rails and set about fixing the wheel.

We were close to one of the shanty towns and Webster told me how more and more people were making their living along the railway. Their days were numbered, however. These old routes would be used for the new tracks, the cuttings widened and all the shacks that hugged the line would have to be demolished. Most of them were tiny places made of tin and wood and bits of plastic sheeting, although a few were more substantial – wattle and daub maybe – some even had wooden balconies.

'Do the people know?' I asked him. 'What the government is planning?'

He nodded.

'Where will they go?'

Webster just looked at me with a grim expression. 'They'll find somewhere,' he said.

When the wheel was fixed we made our way to Lopez. From there it was a short trip in a jeepney to a large concrete barn with turnstiles where a man was taking money. Inside, the place was echoing with screeches and shouts; men yelling at each other and above them the sound of cocks crowing.

This was the Lopez sports centre, run by a man called Buboy Lee. He was in his forties with thinning black hair and a moustache. I told him we'd seen the cock-fighting on TV and thought we'd have a look. He was more than happy to show us around, so we followed him and mingled with punters and cock-owners, who were wandering around with birds under their arms. The centre held fights three times a week and Buboy owned hundreds of the fighting birds himself. He took us to where a man was weighing them so they could be matched with an opponent of equal size. Once a fight had been agreed, the owners took the cocks up to the arena. It was an amphitheatre, a gladiatorial stage. The killing ground was a glass-sided cage with a dirt floor, surrounded by stone steps where a few dozen men were shouting odds at the bookmakers.

On Camiguin they had told us about the knives that were attached to the birds' legs, and now I could see them for myself. Each one was brutal – a sharp, curving blade maybe three inches long. It was set between two prongs that were fastened to the bird's leg, so when it was on its feet, one leg looked like the spiked wheel of a chariot.

With the knife in place the owners paced around each other, letting the birds have a quick peck before they were released – and I was shocked to see how they really went for it, leaping and kicking out violently. It was very nasty, very bloody. The first two birds were so well matched they cut each other to ribbons. After a few minutes both were exhausted, so badly injured they could hardly stand. The referee would pick them up and set them on their feet and it was a case of last bird standing. Before we knew it another pair had been matched. A large white cock disposed of his opponent but got badly cut in the process. His owner won 5500 pesos, but the cock died at his feet. I watched the man stuff the cash in his pocket, step over the dead bird and walk away. The words 'Free Range' were emblazoned on the back of his T-shirt.

It was not my thing at all, but in the Philippines it's a national pastime, having been introduced by the Spanish hundreds of years ago. I imagine that not everyone is into it, but for some people it's a big part of their life. It was bloody and vicious, but at least the dead birds weren't wasted: they were taken next door to the restaurant where they were plucked, cooked and eaten. I suppose it didn't really differ that much from the cruel way birds are treated in battery farms; and I suppose some of the cocks live to fight another day. But I had had enough. It was oppressive in the arena and I was feeling hot and sticky and dirty. The barn had been a cauldron of pulsing adrenaline. What I needed was some air; the wind in my face again. I spotted a feed truck parked across the road and asked the driver where he was going.

'Unisan,' he said, and pointed up the road.

That'll do, I thought. 'Can I get a lift?'

We spent the night at a farm owned by a Filipino senator named Suarez. It's actually run by his son Jet, and since 2001 they've been working on a breeding programme for cattle and goats. The quality of livestock in the Philippines is not the best, and their aim is to distribute breeding pairs of high-quality cattle and goats to local farmers throughout the region.

Jet showed us around, then we sat down to relax with a few shots of the local moonshine: coconut vodka. It was serious stuff. I woke up with a dry mouth, pounding skull and the road to Manila ahead of me.

Jet was delivering a couple of goats to a farmer just outside Lucena and offered Claudio and me a lift. We were happy to accept and climbed on the back of the truck along with the two goats, who seemed truly loved up. They had plenty of hay for the journey but they had eyes only for each other and totally ignored it. All the way to their new home they stood behind the cab, taking it in turns to rest their head on each other.

We dropped them at a bamboo house that stood high above the road and was accessed by a flight of stone steps. Jet assured me that whatever babies the goats produced would be called Charley and Claudio, regardless of their sex. Pleased to know that my name would live on in this part of the world, we got back in the truck and the driver took us to Lucena.

The plan was to make it to Manila tonight, but en route we were supposed to stop at a jeepney factory. Unfortunately I had no clear idea where it was and no idea at all how we were going to get there. There was no sign of Sam or Robin either. I thought Jet's driver might take us but he dropped us at a sprawling, dusty bus terminal in the middle of Lucena.

We grabbed a Coke in a small café and I gazed across the lines of dirty buses. 'I have to tell you, Claudio,' I said, 'even if we knew where we were going, I'm not sure I can face another bus.'

'We could always hitch a lift in that.' Claudio pointed to a massive white limo that had just pulled in. It looked like a Hummer, but stretched to ridiculous proportions.

It stopped right in front of us with the engine idling; the windows were smoked glass so we couldn't see inside. Being the nosy so-and-so that I am, I decided to take a closer look anyway. As I walked over, the passenger window was rolled down. I expected to see some Filipino gangster giving me the evil eye. Instead it was Sam, grinning at me.

'Do you want a lift to the factory, Charley? Or would you prefer the bus?'

The Hummer was, in fact, a Hammer – a replica based on the Nissan Patrol. Looking at it from the outside you would swear it was the American original. Inside was another story – it had leather bench seats and wine glasses that were stuck down with double-sided tape. It wasn't as comfortable as you would think either. The seats were narrow and hard, but hey, this was a limo and who was I to complain? It had been made by the Sarao family who ran the jeepney factory we were on our way to visit. After travelling in the back of a farm truck with two goats for hours on end, it was nice to stretch out and close my eyes before we got to the city.

Sarao Motors Inc. is a large plant on a busy suburban road. Pulling in, we were greeted warmly by co-owner and works supervisor Ed Sarao. A big, amiable guy, he showed us around the various open-sided workshops, and explained how the US military jeep had evolved into the iconic jeepney.

The company had started converting the jeeps in 1955; first taking a military vehicle and reworking it into something more suitable for civilian use. Over time they reconfigured the chassis, stretching it into a slightly larger version, before embarking on the elongated buses they produce now. There were a number of different workshops – the machinery was basic and traditional, but then, as Ed explained, the jeepney is basic and traditional, a vehicle that's simple enough for its owners to repair and service.

He showed me steel chassis together with raw, unpainted coachwork. The seats were wooden bases stuffed with coconut fibres and trimmed in leatherette. The whole vehicle is assembled there at the plant and each one is customised. Ed said that ordering a jeepney is like ordering a tailor-made suit – whatever colour you want, however decorative you want it, all you had to do was say. The average cost is 490,000 pesos, which I worked out to be about £7000.

We had to get across town and Ed very kindly agreed to let me drive one of his creations. It was silver and red with three air horns on the bonnet and God knows how many lights. I loved it – it was really loud and clunky, and when you revved the engine it sounded like somebody farting.

The roads were choked with the most manic traffic imaginable. Behind the wheel with one of Ed's men alongside me, I was crunching gears and hooting the horn, heading for the skyscrapers. It was a mass of snarling metal – cars, vans and motorbikes along with hundreds of other jeepneys. I soon began to realise that 90 per cent of the congestion is caused by jeepneys. They pull out when they want; they stop where and when they want. I was behind this big yellow one that kept cutting up the traffic, pulling over to drop off and pick up passengers. The driver didn't care and didn't indicate – he would just hit the horn and do pretty much as he pleased.

There was a little respite as we crawled to the toll gates and I could see the skyscrapers that encircled the bulk of the city. Manila is one of the most densely populated cities in the world and the closer we got to the downtown area the madder it became. All I could smell was diesel; all I could hear was the harsh grunt of diesel engines. Combined with the heat in the air it was pretty wild. At one junction flowers were struggling to grow in the concrete plinth that formed the central reservation and I saw a street kid flaked out, trying to grab some sleep – a reminder that tomorrow we were going out again with UNICEF.

Some UNICEF projects are easier to deal with, emotionally, than others. The water purifier had been hard physical work but emotionally very rewarding. My visit to talk with the street kids of Manila will stay with me for a very long time. UNICEF has been involved with street kids in this country since 2000, when there were an estimated 246,000 across the islands of the Philippines. Some 50,000 of them were what is known as 'highly visible', meaning they had no relatives and were fending entirely for themselves. The reasons why children end up on the streets are many and varied but poverty, of course, is the root cause. Often it can lead to family break-ups and varying forms of child abuse.

On the morning of 19 July I was introduced to a couple of boys who were living among the market stalls of the Divisoria area of Manila. One of them was Edwin, a young guy with floppy hair who walked the streets as if they belonged to him. He was a thief apparently – a 'snatcher' was how my guide, Butch, referred to him.

Butch had been a street kid himself and was now working with UNICEF as a street educator. His story was slightly different from the others I'd heard, mind you, as he had been born in a decent neighbourhood and to an educated family. But his parents died when he was a child and with most of his other relatives in the United States, he had been brought up by his grandmother. Unfortunately she also died when he was still young, and Butch found himself living on the streets.

Initially he eked out an existence as a newspaper boy, but he couldn't make enough money to survive, so he progressed to thief, drug-runner and finally pimp. He might have ended up either dead or in prison, but thankfully when he was eighteen a social worker persuaded him to go to a shelter run by a Jesuit priest. That shelter changed Butch's life. 'His name was Father Ben,' he told me. 'A good man, very down to earth. He took me in without asking any questions, though of course he knew where I'd come from and what I had done. He gave me food and somewhere to sleep, and because of him I was introduced to faith.'

We were making our way through the market. A multitude of multicoloured parasols shaded hundreds of stalls that sold everything from slabs of meat to cheap children's toys. The streets were heaving with people – on foot, in sidecar taxis and on bicycles. It was hot and sticky and the air was filled with the rank smell of water from the open drainage pool on the other side of some battered-looking railings. It was alongside those railings that the street people cooked and washed; and where they went to the toilet.

'How long were you in the shelter, Butch?'

'In all, six years.'

Getting into that shelter had changed his life. Off the streets and with someone to care for him, Butch left behind the prostitution and drugs and got his act together. He told me that he had been a lost sheep and now he spent his life looking for other lost sheep.

The kids trusted him, and walking those grim little streets I was amazed at how many people seemed to know who he was. There was a quiet purpose about him. His face was weathered from his years living on the street, his hair styled in dreadlocks and tied at the back of his head.

Together with the National Network of Street Children, UNICEF operates what they call an Alternative Learning System. A mobile classroom, donated by the Body Shop, travels through the rundown areas of Manila with the driver showing videos to kids of all ages. Helped by the videos and other media, they perform learning tasks that prepare them for normal education. I did some of the tasks with them – little things like dressing up to go to work, or identifying a life situation from a picture. We did one where I turned my back as if we were playing hide and seek and they formed a tangle of arms and legs that I then had to unravel. It was about problem-solving, and Butch explained that these little tasks were designed to introduce them to options; they asked questions of the children, forced them to make a decision that a formal education would then take to the next level.

He took me deep into Divisoria, where we found Edwin and the other boy I mentioned, who was called Jayson. Edwin was the younger of the two and, as I said, he strolled around confidently with his shoulders back, snapping his fingers. Jayson was quieter and more thoughtful. There was something a little downtrodden about him, a sadness in his eyes that was either missing in Edwin or well disguised.

Edwin lived on a section of narrow pavement between an old

van and the wall of a shop. What few belongings he had were kept in a plastic basket. His father spent the day operating a bicycle and sidecar, trying to make enough money to keep them alive. His mother had left them years before and though they had lived rough ever since, Edwin's father was determined his son would not be condemned to a life on the streets. He was still a young man, very tall and proud looking, but was suffering from TB. With no medication it was all he could do to get through the day. He loved his son and wanted to be with him, but he knew that a shelter would mean the chance of a better life.

I was staggered by their living conditions; the pavement was about two feet wide and there were at least thirty families living along the length of it. Butch explained that there were two types of people on the street: what he called 'street families', like Edwin and his dad; and orphans or abandoned children like Jayson. Everywhere we walked, we were surrounded by girls and boys of all ages. From teenagers to toddlers, they were wandering about with no one to take care of them. I saw a little girl, who could have been no more than five, sitting on her own against a concrete pillar while cars and buses rushed past her. Another kid, a shaven-headed toddler, would try to hold hands with everyone.

It was harrowing and incredibly emotional. Jayson told me that he had left his family because his mother favoured his elder brother and there was no place for him. His father worked in one of the buildings on the street where Jayson slept, but he hadn't seen him for more than a year. He doubted he would see him again. He was determined to go into a shelter, get an education and study criminology. Butch said he was quick-minded, an accomplished thief and would actually make a good policeman.

Jayson took me to the place where he went at night: a meat vendor's stall in front of a beauty salon. He slept on the table where the vendor chopped meat, and told me that for a while the guy had looked out for him. But then he moved on and a new guy took his place. The lady who ran the beauty salon was the previous guy's aunt, however, and she persuaded the new guy to let him go on using the table.

I think quite a lot of the shopkeepers did that – an unspoken kind of guardianship over some of the children. Even so, they had no permanent roof above their heads, they washed in filthy drainage water and they cooked their food on camp stoves among piles of rubbish.

But it was not hopeless. Butch was living proof that the plans implemented with UNICEF were working – he was a link between the world of the street kid and a normal life. I was in awe of him. Every day he would be out there among children who were scavenging the stalls for rotten vegetables – he spent time with them, shared with them until they began to trust him. One of his success stories was a kid called Emilio, who had recently been released from prison after killing another kid in a fight over drugs – as a minor he had not served a full sentence. He could have fallen back into a life of crime and violence, but Butch took him under his wing and showed him he really did have a choice. Butch and UNICEF gave Emilio and others like him another chance – he was free of drugs, he had a job and with it, thankfully, some hope at last.

14

Mad Dogs and Some Englishmen

AFTER A DAY ON THE STREETS of Manila, getting on a motorbike and blowing away the cobwebs was just what I needed. Tomorrow was Saturday and we'd lined up a day riding Harley-Davidsons with some boys from the Mad Dog Motorcycle Club. The club's president, Big John, had invited us over to the clubhouse tonight for a couple of beers.

The clubhouse was known as the Handlebar. It was given away by the lines of Harleys parked outside and the sign, of course, bearing a set of ape-hanger bars. To be honest, I was a bit nervous about riding with them – a bike club like this in a city like Manila . . . and I would be riding one of their precious Harleys . . . The last thing I wanted to do was trash it.

This outfit was not unlike the Hell's Angels. Motorcycle clubs, or 'MCs' as they are known to the police, have something of a reputation. I knew that this one had had some problems in the past (something to do with a previous president having been assassinated) so it was with a little trepidation that we rolled up.

Big John greeted us. He was a huge man with a bald head, wearing the obligatory leather waistcoat bearing his club's insignia. He was intimidating to look at, but he was friendly and inside we were made very welcome.

It was Friday night and lots of members were drinking beer, shooting pool and smoking cigarettes. One guy from Sweden was having a tattoo added to the many he already had; a couple of 'prospects' were wandering around wearing dog collars. Big John explained that any would-be member had to wear the collar at 'dog functions' for their six-month probation period.

The atmosphere was buzzing and the chat the same as that of bike lovers anywhere in the world – it was motorbikes, motorbikes and more motorbikes, in this case customised Harley-Davidsons. The members were from all over the world, a real mix of ex-pats and native Filipinos. They were a variety of age groups as well, although I reckon most were over forty.

The bike I would be riding had been built by Danny Stewart of radkustomcycles.com. Danny was an Australian who came to the Philippines for a holiday ten years ago and never went back home. He could certainly build motorbikes and for me he had a chopped Harley with massively long forks, a low-riding saddle and a side stand in the shape of an upturned finger.

'Fantastic,' I said as I tried it for size. 'I'll be fine. Just as long as you look after me and don't drag me off somewhere to beat the crap out of me, like bike gangs are supposed to.' The boys promised that nothing could be further from their minds . . .

We all hooked up again the following morning. There were about thirty members coming on the ride – the brotherhood was sixty strong but not everyone could make it because of family or work commitments. Big John rode up front and I joined him for a while. He told me that he was from Canada originally, which explained the maple leaf he wore on his colours. He had come over with a construction company, working on a contract that ran out in 2002. By then he had fallen in love with the place, so he stayed, formed his own company and was doing very well. There was another John in the group, John Morgan from England, who had been in Manila eleven years and had no intention of leaving.

One of the Filipinos, a man in his fifties whom everyone called 'Boy', asked me how I had slept the night before.

'I slept OK,' I told him. 'Except I woke up in the middle of the night and I had no idea where I was.'

'I know the feeling,' he said. 'I spent a long time in the corporate world, flying all over the place. I would fall asleep on a plane and wake up not knowing if I was going to my destination or coming home again.'

It was interesting listening to him. There he was with his colours and his bandanna, his rumbling old V twin; a man who had been riding bikes since he was ten and had his first Harley, a 1977 shovelhead, twenty-six years ago. For years he had been a suit-and-tie man immersed in the rat race; now he was a club member and for the first time in his life felt that he belonged. That's how it is with groups like this: it's mostly about friendship, camaraderie; like-minded people who look out for each other. Tribal, perhaps, but a brotherhood nonetheless.

The Mad Dogs came from all walks of life and it was wonderful riding together in convoy. I was reminded of that first day in Sydney, only this time I was on a chopper that grounded out in the corners and I really had to tug on the bars to get it turned. We were heading for Angeles City, a tourist spot that evolved from its proximity to the Clark Airbase. Until Mount Pinatubo erupted in 1991, Clark had been the largest US airbase outside the United States, but after the eruption the Americans pulled out.

Side by side we rode the back streets to an underpass and the main freeway, where we filtered between vans and trucks and cars. I have no idea why anyone would want to drive a car when they could be enjoying the freedom of a motorbike.

I was in my element again and I was happy. Riding along with a whole new group of people I would never have got to know in any other circumstances. In addition to the Swede I mentioned, who had been a commercial diver, I met a Scotsman from Dundee and a tall, rangy guy in his sixties called Bob Hunnicut. Bob was from Texas originally, a former US marine turned traffic cop, who had ridden motorbikes for eleven years with the Texas Highway Patrol.

'Don't ask me why I became a cop,' he said. 'Too nervous to steal, I guess, or too lazy to work maybe. Something like that anyway.'

We rode up country to Angeles City and the Big Hat Bar that was the Dogs' home away from home when they were up this way. It was run by a good friend of theirs called Greg, a pony-tailed Aussie in his fifties. He looked at me a little strangely when I told him we were travelling to Taiwan by boat. The bar was sort of outside, open on one side though covered by a roof, and some of the guys rode right inside. It had started to piss with rain and there was room for a few bikes among the pool tables. As the engines were cut I asked Greg whether the Dogs behaved themselves in his pub.

'Oh yeah,' he said, 'they're good as gold, Charley. They can get a little raucous of course, but then they're boys, aren't they? I've known them for years and when they're in Angeles City, this is the doghouse. Are you staying in town tonight by the way? The boys taking you to Fields Avenue, are they?'

'Fields Avenue?' I wasn't sure where he meant. Then it clicked. 'Oh, you mean the naughty three miles I've heard so much about. No, I'm a married man, Greg, and anyway, tomorrow I'm up in a plane.'

'Is that right?'

'Yes,' I said. 'I'm planning to have a few quiet beers then tomorrow I'm taking an ultralight up to Subic Bay.'

'A few quiet beers, right, right . . .' He peered at me in disbelief. 'An ultralight though, that'll be amazing.'

'I hope so. I'm not the best when it comes to small planes. I like to think I am, but that's not the reality.'

He slapped me on the shoulder. 'You'll be fine, mate – a fella like you? I'm sure.'

I hoped so. As much as I was excited about the ultralight, I was plagued by memories of the Spitfire in Australia. I wasn't helped by a story Terry told me either. Terry was the guy I would be flying with and we met up with him later that afternoon when we took a drive into the countryside to try to find the airfield. It belonged to the Angeles City Flying Club and was in the middle of nowhere. We found it eventually, though, and Terry showed me his ultralight. It was small and red with a bubble cockpit and the seats set side by side. A few years back he had taken a travel-show presenter up for a brief flight, but the poor guy was terrified of being in the air. His fear was so great that after just a brief spin, they landed, stripped him of his clothes and put them on his cameraman. They used someone else to film while the presenter stayed firmly on the ground and his cameraman took his place up in the air. It worked apparently, and when the TV show aired no one was any the wiser.

That wouldn't happen to me. I'm not scared of flying. I love small aircraft; I just get sick. Terry told me that the weather forecast for the next day was not looking that good, though he was hoping for a brief window of opportunity so we could get to

Subic. It was only forty-five minutes in the air and he was confident we would be OK.

Fortunately he was right and when we arrived the following morning there were three planes ready for us. I would be flying with Terry, Claudio with an American pilot called Pete, and Robin with a really funny German guy called Helmut. Helmut had been in the German air force, but not as a pilot. I asked him why he didn't fly and he told me he only lasted four years because he had never liked doing what he was told. He had worked as a technician and only took up flying when he left the air force.

Surprisingly perhaps, given my track record, I was suddenly really looking forward to going up. Whereas with the Spitfire I'd been cramped in the back and sweating buckets, this ultralight had a cone-shaped windscreen and no doors. I would have the wind in my face and hopefully I wouldn't get sick. I couldn't wait. While they fuelled the planes I was scampering around the airfield like a kid. It was a gorgeous place – the landing strip was beautifully mown lush grass and there was a swimming pool and a couple of cottages that were rented out to people learning to fly.

Terry had the calm assurance of all good pilots. He was an ex-pat from the UK who had lived out here for twenty-five years. He told me he had married a Filipino woman with a daughter from a previous marriage and subsequently they had another daughter of their own. Once I was strapped in, I settled back as he spoke to the tower. A few minutes later we were airborne. I loved it! Sitting there with no doors, I could feel the cool breeze blowing across me. The little two-stroke engine produced just under 70 hp and we cruised at around 90 kph at an altitude of 500 feet. The plane was a RANS S-12, one of the most popular ultralights around, and Terry told me that a good second-hand one cost only about £10,000.

Leaning over, I said, 'I love the fact there are no doors, Terry. It means I'll have a really clear view of the ground when we hit it.'

'We're not going to hit the ground,' he assured me. 'We're going to have a really pleasant flight.'

Climbing above the trees, we headed for the mountains, where I could see the conical dome of Mount Pinatubo, the volcano that had caused the Americans to leave the area nearly twenty years earlier. It was stunningly beautiful scenery, the mountain dominating the smaller peaks, the valley spread with paddy fields that glimmered in the morning sunlight. We flew over an ostrich farm and later a massive resettlement area with millions of crammed together huts housing refugees from natural disasters while their towns and villages were being rebuilt.

'Thank you so much for this,' I said. 'It's fantastic, really.'

'Are you enjoying yourself, Charley?'

'Just a bit, yeah.'

'I'm glad.' He was smiling now. 'I took this one chap out in the other plane – the X-Air that Pete's flying.' He nodded over his shoulder to where Claudio was filming from behind Pete in the second plane. 'I asked the passenger if he was having a good time, and all he did was grunt and say it was all right. All right, I thought, I'll show you all right, mate . . .'

'What did you do?'

'I stalled the plane and yelled, "Oh shit!" into the microphone. The poor bloke just about crapped his pants.'

'Stalled it?' I asked.

'I'll show you.' And with that he let the revs drop until there was no sound from the engine at all and the nose began to dip. Then, as he pulled on the stick, the engine kicked in once again. 'I do it all the time,' he said, 'but he didn't know that, did he?'

We flew over the northern tip of the Bataan peninsula where, in 1942, a Japanese general called Masaharu Homma forced thousands of American and Filipino POWs to march seventy miles from Mariveles to San Fernando. If they faltered, his soldiers killed them; when some tried to fill water canteens Homma set up machine guns and shot thirty at a time. If anyone so much as looked at a guard, the guard could bayonet him to death. The march took nine days and one thousand men died. In 1946 Homma was tried for war crimes and executed.

After flying in across the bay we landed at Subic. This was the quietest international airport I've ever seen. During the Vietnam War the US had forty thousand men here and B52s would land to refuel. Now the only planes were the ultralights, and the apron and terminal buildings were deserted. It was weird, like a ghost airport or something . . . really strange.

Thanking the guys for a fantastic flight, we found a taxi to take us to the yacht club, where hopefully the captain of the boat to Taiwan, Derek, would be waiting. I had spoken to him last night and discovered that the vessel was a converted trawler. I hadn't seen any pictures, but her name in English meant 'No Problem', and he assured me she was perfectly seaworthy. The only issue was the weather. We had known about the monsoon season for a while now, but a typhoon had just swept across the area we would be sailing through. The fact that it had come and gone sounded quite positive, though, and by the time we arrived at the yacht club we were feeling pretty encouraged.

I really did not want to fly to Taiwan. The Boorman boat curse notwithstanding, this was an expedition across land and sea and I'd seen enough commercial aeroplanes already. Fingers crossed, the weather would be with us.

The yacht club was upmarket – it looked like a five-star hotel. The marina was marked by a series of floating pontoons, with some very expensive-looking motor cruisers tied up against them.

'One of those would be nice, Claudio,' I commented, as we made our way down to where the trawler was berthed. We could see it now – a huge boat with a bridge and everything; it was way more substantial than the boat I'd been on from Timor to Darwin. It was painted white with a pale blue hull and sat high in the water. As we approached, Derek came down to meet us. He shook our hands and welcomed us aboard.

It was a great boat, very spacious below deck with three decent cabins, although one was better than the others – more comfortable and further from the engines. I had my eye on it right away. The captain's cabin in the bow was on offer too, but Derek said it was no good at sea because of the way the prow slapped through the waves. Derek was English, in his forties and had been skippering the boat for a year. He introduced us to the crew, two boys called Sting and Mark, and a girl whose name was Ping. This was a good boat, well fitted and organised. I had a positive vibe, and if only the weather would hold this would be great.

Taking us up to his office on the bridge, Derek showed me a laptop he had hooked up to the ever-changing weather charts.

'We've got a bit of a problem,' he said. 'I'm afraid we're going to lose at least one day.'

My heart sank. 'Why? I thought the typhoon had gone through.'

'It has. Right now it's heading for Hong Kong but it could turn left or right and it could just as easily come back. I want to make sure it's well clear so we have the time we need to get to Taiwan.'

He showed us our position on the chart. 'It's four hundred and twenty miles,' he said. 'Two hundred along the coast here in the Philippines, the other two hundred on the open sea. Right now there's a patch of low pressure developing in the southeast which I'm keeping an eye on. The monsoon is southwesterly, which means the winds and the current are along the port side all the way. If it were northeasterly we'd be sheltered until we left the tip of coast.'

'How long does the crossing take?'

'Two and a half days. We do about two hundred miles in a twenty-four-hour period, so if the weather is OK then it shouldn't take any longer than that.' Again he indicated the map. 'What I might do is run up the coast for the first hundred miles to a place called Bolinao Bay; it's sheltered there and we can sit out any weather if we have to.'

'That sounds great.' I liked Derek; clearly he knew his stuff and there was no way he was going to risk anything with the monsoon. I liked the idea of Bolinao Bay too; he told us it was really beautiful and with dive gear on board, if we did have to sit it out there would be plenty to do.

It was settled then. We'd keep our fingers crossed for the weather and all that was left to sort out now was which of us got Cabin No. 1.

Claudio came up with a way of drawing lots – a complicated method he called the Buddha system. Taking a piece of paper, he wrote down our names, mine at the top, then Robin's and finally his own. On the right-hand side he wrote the numbers 1, 2 and 3, with 1 on the same line as my name, 2 next to Robin's, and 3 next to his. Then he marked the space between the name and number with some vertical lines and told us to do the same. That done, the trick was to connect your name to a cabin number by drawing horizontal lines to join the vertical ones.

I was immediately suspicious, especially when he told us his dad had taught him the system. But it was that or drawing straws, so we gave it a go. Of course, my name came out at Cabin 3, Robin stayed at 2 and Claudio landed on 1. It was fixed, it had to be. Claudio was just too smug, but there was nothing we could do but accept it, and he settled down in the quietest, most comfortable cabin, just as he knew he would. I suppose that's democracy for you.

Up on deck I went to the bow and gazed across the flat waters of the natural harbour to where it looked a little rougher out to sea. Coming alongside, Derek leaned on the rail.

'That's not good,' he said, 'water like that. If it looks lumpy from here you know it's going to be serious when you get out there. What you want is a mill pond as far as the eye can see.'

Things didn't get any better. In fact they got much, much worse. In the early morning all was still, but around eight o'clock it began to rain. The wind picked up, the harbour waters began to swell and it rained and rained and rained. Looking at the weather charts, we could see that the typhoon, which had been heading for Hong Kong, had turned its fury on Taiwan instead and was battering the coast. In the meantime we had the weather systems created by the southwest monsoon as well as another large depression working its way up the east coast. Derek said it would settle right over the northern tip of the island and another was beginning to take shape in its wake. Deep down I already knew we were going nowhere by boat.

I was gutted to the point of depression. It had struck again, the hex, the curse . . . whatever it was. I just could not seem to get it together with any kind of boat.

*

I refused to give up hope entirely, however, and we decided to wait one more night. To pass the time we crossed the harbour in a Rib to find Ocean Adventure, a sea-life centre. I pulled on a wetsuit and in stair-rod rain descended into the depths of the lagoon, where almost immediately a bottlenose dolphin swam up and peered into my eyes. I mean *right* in the eyes. In that moment the worry and the woes I'd been feeling just seemed to melt away.

The dolphin floated with its nose pressed to the palm of my hand and span around like a top, then I grabbed a handful of dorsal fin and it took me for a ride. On the surface I held on to its flippers and belly up it took me across the surface. It was amazing. I'd never swum with dolphins before but now I could see there is something about them, as if they can address issues you're not even aware you have. No wonder you hear of people with serious depression swimming with these animals and feeling so much better. They are warm-blooded like a human and the contact you have with them is like that you have with another human; only they're not human, they're more . . . fundamental somehow. It's hard to explain. But it was wonderful.

I also met a small, black whale with a bulbous nose and the same type of teeth you find in a killer whale. In fact, the species is named the false killer whale because they look like young orca. This one lifted its head out of the water and danced with me – with my hands on its flippers we whirled like a couple of waltzers.

It was incredibly therapeutic. Later, when we got back to the boat, Derek told us that two more typhoons were on the way, and I just kind of accepted it.

'I'm sorry,' he said. 'But a crossing like this is one hundred per cent about safety and I'd be a fool if I tried to take you out in the kind of weather we're having right now.'

He reckoned that we would be marooned here for at least five days and we could not wait that long. We would have to fly. I was desperate not to return to Manila so I called a guy we'd heard about who freighted large animals. His name was Joi and he told me he would happily fly us to Taiwan. He had a variety of planes but said that regardless of which one he used, it would take at least three days to obtain the correct landing permits. That was no good. If we were going to wait three days for a plane, we might as well wait five and sail as we had originally intended. Gutted now, I realised there was nothing for it. Like it or not, we were going back to Manila.

15
The Path to Enlightenment

Taiwan Strait

TAIWAN

East China
Sea

Sun Moon Lake

Alishan
Mountains

Chiayi City

Tainan City

Fo Guang Shan
buddhist temple

Kaohsiung

From Manila
via Hong Kong

Kenting

South China
Sea

SO IT WAS on the evening of 14 July that we finally landed in Kaohsiung, Taiwan. There was a bit of drama with our booking in Manila but eventually we made it. In the airport we met some Bulgarian gymnasts who were competing in the World Games, due to begin in Taiwan in a couple of days' time. These games showcase sports that are not at the Olympics. Never having been to that kind of event before, I had a go at blagging a couple of tickets to the opening ceremony, and succeeded. Outside we met up with Sunny, a lovely Chinese woman who was going to translate for us.

Over the last few days my energy levels seemed to have dropped a little. When we set out on this adventure I was full of beans and could keep going all day, but now I was finding that I was just bushwhacked come about three in the afternoon. The constant moving takes it out of you and the different beds – indeed the lack of beds some nights – all takes a toll. I'm not saying it's hard work – it's too much fun to call it that – but a couple of months on the road can wear you down in the end.

I really didn't know much about Taiwan. None of us did – not even Claudio, who knows most things about most places. But I had done a bit of research before we left and discovered that Malay people had settled on the island centuries earlier. The first European settlers were the Portuguese in 1544. They named it Formosa, which means 'beautiful island'.

Kaohsiung is the second-largest city and it was something of a culture shock after Indonesia and the Philippines. It was so modern, the roads not bunged up with jeepneys or motorbike taxis; everything felt clean and new. When I looked around it was hard to find any vehicle more than ten years old.

The plan was to be back in Kaohsiung for the opening of the World Games, but we would spend our first day at a place called Kenting on the southern coast of the island. This was where we had planned to arrive if the boat trip had gone ahead. The typhoon had put paid to that, but for every negative there is a positive, and for Taiwan's burgeoning surf industry the outgoing storm had left plenty of huge waves.

We met up with a surf dude called Afei, who said he would be delighted to teach me to ride a board. I'd been planning to try it with Dare Jennings when we were in Australia, but the weather had put paid to that too. It was about time we had a little payback from the weather, and perhaps this was it.

I was excited. I reckoned we deserved a day or two just kicking back and having fun after all our travels. We caught the bus to Kenting. It was due to leave at 9.50 a.m., but it set off about five minutes before with just us and a couple of other passengers on board. That would never have happened in the Philippines; there the buses don't go anywhere until they're full. Again, the roads were amazingly clear, though the city limits seemed to go on for ever. The driver was quite chatty, telling me how he and his wife liked to travel; they had been to Japan, which he liked, and they were about to go off to the Philippines.

When finally we did leave the city behind, we were into familiar landscape, similar to what we'd seen in the Philippines. The countryside was verdant with palm groves and rice paddies – the only difference here was that the farmers harvested the rice with great box-shaped machines instead of by hand.

Afei met us at the bus stop. He was a typical surf dude, tall and slim with long hair, baggy shorts and the obligatory flip-flops. He greeted us with a big smile and warm handshake and loaded us into his VW van to drive to his surf shack.

'So how long has surfing been big in Taiwan, Afei?'

'Only for the last two or three years. Ten years ago there were just a few people surfing, though we've always had the waves for it, especially in typhoon season. A couple of years ago, though, it just took off.'

His shack was a really cool V-shaped bungalow, made of wood and painted purple. It straddled a patch of ground between two concrete buildings, directly across the road from the beach. Inside it was humming with people and a black Labrador was sniffing around. Surfboards were stacked in vertical rows and there was a rack of wetsuits, T-shirts and the little rings that attach the board to your ankle. Out front on the patio some people were waxing a couple of boards ready for the water.

'Have you ever surfed before, Charley?' Afei asked me.

'Once, in Cornwall, years ago. I had to wear a really thick wetsuit because it was so cold.'

'Not here,' he said. 'We sell them, but you don't need a wetsuit here.'

A blonde girl called Erica was hovering around. Afei had painted a mural of Bob Marley on her board and she told me proudly that she would turn professional within a year.

'Really? Has Afei been teaching you?'

She nodded. 'He's teaching me now.'

'So how many lessons have you had?'

'Three,' she said, proudly.

Afei decided that the waves were too big here and suggested another spot twenty minutes up the road. Back in the van we made our way to a small cove where the waves were smaller and a bunch of people had gathered with their boards.

We laid our boards on the sand, and Afei taught me how to push myself from prostrate to my feet in one smooth movement. He showed me the correct place to stand, where to put my feet and the right arm position. After performing a few exercises, I was ready to hit the waves.

Paddling out, I waited for a wave. Afei was chest-deep in the water and when the right one came along he gave my board a shove and yelled at me to stand up.

Up I got. And immediately peeled off to the side.

The next time I got my balance and stayed upright until the wave broke. And then I fell off. Very quickly I worked out that the longer you were on your feet, the more you learned. That might sound a bit obvious, but when you're upright you quickly get the feel of the board.

Trying again and again, I eventually managed to ride a few breakers all the way to the beach.

Now I understood why you see surfers spending such a lot of time just lying on their boards. It's very tiring and if you catch a good wave you need to take a breather afterwards or you run out of energy.

Afei was a great teacher. He was very laid-back but really enthusiastic and he loved his job. He said the sheer excitement of his students rubbed off on him, and he couldn't think of any other work where people smiled and laughed quite as much.

When the surfing was over Claudio and I had a go on a couple of bob bikes – tricycles on skis, like a sort of hand-held hydrofoil where you stand up and bounce to make them go. Weird things . . . mine kept sinking. After that I was strapped inside a massive plastic ball with Afei and sent tumbling down a hill. Don't ask me why I did that! I mean, I climbed a hill, got inside a ball and bounced all the way down again. I hate stuff like that – it makes me feel sick and that bloody ball put me out for the rest of the day. But it was a dossing-about day, wasn't it?

That night we had a barbecue at Afei's place and first thing in the morning we headed back to Kaohsiung. The World Games weren't opening until the evening, but I was hoping to see some dragon-boat teams going through their paces during the day.

The games have been running since 1981 and feature sports that either might become or once were Olympic events. The venue for the water sports was Lotus Lake – a beautiful spot where the shores were lined with the most elegant Chinese pagodas. Here they would hold the dragon-boat racing, the water-skiing and canoe polo, which up close looked really quite brutal. The Spanish team were practising in a small arena separated from the main lake by a network of pontoons, and looking on with his arms folded was one of the officials from the German team. He was a big guy with blue eyes and a bald head.

'So who do you think will win?' I asked, sidling up.

'The Dutch maybe,' he said, 'since a few years now they have been the strongest.' He gestured. 'The Chinese are always strong but we don't know if they're sending a team.'

'It looks like the rules are similar to water polo.'

'They are,' he said, 'only it is much faster and the goals are taller.'

The canoes were small and clearly very nimble. The players used the paddle not only to manoeuvre but to pass the ball and shoot. Even practice looked frenetic: two guys were fighting for the ball, their boats clattering into each other. The German told me there were eight players in each team, though only five were on the water at any one time. The game lasted only twenty minutes and you could change the players as often as you liked.

'What about Germany?' I asked. 'Have they got a chance?'

'Germany only has a women's team this year,' he said a little sadly. 'The men's team did not make the qualification.'

Across the lake I could see teams practising in the dragon boats and I wanted a closer look. The boats are like large open canoes where twenty paddlers sit in pairs with one person at the back to steer and another up front beating the stroke on a drum. It's an ancient sport, going right back to the fourth century AD when a famous Chinese poet named Qu Yuan fell foul of the Emperor. He was so out of favour that his only option was to take his own life, so he decided to drown himself in the River Mi Luo. The local fishermen heard what he was planning, however, and desperate not to lose the one man who stood up to tyranny, they went after him, racing their boats and beating their drums to scare away the fish.

I could hear the drumbeat as the American team raced across the water. A little earlier we had met their leader, a lovely lady called Kim who said I could have a go at paddling. Kim was in her fifties and had been a paddler herself for fifteen years, but injuries had forced her onto the sidelines and now she was the mama of the team. An event organiser by profession, she knew how to make things tick. Locating a twin-hulled jet-ski that took passengers, we made our way across the lake to see them.

The American team was made up of a dozen men and eight women, and their boat was provided by the International World Games Association, as they all were. Kim explained that there are four different races: two hundred metres, five hundred metres, one thousand metres and, the daddy of them all, two thousand metres.

'That's a chariot race,' she said, 'the one we all want to win. It's four lengths of the lake, Charley, five hundred metres each length, and there are three turns. Each team starts at a ten-second interval and when you catch up . . . boy, it can be messy. You're not supposed to touch other boats, but when you hit the turn side by side . . .' She whistled. 'It can be ugly, believe me.'

It sounded fantastic. Keen to have a go, I took a seat behind a really buff-looking guy called Gerry. We were on the left-hand side of the boat and he showed me the stroke. My right hand had to stay high, with the left gripping the paddle almost at the blade.

'We're going to practise the fast start,' he told me. 'Reach all the way forward and dip the blade, and when I yell "go" we go – three short strokes then ten long. You got that, Charley?'

'I think so,' I said.

The girl at the front began to beat the drum and our paddles dipped. Gerry prepared to start.

'A-TTEN-TION,' he yelled. 'GO!'

Off we went, three short strokes and into the ten: it's vital that you keep the rhythm, because if anyone misses a stroke it's chaos. Of course, being the novice, I was bound to miss a stroke. At one point I found myself going down when Gerry was coming up, and I whacked his well-muscled shoulder with my paddle blade. It didn't seem to bother him, but I was off the rhythm now and it took a moment before I could get back in time. I did all right actually – it was just a few hundred metres across the lake, but not bad for a beginner.

Back on the dock, I spoke to a couple of huge guys with muscles in places I didn't even know existed. They were fifty-five and fifty-four years old and had been racing dragon boats since 1985. One had six children all under fourteen, all conceived in the boat, or so he said. The other looked like Arnold Schwarzenegger in his heyday. I'm serious, they were ripped, the pair of them.

I loved the boat and just hanging out with the team; I could feel the buzz, the camaraderie and the will to win. They were having a lot of fun too and it struck me that the athletes at these games weren't under the same kind of pressure as Olympians; there was plenty of competition, but winning wasn't everything. Kim said they had been trying to get the sport into the Olympics for years now and had been hoping for Beijing. But with such big teams it was difficult logistically and the only way it might be possible was to use smaller boats with only ten people paddling. What I found most amazing, having witnessed first hand how good they were, was the fact that the American team came from at least ten different states and they hardly ever got to train together.

We ate lunch in a busy street where the shop signs were hanging vertical banners with Chinese characters. I was looking for something traditional when I saw a toilet bowl fixed to a wall and above it a sign that read 'Modern Toilet' . . . believe it or not, it was a restaurant. The tables were made from toilet cisterns, the seats were toilet bowls and the food was served on plates shaped like urinals. So not remotely traditional, but so mad it was worth checking out. Everywhere you looked there was a reference to shit or piss, from a massive dangling ornamental turd to swirls of mock poo on the window sills. Appetising. Taking a seat on a toilet, I was served from both a urinal and a hospital bedpan. It was bizarre, and I asked one of the waitresses what it was all about. She told me that when the owner was a kid he was particularly naughty and his teacher used to punish him by making him clean the school toilets. It happened so often that the toilet block became his home away from home and when he grew up he decided to portray the toilet in a more positive light. So he started this restaurant. As you do.

The opening ceremony for the World Games was held at the most spectacular stadium. The stands looked as though they had been woven from lattice ironwork and the whole thing was powered by solar panels. We were treated to dancing and a light show before the teams were introduced. The President of Taiwan was roundly applauded and I was reminded that this is a politically sensitive country. Outside I had noticed banners proclaiming: 'Taiwan is Independence', yet all the competitors we had spoken to referred to the country as Chinese Taipei.

Taiwan sits between the South China Sea and the East China Sea, and Kaohsiung is the largest port in the country. According to Felix, the young translator who would be accompanying us to the Buddhist temple at Fo Guang Shan, there is evidence of human settlement here going back thirty thousand years. In terms of colonial influence, the island was Portuguese from 1544 until 1624, then Dutch until the Chinese invaded in 1662. After that the territory was batted back and forth between various dynasties, including the Great Qing in the 1870s. Japan had had its eye on the place since 1592, mind you, and when in 1874 Paiwan aborigines beheaded the survivors of a Japanese shipwreck, it finally invaded. In 1895 the island became an official Japanese colony.

We hooked up with Felix the morning after the opening ceremony and I asked him how he thought it must have been for his country, becoming Japanese after being under China's control for so long. He was a young guy, but he knew his history and as we rode north on a couple of rented scooters he told me all about it.

'Originally, we were enemies,' he said. 'The Taiwanese did not want to be a colony. But in some ways the Japanese were good for the country. Before they came the harbour at Kaohsiung was very small, and they made it much bigger and more important. They also built the road system and infrastructure; the capital city is like a chessboard.'

'You mean a grid system?' I said.

'Yes, that's right; a grid.'

We were riding in the scooter lanes, having picked up the bikes from a shop in the middle of town. Evidence of the Japanese grid system was all over this city; the roads were wide and well ordered and with the English translations of Chinese characters it was easy to find your way around. It was a bike-friendly place – the scooter lanes were nice and safe and the cars kept away from you. Riding alongside Felix, it was easy to hold a conversation; there was plenty of traffic but we seemed sheltered from it.

'So they did some good then, the Japanese?'

'In some ways, yes, but during the Second World War they were frightened that the Taiwanese would fight with the Chinese so they made the people worship the Japanese shrine. And they made them learn Japanese and take Japanese names.'

'And after the war?'

'Taiwan was given back to China. During the civil war in 1949, people like the monks at Guang Shan retreated here from mainland China.'

'So what is the main religion here then?'

'It's a mixture. Buddhism, Taoism and some Confucianism as well.'

The monastery was an hour north on Highway 1 – the first real road to be built in the country. In truth we didn't ever seem to leave the city. Guang Shan was no more than an extended suburb. We did pass through a little countryside here and there, following the Laonong River, at 137 kilometres the second longest in the country. The suburbs were less salubrious and well heeled than the downtown area and the buildings more traditionally Chinese.

At Guang Shan the river was spanned by an enormous bridge, and long before we got anywhere near the monastery the horizon was marked by a massive golden image of the Buddha, dwarfing everything around it. Pulling over for a moment, I just stared and stared. Felix took me down to the river, rather than going straight into the monastery. We rode under the bridge and beyond the enormous storm drains to the headland, where the monastery buildings with their white pagoda towers seemed to cover the entire mountain. This was the back of the complex, a mass of perfect-looking buildings that sprawled across the headland. We would be spending the night here and I couldn't wait. Keen to have a look now, we rode back to the main gate. In many ways the size of the statue was a fitting emblem as this is the headquarters of the International Buddhist Progress Society. They promote a form of humanistic Buddhism that places great store in being relevant to the modern world. Because of that, they encourage visitors from all over the world.

The main gate opened into a massive courtyard bordered by trees. An enormous white arch spanned the flight of steps that led to a second gate.

A monk was waiting to greet us. His name was Hue Shou and he was from Austria originally. He had been in Taiwan for nine years and a monk for eleven. He was a lovely guy, very witty and very insightful, and was the designated host for European guests. Before he devoted his life to the order he had been what he called a lay Buddhist, back home in Austria. He had lived a normal life, with a girlfriend and a son. In fact, his son was with him in

Taiwan, though not living at the monastery. The boy's mother died before Huc left Austria, so it was only natural that he brought his son with him. The Buddhist organisation is one of the largest charities in Taiwan and Hue's son lives in the orphanage attached to it. He was excelling at school and was something of a basketball star, apparently. He had already been on TV and had won a prestigious Nike award for the most valuable player.

As we walked up the steps to the gate, Hue told me the monastery was like a small city. It covered a huge area, with hundreds of beautifully designed buildings and all of it perfectly maintained. The buildings were different colours, white and cream and beige, but they complemented one another, creating an ambience of total tranquillity. The walkways were paved, and the lawns lined with shrubs and stands of trees that reminded me of bonsai. Beyond the second gate, the path was bordered by grassy terraces where five hundred white statues were huddled.

'They were placed here in honour of the first five hundred enlightened and liberated disciples of Buddha,' Hue told me, 'the monks who made up the first Buddhist council.'

It was an awe-inspiring place, vast and quiet and very peaceful. We passed beyond a third gate and Hue took me to the meditation hall. The sign above the door was written in Chinese characters and translated as 'The Gate to the Sane World'.

'There are two types of meditation,' he told me. 'Concentrated meditation and inside meditation. Concentrated meditation is where you focus your mind on one thing, like watching your breath, for example. You breathe in and out, every breath is counted and that is a way of sharpening your mind. Your mind is a tool that needs to be sharpened all the time and in so doing, it calms you. If you lose count of the breaths, you have lost concentration, so you begin again.'

It sounded fascinating. 'And the other type, inside meditation?' I asked him.

He smiled now. 'That is where you investigate yourself, Charley. When you're concentrating you can experience a state of incredible happiness, but that is only a side-effect of the tool-sharpening process. When you investigate, you look in on yourself. You investigate what is going on deep within the person you are. You consider things like greed and jealousy, hatred; emotions that can only lead to unhappiness. In order to be happy you have to know the problems that lead you to unhappiness and get rid of them.'

I was really intrigued now. I have never been one for any kind of structured meditation, but I understood what he meant. Over the years I've noticed that when I'm riding a bike all day, as I did on *Long Way Down*, my mind drifts off in all kinds of directions. There's no one talking to you, no influences other than what's happening on the road, and I find myself meditating on all sorts of different things. Hue understood exactly what I meant.

'Of course,' he said. 'You are within yourself. You are alone with only the road ahead; it's the perfect kind of meditation. That's great; there are many different methods of meditating, many different ways to create feelings of non-greed, to achieve a state of mind where you are happy for people who have more than you and not jealous of them. There are ways to create feelings of compassion for people you might otherwise really dislike.'

I enjoyed his company. Together we walked round the complex, pausing before a wall inscribed with so many vertical Chinese characters that from a distance they looked like rain.

'I had one guest from America who told me it reminded him of *The Matrix*,' Hue told me.

'Yeah, I can see what they meant. You know it's funny,' I said, 'when I came out of the cinema having watched that movie, for a moment . . . just a moment . . . I wondered if the street outside was real.'

'Did you?' Hue arched one eyebrow. 'So what had you been smoking?'

They taught sutra calligraphy at the monastery. Taking a seat in the hall, I had a go at it myself. It was a simple method where, initially at least, the characters are traced for you and you sort of colour them in. It gives you an initial feel for the art, a confidence in your penmanship, and progress is built from there.

I'm not sure what I had expected to find here – enlightenment, a really deep sense of spirituality, perhaps? But that's not how it was. I can't put my finger on why, but for all the chanting and the symbols, it did feel just a bit commercial. There were gift shops and the pilgrim lodges where we were staying felt exactly like hotels.

The morning meditation service the next day was held at ten to six in the great Vow Shrine, the most decorative building in the complex, designed to resemble a Chinese emperor's palace. Hue translated the characters inscribed above the door: 'Precious Palace of a Great Hero', Buddha who had transcended suffering.

It was a beautiful morning – albeit hot and humid. It was always hot and humid in this part of the world. But the sun was up and as we walked to the shrine I saw lines of people making their way to the service. It was not just monks, but lay people wearing similar robes to the monks, people who had in some way devoted themselves to the order. Entry was marked by the chimes of a single bell and, once the gathering was assembled, the singing and the chanting began. Drums were beaten, and the chimes rang out from lots of different bells. There must have been six hundred people in the hall, the service lasting about half an hour. I have to say, it didn't feel especially spiritual to me. It was a nice service, but I had felt closer to my spiritual side riding along the river bank, looking up at the pagodas.

Once the service was over, we trooped to the dining hall for a monastic breakfast; a simple meal of bread with peanut butter and vegetables. The meal was eaten in silence; waiters wearing surgical masks served us and it felt very formal and sanitised. I imagine the masks were due to the ever-present fear of swine flu. I was disappointed. As I said before, I'm not sure what I had expected, but I had not expected to feel like this. Hue was very knowledgeable and very funny, and through him I learned a lot. But the experience itself was nothing like as introspective and spiritual as I had hoped it would be.

Never mind, I had no plans to become a monk anyway. It was time to get going, and down by the main gate I found a delivery truck waiting for me. The driver's name was Lo Bo-Ya and he spoke good English. He made deliveries to the monastery a couple of times a week, but now he was travelling north and said he would gladly take me to Tainan City. I told him we were looking for a cricket farm that was located somewhere on the outskirts. He asked to see the address, then said he knew the area and would take me all the way.

That was terrific, a perfect start to the next stage of the journey. And by the way, when I say cricket, I don't mean anything to do with the game. I mean the large winged insects that make the chirping sound. They used to be something of a delicacy here apparently, though nobody really eats them any more. The ones we were going to see were fighting crickets and I hoped they wouldn't be as bloody as the cocks in Lopez. Somehow I didn't think they would. I just couldn't see any way of finding a knife small enough to attach to a cricket's leg.

Lo Bo-Ya was very chatty and as we drove north on perfect roads he told me he was into camping, so he and I spent the journey discussing tents and sleeping bags and being out in the cuds. I told him about camping with Ewan in Russia and Ethiopia and he said he would love to do that. His girlfriend hated camping though, so whenever he had some time off they argued over what to do.

The cricket farm was in the suburbs of Tainan City, in a modern apartment building close to a restaurant. It was a nice area, very clean and quiet. Ango, the cricket farmer, wandered out of his garage as the van pulled up.

I knew nothing about the sport other than it was older than cock fighting. In this part of the world it can be traced back to the Tang dynasty. It's perfectly legal, though betting on it is not, and quietly Ango told us how now and again a bunch of guys will get together in some darkened basement to bet on the outcome of the fights. I assume the fact that the police might raid the place only adds to the sense of adventure.

Ango was a bit of a cheeky-chappie – you know the kind of person, he had a real sparkle in his eye. He took us into his garage and showed us how he farms the crickets. There are around 200,000 of them, and he rears them from eggs to the point where they have shed their skins a bunch of times and fully grown their wings. I had no idea, but there are nine hundred different species of cricket and the chirping sound is only made by the male. It does so by rubbing its left hind leg against its right, which has a kind of scraper on it. According to Ango, every species makes a different sound.

The ones he bred grew pretty large and they were black. Once the eggs were hatched, he moved the larvae into a large plastic container filled with rolled-up newspaper and sawdust. Then, after a week, he would move them on to another container and replace them with another batch of larvae. He did it with military precision; from week one to week eight, he knew exactly what stock he had.

'But how do you know which cricket is going to be any good at fighting?' I asked him.

'Experience,' he said; 'experience and selective breeding.'

'You mean sort of cricket genetics then, is that it?'

He nodded. 'You can tell the good ones because they have a big head and small tail, and once you have a pair that both fight they can be mated to produce more fighters.'

This was fascinating. A Taiwanese man engineering *super crickets* in his garage. He told me that not even a big-headed, small-tailed cricket will fight just for the hell of it, mind you; it has to be coerced and coaxed . . . really pissed off, basically. And he did this by tickling it with a prod made from cat's hair.

We moved next door to the restaurant where a group of families were gathered. Ango set up the fighting arena to show me what went on. The crickets were placed in a narrow Perspex cage that was split by an opaque partition. Taking a pair of cat-hair prods, we tickled our respective gladiators into action. With their hackles well and truly up, the partition was removed and they wasted no time in piling into each other. Ango told me that they were always evenly matched – they had to be weighed, just like the cocks, so neither had an advantage. It was a wrestling match, lots of flipping each other over and butting heads, until finally one of the crickets succumbed. Fortunately it was not a fight to the death. When one cricket had had enough he would scuttle away while the victor celebrated by scraping his legs and chirping.

It was much less cruel than cock fighting. Indeed, this little demonstration seemed quite tame. Watching Ango, I could see how much he was into it. As soon as those two tiny chaps went for each other, his eyes lit up and I could imagine what he must be like if there was money on it.

He invited us for lunch and, before we ate, I took a moment on my own to collect my thoughts. I wasn't sure what I thought of this place; it was thoroughly modern, and so unlike the last three countries we had been through. I could see from the map why so much of the population occupied the western side of the island – the east was very rugged and mountainous. And of course it was at Kaohsiung that the Japanese had made so much of the harbour. I suppose with all the goods being landed there, it was inevitable that most of the settlements had grown up in the west.

Ango liked his crickets stuffed with garlic, dipped in batter and fried with chillies and green onions. They were served on a square platter garnished with slices of orange, and the wings stuck to your tongue when you crunched them. I took a plateful into the restaurant to see if any of the locals fancied them; it's been a long time since most people considered them to be the delicacy Ango still believes them to be. Funnily enough it was the kids who got stuck in; they didn't seem put off at all and some of them grabbed some chopsticks and tucked right in.

Our next stop was a bullet train that would take us to a tea plantation in the Alishan mountains, a thoroughly modern mode of transport that I planned to juxtapose with a thoroughly traditional one. The locals use bastardised motorbikes to carry fruit to market – it was another trike affair, with a trailer built on the back. I had managed to blag my way into riding one across Tainan City to the station. It was powered by a Kawasaki engine that had been converted to shaft drive and the gears were shifted by hand, using a lever behind the driver's right leg. I think its top speed was about twenty miles an hour and the whole thing was a real mish-mash – the trailer, the engine, the way they cobbled together the shaft drive. It was rather incongruous set against the backdrop of modern Taiwan. But it was traditional, and as I was going to be taking the bullet train, I thought it would be cool to arrive at a modern station on the most home-made form of transport in the country.

By now I was feeling pretty tired and perhaps just a tad irritable. It had been an early start and I'd felt a little let down by my experience at the monastery. I was missing my wife and kids, too. They had been on holiday in Spain for a couple of weeks, something we used to do every year with Olly's parents. It was a few years since we had been now and, far away in Taiwan, I couldn't help feeling I was missing out.

I forced myself to snap out of it. Travelling the world, as I'm fortunate enough to do, is a great experience, and it's hardly clocking on and off a nine-to-five job. Strangely, perhaps, the train helped my mood. Leaving the trike in the heat-soaked afternoon, I stepped into an air-conditioned station and from there onto a sleek, space-age train. It was surprisingly refreshing.

The train was so quiet I didn't even notice it pulling out of the station. One minute we were sitting there and the next we were flying along a track built on a viaduct, with a motorway running underneath. The line runs for just over two hundred miles from Kaohsiung to Taipei City, but we were only going as far as Chiayi. From there it was a bus into the Alishan mountains, part of a national park in Chiayi County, famous for its traditional villages, temples and tea. There are twenty-five mountains above 2000 metres, the highest Da Ta Shan at over 2600 metres. I hoped the air would be cooler up there.

It was. After hitching a ride in a Post Office van from Chiayi, we spent the night at a tea plantation. Waking early, I worked out that today, 19 July, was our sixty-third day on the road and there were only three weeks of the journey left. For a moment it was hard to take in.

Downstairs I spoke to Lo Hsiu-Mei, the lady who owned the plantation. She was in her fifties and one of the top ten women farmers in the country. She is completely absorbed by her way of life. This area is relatively new in terms of tea production: the first plantations here were started in the 1920s, whereas most Taiwanese tea plantations date back to the early 1800s. Lo Hsiu-Mei told me that Alishan originally produced black tea only for the export market, but these days there are many different types. This place is close to the Tropic of Cancer and is perfect tea country: the atmosphere is cooler than the lower ground, and the air moist. The climate creates the right environment to keep the bitter elements in the tea leaves to a minimum, while naturally increasing the soluble nitrogen that helps it to taste sweet.

I thought it was amazing that we were picking tea at 9 a.m., and an hour and a half later we were in the shop drinking what we had picked. It had been cleaned and dried, the leaves refined to the point where it was ready for sale. It was very much a family business and I was impressed by the way they all pulled together. Lo Hsiu-Mei's three sons worked the plantation with her, and she had a grandson which meant the next generation was involved as well. It was a beautiful spot, high in the mountains, the tea planted on lush, green terraces with the mist draping the landscape. Given how much cooler it was, I was loath to go down to the valleys again.

But we had to, and Lo Hsiu-Mei's son Chan-Kjao kindly gave us a lift to the railway station at Fenchihu. From there we were taking a train back to Chiayi and hopefully a local plumber would be there to meet us. We had arranged for him to drive us to the Sun Moon Lake and I was looking forward to meeting him. Not because I needed anything fixed, but because he was indigenous Taiwanese.

I was still thinking about the monastery and how flat it had left me feeling. The more I thought about it, the more disappointed I became, and I began to wonder if that was indicative of my mood, or if my mood was indicative of that. We would see other Buddhist temples in Japan and I was looking forward to comparing them.

The station was busy and we had to wait for the train. It was an hour at least to Chiayi and we'd be hungry by the time we got there, so we bought traditional lunchboxes from a little kiosk café that had been going since the 1930s. They cooked chicken or pork on the premises and sold it with spicy rice. The guy running it told me that his father had been there before him and his grandfather before that. In addition to the lunchboxes they sold rice pancakes filled with a mixture of ice cream, nuts and a hint of coriander that were absolutely delicious.

Finally the train rattled in – an old box-fronted diesel. Spotting the camera, the driver invited Claudio and me up to the cab and told us he had an English friend called Andy he was desperate to say hello to. So, Andy, if you're reading this – your man in Taiwan says hello. I couldn't grasp his name, he was speaking so quickly, telling me he had been driving this train for thirty years and rarely took a day off. He told us this had cost him his marriage.

The Japanese built the line so they could log this area. The tracks encircled the mountain, the train descending in spirals through thick forest where the trees overhung the rails so densely that if you stuck your head out of the window you'd be slapped in the face by leaves. Halfway down, however, we had to get out and walk. A few years previously the area had been hit by a typhoon that ripped away a great chunk of the mountain and took the train tracks with it. We had to walk five hundred metres on a twisting path through bamboo to another station and another train. It was pretty cool, actually: a train trip, a bit of downhill hiking and then another train.

Finally we arrived in the bustling and modern Chiayi City, where Yang the plumber was waiting. His van was our way of getting to the Sun Moon Lake where we would camp for the night. Despite the fact it had rained every night for the last fortnight, I was up for camping – a bit of fresh air and a night under the stars. I was thinking campfires and wilderness, a break from all this modernity. It had only been a couple of days, but after the Philippines and Indonesia it was more of a culture shock than I'd expected.

Yang was in his early fifties with hair the colour of slate. He told me he was very proud of being of aboriginal descent. Far from being a dying race, he said that his culture was alive and well. The government was keen that all peoples of indigenous origin should be fully integrated, without losing their culture, which was Malay islander, historically. Yang's people had been in Taiwan for four thousand years, and his grandparents had spoken a similar language to that spoken in Malaysia today.

The aborigines were a tough, resilient people. The early tribes cultivated their own crops and fished the waters off the coast. The Chinese tried to settle here many times, but the tribes were so fierce they were always driven off. The Chinese settled in the nearby Penghu Islands in the thirteenth century, but the only people who came here were fishermen.

Halfway to the lake it started to pour with rain and I sat there trying to envisage putting tents up in this kind of deluge. I had been hoping for some good open country, but we were driving on a three-lane motorway and the closer we got to the lake, the busier it seemed to become. When the lake first came into view the rain had ceased, but the road ran right alongside the water and the traffic was very heavy. Far from being open country, there were buildings everywhere – restaurants, hotels, even a new white terminus for the cable car.

The campsite was run by Ling and his wife Chen, a young indigenous couple who were friends of Yang. They were very welcoming and as it had started raining again they invited us to take shelter under a large-framed canvas tarpaulin where their kids were playing. It looked like part of their home, with a few weather-beaten sofas arranged in front of a massive TV. Books, children's toys and bits and pieces of bric-a-brac were everywhere. It was dry though, and with the rain teeming down they told us that if the tents were no good we could sleep on the sofas.

It was very kind of them, but I wanted to camp. I didn't care about the rain or the traffic or the fact that this wasn't in the least bit out in the wilderness. We got the tents up without our gear getting soaked, then ate spicy steamed rice barbecued in bamboo sleeves with Ling and Chen. By the time we had finished, the rain had stopped, and after a long and hectic couple of days, I was more than happy to crawl into my tent and get my head down.

16
Betel Nuts and Beauties

East China Sea

Taipei — Hsuehshan tunnel

Jhungwei

Su-ao

Taroko Gorge

Puli — Meifeng Farm Lodge

Shueishe

Sun Moon Lake

TAIWAN

Taiwan Strait

South China Sea

FORTUNATELY, THAT WAS the last we saw of the rain and I ended up getting a pretty good night's sleep. The main problem was the massed ranks of black mosquitoes eager to feast on my blood. Like someone trying to deter a vampire with garlic, I applied plenty of Deet and thankfully it kept them at bay for most of the night. And I suppose I should have expected a few mozzies, given we were in lush grass and moist air, camping beside a lake.

If you ignored the large buildings surrounding the lake, it was quite beautiful. The water was very still, the only ripples caused by fish jumping close to the shore. Dotted here and there around the bank I could see a number of fishermen's huts with moorings for their boats. It was a gentle place and a good spot to spend the night. Much as I like a comfortable bed, there is something invigorating about being in the open air.

I was keen to press on; today we were making for a farm at Meifeng, high in the mountains that form the central spine of Taiwan. We were crossing to the mountainous east coast before taking a train north to Taipei and I was keen to see the difference. I guessed it would be pronounced – 90 per cent of the population live on the western side of the mountains.

With our camp packed away, I crossed the lake in Yang's fishing boat – a narrow skiff made of plastic but built in the traditional style his ancestors would have used. In those days the lake was stocked naturally, but today small fish are brought in from local hatcheries. As we made our way across I noticed islands of vegetation bobbing on the water. Yang explained that these would encourage the fish to lay their eggs underneath and so breed naturally in the future.

He dropped me at the jetty at Shueishe, where a mountain bike was waiting for me. I hadn't cycled yet on this trip, and I wanted to get some exercise. I had entered the Royal Parks half marathon in the autumn and so far hadn't managed to get in much training.

A Taiwanese manufacturer called Giant had loaned me the bike, which was made of carbon fibre and weighed just eight kilograms. The brakes were state of the art and it even had an odometer to tell me how many kilometres I had covered. I planned to do only about twenty – which would get me as far as Puli bus station – but I was not as fit as I wanted to be and I thought I might be a bit stiff come tomorrow morning.

I was not riding alone. Our translator Sunny had found a companion for me, a sixty-ywo-year-old guy called Tim who had become a keen cyclist since he retired.

'Sixty-two?' I said. 'He'll never keep up with me.'

'He might, Charley,' she said. 'He's just cycled round Taiwan in ten days.'

Bloody hell, I thought; this could be embarrassing. Forty-two-year-old Charley Boorman, veteran of *Long Way Round* and the Dakar, outpaced by an old codger from Chinese Taipei . . . I'd never live it down.

Tim was waiting for us a little further down the road. He was a lovely guy and clearly the cycling had paid off – he was very trim and fit and didn't look anything like sixty-two in his orange Lycra cycling shorts and trainers. I was wearing my favourite baggy shorts, *By Any Means* T-shirt and flip-flops and I had picked up a cycle helmet too, just in case.

We set off riding side by side and for a lot of the journey it was downhill. That was perfect because going downhill I was way ahead of Tim. Going uphill, however, was a completely different story: he was brilliant, up on the pedals with his legs pumping like a veteran of the Tour de France. He told me he had only had this bike for a couple of months and already he'd put over nine hundred kilometres on it.

'I ride two hours every day, Charley,' he said. 'Sometimes I climb as high as three thousand metres.'

Christ, I thought, that's more than twice the height of Ben Nevis; no wonder I was struggling to keep up.

It was good to be in the open air on good roads, pedalling along merrily. There's no question you see more of the world on a motorbike than you do in a car, and more again on a bicycle. It's all about pace; the slower you're travelling, the more you're going to see. On my bike I got to see plenty . . . particularly as I climbed the same hill twice. Tim was yelling at me to head for the peacock gardens, but I went the wrong way. I heard him all right and I saw the gardens, but I just thought it was some tourist attraction that I didn't want to see. But of course it was the only way to go, so I had to double back and re-climb one of the steepest hills we had seen. Puffing and panting, I told myself it was worth seeing twice – the hillside climbing steeply, the trees broken only by a glimpse of an old landslide and a Chinese pagoda. Yes, it was definitely worth seeing again.

As we came into Puli, Tim rode up alongside me. 'This town is a very good place,' he said, 'famous for the three Ws.'

'Really?' I said. 'What are they then?'

'Well, first there's the water. The water in Puli is very good to drink. Then the wine, that's also very good to drink.'

'What kind of wine is it?'

'Shaoxing wine. A type of rice wine. The Japanese like it very much and use it all the time for weddings and other ceremonies.'

'What does it taste like? Sake?'

'No, I think it's more like whisky.'

'And the third W, Tim, what's that all about?'

'Women,' he said with a wicked glint in his eye. 'The women of Puli are the most beautiful in Taiwan.'

I explained that I was happily married, so the women of Puli were of no interest to me. The wine, though, was a different matter. A little later at a busy restaurant in the heart of the town, I decided it tasted like a cross between soy sauce and sake – a little harsh but quite sweet at the same time.

The restaurant was run by a guy who played Spanish guitar. Strumming away, he told me that he used to be a farmer but had lost his farm in a devastating earthquake nine years previously. He moved to the town and opened this restaurant, which he decided to give an Andalucían feel. As well as the guitar, the decor included a mass of Spanish posters plastered on every wall. With Sunny's help I managed to work out that his love of all things Spanish came from when he was a boy and used to fantasise about flamenco dancers. So much for the beauty of Puli women then. I asked him if he had ever been to Spain.

'No,' he said sadly, 'but I intend to.'

'You'll love it,' I told him. 'The wine is good and the women are very beautiful.'

After lunch I parted company with the super-fit Tim and his bicycle. He showed us to the bus station and we got aboard a pretty ropy-looking bus that would take us into the mountains. I was quite glad – this old jalopy was reminiscent of the buses on Sulawesi and anything but modern. It was as close to a traditional, modest form of transport as I was likely to find in such a technologically advanced country.

The bus driver let us out at Meifeng farm lodge, where we were spending the night. We were much higher up now and the air was much cooler, giving the place a strangely alpine feel. The lodge, a sprawling white building with a chalet-style roof, looked anything but Chinese; if you shifted it to Switzerland and started yodelling no one would have batted an eyelid. I discovered apples and tea plants clustered on the terraces, lots of vegetables and a greenhouse where a woman called Li Mei-Ling was dead-heading flowers. She spoke some English and I asked her about orchids and tea, and the different kinds of vegetables she grew.

She told me she had been working on the farm for twenty years and, much as she liked fruit and vegetables, tending the flowers was what she did best.

'What's your favourite flower?' I asked, thinking she'd say 'orchid' or something equally exotic.

'The cabbage flower,' she said.

'Oh, right. Do you eat it?'

Shaking her head, she laughed. 'No, you don't eat it. It's food only for the eyes.'

On the morning of 21 July I was up early, listening for the distinctive sound of dirt bikes coming up the drive. After boats and bicycles, buses and trains, today I would negotiate the rest of the central highway with a bunch of bikers. I could hardly wait and by the time the bikes arrived I was as excited as a little boy at Christmas. There were four of them, led by Clint, a forty-four-year-old doctor who worked in the local emergency room and had been on duty for the last twenty-eight hours. Then there was Sam, an older guy who spoke no English, and Joseph, apparently one of the most famous motocrossers in Taiwan. He looked about twenty-five but was actually forty, and I was amazed to discover he had been riding for only five years. The fourth member of the team, June, was one of the few women racers in the country. When she wasn't racing against the men, she ran her own internet café. The most important thing was that they had a bike for me: a Yamaha 250.

I was in my element, doing stand-up wheelies as we left the farm. The roads were fantastic and from the back of the bike I began to see the real beauty of this country: tea plantations and alpine forests, rich mountain farmlands that reminded me of my dad's place in Ireland. Landslips and mudslides were commonplace up here and the roads were tight and twisty. In some spots the height of the drop sent a shiver through me. It all added to the buzz, though – these were some of the best roads I had ever been on and it felt great to have the adrenaline pumping.

Although we were on tarmac most of the way, we did find a spot where we could ride off-road. Clint had taken the lead and after a few miles he came across a narrow stretch of tarmac that cut through the jungle. This in turn opened on to a mountain cut into terraces and interwoven with a string of dirt roads used by trucks to pick up the produce. We had a great time messing about, before eventually dragging ourselves away to head east and up into the clouds. For the first time since I had left England, I was cold: we were so high there was a nip in the air and the clouds swamped the road in places. For a few miles the visibility was poor and we had to keep the pace right down; then all at once the sky opened and I could see the spiralling blacktop all the way to the valley. I put my foot down and for a quarter of an hour I was in the zone, riding as hard and fast as I could with no thought in my head save for taking the oncoming bend.

We stopped for lunch just as the clouds burst and in no time the whole mountain was soaked. The rain came down like a monsoon; I'd never seen anything like it, even when we were in Cambodia last year. Within minutes the surface of the road was flooded and the hillside a mass of tumbling streams. I could see how easily the land would become mud and how that mud would become a slide and what kind of devastation that could cause. Indeed, further down the hill there had been a recent big slide and they were only letting traffic through during the first fifteen minutes of each hour.

Eventually the sun came out and by the time we had gone a few miles the tarmac was bone dry. It was mesmerising; we took hairpins that made your hair curl, crossed bridges over fast-flowing rivers at the bottom of terrifying gorges. We rode beneath savage-looking cliffs and into jungle where the trees were so dense it was almost like riding at night.

By the time we stopped in Taroko Gorge, it was all Clint and the others could do to prise the keys to the Yamaha from my hand. I'd had the most brilliant day.

Taipei is situated on the northern tip of Taiwan, and to get there we would go through the Hsuehshan Tunnel. After a night in Taroko, we were catching a train north to Suao, where I planned to take a dip in one of the world's few natural cold springs. In fact, they occur only in Taiwan and in Italy. I had visited plenty of hot springs in my time, but never a cold one. Though at a constant twenty-two degrees Celsius, these didn't sound that cold.

We were on the road at 7.45 a.m. and already I was sweating. The sun was blazingly hot and now we were back at sea level the humidity was close to 100 per cent. As I made my way to the station, the thought of taking a swim in cool water was suddenly very appealing. We had spent a quiet night in Taroko, a gentle place with hardly any traffic. In the station I looked on the map at where we had been yesterday and thought again about just how amazing that road had been. I couldn't remember a single straight; it was bend after bend – on a supermotard bike it would have been even more awesome.

On the train travelling north we passed through a series of small towns much like the one we had just left and I could see for myself how few people lived on this side of the island. The Japanese had established their port at Kaohsiung and everything spread out from there – the roads, the cities – all the way up to Taipei. And because the land was so mountainous, crossing from west to east would have taken for ever. Over here it was very quiet and peaceful; when we arrived at Suao an hour later, it was just as sleepy as Taroko had been. The station was awesome, though. Whoever ran it must have had a real passion for art, because crossing the bridge to the main entrance we saw painting after painting hanging on the walls: the *Mona Lisa*, Van Gogh's *Sunflowers*, Rembrandt, Monet, they were everywhere. Not the originals, obviously . . .

Once outside we hopped in a cab to take us to the cold springs. I didn't know what to expect; sometimes these places can just be a hole in the ground and sometimes they can have entire spa complexes built around them. I suppose this one was half and half. The water gushed from various pipes into a kidney-shaped pool lined with natural stones. There was a brick wall to one side, with the jungle scaling the hillside above it. There were changing cubicles and showers, but it was all in the open air and it had a Victorian kind of ambience. I changed into a pair of swimming trunks, wandered over to the stone steps and went in. God it was cold! Twenty-two degrees? It felt more like seven!

After a few minutes my overheated body adjusted and I was glad of the cool; it was nice to wallow for a while. We had heard that today there would be an eclipse and, as I lay back in the water, the moon slowly crossed the sun. It didn't get properly dark, but everything faded to a weird kind of half-light as if someone had slipped a filter over the sun. I had experienced only one eclipse before, in Cornwall years ago, and I remember everything had got much darker. As the light dulled, the sheep and cows had become confused and started lying down as if settling in for the night. It wasn't like that here, but with the falling water, the old brickwork and the jungle surrounding me, it was still quite a moment. Having said that, the magic was ruined slightly by the smell coming off the water. It's supposed to be odourless, but there was a definite whiff of sulphur.

Nicely refreshed, it was back to the station again, only this time we walked. It wasn't very far, less than half a mile, and it was pleasant to take in the quiet streets and the smiles of the people.

I'd noticed that everyone in Taiwan had seemed genuinely pleased to see us; they would wave and say hello and ask us where we were from. Sunny said it was more difficult to make a living here in the east, and over the last ten years places like the cold springs had helped put them on the map.

Our next train took us north to Jhuangwei, where we grabbed a bite to eat before meeting up with a man from the Highways Agency. These were the people who looked after the Hsuehshan Tunnel – the longest in the country and the second longest anywhere in Asia. I thought someone had told me it was 120 kilometres, but this guy explained that it was actually just 12.9. I couldn't help but laugh. I don't know where I got the figure, but thinking about it, that would have been a bloody big mountain! Just under thirteen kilometres sounded much more like it. On average 2200 cars pass through Hsuehshan every hour; some nineteen million a year. It is part of Highway 5, a fifty-five-kilometre stretch of road.

As we drove up from Jhuangwei the Highways Agency guy explained that the tunnel had been built with the specific purpose of trying to redress the east–west balance. It used to take at least two hours by road from Taipei to Yilan County but now it was just a thirty-minute journey. Sunny, who lives in Taipei, told me that it makes all the difference. Gradually the east coast is opening up and people who live in the capital can have weekend breaks in places like Suao.

The tunnel took fourteen years to build, a central pilot bore hole with twin tunnels either side to carry the traffic. I've always wondered how these passages underground actually function – how they're maintained and who responds when something goes wrong. Every time you go through one you see all those little metal doors, don't you? Where do they go? What's behind them? Finally I got to find out.

When something went wrong in this tunnel, the highway emergency teams were summoned. If a car caught fire then eight fire-fighters with state-of-the-art equipment responded from a station a couple of kilometres south. We were invited to pay them a visit, and the fire chief showed me all the gear, including a Suzuki motorbike with water tanks, compressed air and a reel of hose mounted on the back. I rode it around the car park and tried to imagine high-tailing it to a burning car with all that equipment making it top-heavy.

While we were there the fire-fighters invited me to join them in a quick drill. When a call came in I had to pull on the protective clothing and jump into the fire engine. I managed it in one minute and ten seconds, which was not half bad. Although, I only had to put on the jacket and helmet – the boots and trousers, which come as one, were too small for me, so I stayed in my own gear.

We took a maintenance truck into the tunnel. The driver told me that when they were building it the construction workers encountered quite a few problems, not least of which was when one of the support tunnels collapsed. They had to contend with six major fault lines, ninety-eight fracture zones and thirty-six high-pressure underground water courses. During construction they hit at least one of those water courses and had something like 750 litres of water pouring in every second. During the fourteen years the tunnel took to complete, twenty-five people were killed.

Inside the control centre we watched on monitors as a car broke down. In minutes the police arrived and a minute later a tow truck. The lane was closed, the car loaded up and the lane opened again inside ten minutes. Any longer and traffic jams would build up, something the controller refused to allow. It was a really slick operation. Only cars are allowed in the tunnel, though, which makes it easier. (Big trucks were banned after the Mont Blanc tunnel fire in 1999.)

Highway 5 is watched over by one hundred traffic cops. At the end of our visit to Hsuehshan we met one of them – a young officer called Warrent – who offered us a lift to the capital in his BMW.

Perfect, Taipei at last. It is always exciting to arrive in any capital city, and this time we would be arriving in style, in a very fast police car. It was white with red chevrons on the bonnet and boot, red and blue lights on the roof and an iron bar fixed to the floor where they handcuffed the bad guys. Warrent had been in the job for three years and clearly enjoyed it. I asked him if he fancied becoming a city policeman, a detective perhaps, but he wanted to remain with the highway patrol. He drove us into the capital and dropped us at the foot of the Taipei 101, the world's tallest building.

I would be making the crossing from Taipei to Japan on a boat, but before then I had a few days free and was really looking forward to exploring the city properly. Taipei lies in the valley of Danshui, surrounded by mountains, and is one of the most densely populated cities in the world. I had a feeling it was going to be an interesting few days. But as I said goodbye to Warrent I had no idea just how eventful my time there was going to be.

The first morning was hot and muggy with clouds smothering the skyscrapers; I could barely see the top of Taipei 101. Jumping on the Metro and than a local train, we headed out to National Central University at Jhongli, where I had been invited to take a look at a motorbike powered by compressed air. It had been developed by a mad professor called Allen. Okay, he wasn't exactly mad, but with his longish hair and glasses he was just as I'd imagine an engineering professor. His bike – a standard moped – had been fitted with a tiny engine, powered by twin tanks of compressed air strapped on the sides. It was basic, but pretty amazing nevertheless. I asked Allen about the tank capacity.

'At the moment it can take ten litres each side. Those are the smallest tanks we can get. Anything bigger would be too big for the bike.'

'And how far will the bike go on that?'

'About two kilometres.'

It didn't sound very far, but this was just the prototype. 'At the moment the pressure in each tank is only 110 bars,' Allen explained. 'We can increase it to 250 maybe. When I am finished the bike should go fifteen or twenty kilometres.'

That was still not very far, but the bike was simple to ride and as I took it for a spin I decided that in London it would probably be enough to get you to and from work. And it was so cheap – all you had to do to fill up was pull into a garage and plug in the air hose. I loved it; it was so innovative. Allen had developed it because the pollution in Taipei is so bad. Riding along you could hear the engine hissing away like something from *Chitty Chitty*

Bang Bang – it was incredible that this little bike ran on something as simple as compressed air.

Allen wasn't the only motorbike manufacturer in Taipei. From the university we went to the district of Hsinchu and the hi-tech Sanyang (SYM) scooter factory.

We were shown around by Yang, the overseas marketing manager, who told us he would lend us a couple of scooters to ride back to Taipei. He was full of smiles and really enthusiastic about the plant. He told me they produce one thousand finished scooters every day; a completed model rolls off the production line every fifty-eight seconds. I know because I timed it.

The factory floor was colossal, with great banks of CNC machines making every working part of the finished scooter. There didn't seemed to be many people around and it felt a little weird being among all those machines making crankcases, pistons and bodywork panels all by themselves. Not very long ago, this would all have been done by hand.

There were some people working in the factory, plenty of people, it's just that they were further down the line. Once all the parts of the bikes came together, a line of workers in grey uniforms and baseball caps assembled them. There were bits of bike on different conveyors, starting with the frame and the engine then right down to the brake levers and indicators. When the bikes are finished, they're fully checked to make sure everything is working, then taken outside and loaded onto pallets.

The warehouse is racked from floor to ceiling and can store ten thousand scooters. I watched awestruck as hydraulic lifts hoisted the pallets to shelves way above my head. In Australia I'd witnessed the birth of a Spitfire engine and now here I was in Taiwan at the birth of a motorbike.

The scooter Yang lent me was a 300 cc SYM. I was delighted to be on two wheels and took off through the suburbs, weaving between the cars with the wind in my face. It was a very nice machine, bigger than most with a good screen and decent-sized wheels so the whole thing felt stable. Ideal for bombing about the city.

Taipei lay ahead of us, clouds still massed over the skyscrapers. It was hot and very close and I rode in shorts and flip-flops.

Claudio was filming from another bike and he told me that Sunny had mentioned something about girls selling betel nuts to passing motorists somewhere along the road from Hsinchu. Chewing betel nut was very common here, just as in Papua. I saw loads of people with red lips from the juice.

'What kind of girls? What do you mean, Clouds?'

'Pretty girls. Girls who aren't wearing very much.'

'Let's take a look then.'

We rode right through that part of the city, suddenly coming upon rows of brightly lit kiosks where girls wearing lingerie and not much else were walking out to cars and trucks with trays of betel nuts and drinks. Sunny told us that the girls, known as 'betel-nut beauties', are something of an icon in Taiwan, where they've been a fixture since the original Shuangdong betel-nut kiosk first opened in the 1960s.

We got off the bikes and started to film one girl, but she immediately got very upset. Within seconds a young guy with cold eyes and stained red teeth was right in my face. He looked wired on the caffeine-like buzz you get from chewing too many of the nuts. He covered the lens with one hand and started yelling in Chinese.

'He doesn't want you to film, Charley,' Sunny told me.

'Clearly,' I said. 'But what's he so pissed off about if it's only betel nuts the girls are selling?'

The guy was glaring at me, one hand balled into a fist. He looked as though he was going to rip the camera from Claudio and smash it.

'Maybe that's not all they're selling,' Claudio muttered. 'Come on, Charley, let's go.'

By the time we got back to the hotel I was pretty tired and would have happily settled down to a quiet evening. But Sam had heard about the city's night markets and insisted we go and find one.

'We'll have some dinner,' he said, 'deer penis, a bit of snake skin maybe.'

'What?' I stared at him, thinking I must have misheard.

'Didn't you know? The men here like to eat deer penises because they think it makes them virile.'

Interesting place, Taiwan. Here I am eating ice cream from a urinal . . .

. . . And here I am about to judge some 'cricket fighting'.

Picking tea on a plantation in the beautiful Alishan mountains.

The Dirt Bike club. From left to right: Clint, Robin, Sam, me, Joseph, Li Jane-Liu, Claudio and (other) Sam.

Hitching a ride on an old box-fronted diesel train at Fenchihu station.

Scooter heaven! At the Sanyang scooter factory in Hsinchu.

Sports bike riders gathering at Lungtan Taouan County.

'The Stig of Taiwan' races on the Lungtan Speedway.

Okinawa – our first stop in Japan. Talking with Yoshitaka Agarie, who was on the island when the American troops arrived in 1945.

The Genbaku Dome, Hiroshima.

Holding a paper crane – a symbol of hope – in Hiroshima.

Sashimi, anyone?

Does my bum look big in this? Paragliding on Mount Fuji.

With the guys from Jene Choppers. Norio Nida – the guy in the middle – is a designer of true genius.

'Mucking around with the 'Cosplay' girls in Yokahama.

With my Samurai brothers – Claudio, Sam and Robin.

Arriving in Tokyo on a classic
Japanese Bratstyle motorcycle.
Happiness is made of this!

Oh God, this was the last thing I needed. But it seemed I didn't have a choice. Sam dragged me down a brightly lit side street to a restaurant where a young woman wearing a headset and microphone was trying to persuade people to come in. Coiled in front of her on the counter was a very large, very live, golden python.

Inside they had all kinds of snakes, as well as the live mice to feed them. Reluctantly taking a seat at a table, I noticed shelves arrayed with jars of what I assumed must be deer penises bobbing around in alcohol. Before I knew what was happening, a waiter was hanging the golden python around my neck.

From then on it got steadily worse. Apparently Sam thought I still needed to pay for coming second in that trike race in Cebu. First off they brought me a dried snake's penis – all bumps and spines and on a stick, of all things, like a lollipop. Yeah, right, I was really going to chew on that. Next came a glass of snake's blood, followed by cobra soup. After that the waiter (who thought all this was perfectly normal) brought me a glass of snake's bile and honey. I was beginning to feel sick.

The waiter assured me that the bile and honey would keep me young. I told him I thought it was all a load of bollocks. Then he presented me with a plate of snakeskin and gravy. I sat there with a slimy piece of diamondback dangling from a pair of chopsticks – it tasted rubbery, like very chewy octopus, and I told the waiter it would be better fried with garlic and chilli.

'That's how I like my crickets,' I said, 'fried with garlic and chilli.'

Apparently, although the snakes in this establishment were alive, the restaurateur was no longer allowed to kill them in front of you, which is something, I suppose. I don't mind snake, actually. I've eaten it before and it tastes like chicken. But then everything tastes like chicken, even squirrel.

In response to my complaint about the snakeskin, the waiter fetched a jar of turtle bollocks fermented in alcohol and a bowl of turtle soup with a foot floating in it.

'Any minute now I'm going to vomit,' I muttered.

'Fine,' Sam said. 'It'll make good television. In the meantime, here's some turtle blood and a glass of turtle ink. That's really rare, Charley, so make sure you drink it all.'

17

Madness, Mayhem and M13

WE WERE DUE TO LEAVE Taiwan in just a couple of days, having finally secured passage on a boat that would get us to Japan. We had attempted many boat trips on this journey and few of them had worked out; from illegal fishing vessels to converted trawlers, so far we had been thwarted at every turn. This time we knew we would make it, though, because we had decided to join a cruise liner.

I know, I know, a cruise liner is hardly roughing it, but we had to make sure we actually made it this time. I could hardly believe that we only had a couple of weeks left of the entire trip. It's at this point in any journey that I find myself torn emotionally. I'm keen to reach our final destination, not to mention desperate to see Olly, Doone and Kinvara. At the same time I can't help feeling sad that the adventure is coming to an end . . . at least till the next time.

Today I wanted to visit Taipei 101, which might not be the tallest building in the world for much longer. Its rival, the Burj Dubai, is already technically taller, but the guys who adjudicate this kind of thing reckon it needs to be fully occupied before it can be legitimately entered in the record books. So until the Burj is entirely finished, 101 still has the record.

The building is in Xinyi, the modern government and financial district, as well as where much of the city's entertainment is located. En route I stopped for breakfast served from the back of a car. Two friends called Jason and Chien had set up this mobile catering business a couple of years ago, bringing hot food to the business district. They offered me black eggs, but having tasted them before I had to decline. I really don't like them. They're fermented in ammonia, which makes them go black, and they taste and feel rubbery. That's bad enough, but what really puts me off the most is that they used to use horse piss to create the ammonia.

So after a nice, safe bowl of rice porridge, I headed for

101. At one hundred and one storeys, it was hard to miss. Standing almost 1700 feet tall, it's roughly the same height at which an aeroplane starts to make its final approach. Mind boggling.

I felt dizzy just looking up at it. It's styled like a pagoda with five additional storeys below ground level. Not only is 101 the tallest building in the world, it has the world's largest counter-balance damping system. You can see it when you get up to the topmost floors – a massive golden ball comprising different layered weights that are designed to counteract the building's movement in strong winds.

The building also holds the record for the world's fastest elevator. It whizzes up to the top in thirty-seven seconds – unbelievable! The lift is pressurised like an aircraft cabin and the outer skin is made from the same kind of heat-resistant ceramic they use on the space shuttle.

Unfortunately, on the day we visited the very top floors of the building were closed and I was only able to get up to level 89. That was all right – it was high enough for me. I stepped into a spacious foyer with glass walls offering the most outrageously dramatic views across the city. Funnily enough, it wasn't so much the views that brought home the height of the place as the window cleaners. I had wondered how on earth they cleaned the glass up here and had been thinking that it was probably done electronically. Then I saw one of those cleaning platforms with two guys scrubbing away with spray guns and squeegees, 1700 feet above the city.

Every year at 101 they hold races to see who can run up the ninety-one flights of stairs to the outside observatory the quickest. Just the thought of it was enough to make my leg muscles ache. But being the bold adventurer I am, I was keen to try it. Not the full ninety-one, mind you . . . ten or so perhaps, just as a taster.

I would need someone to race against, so of course I thought of Claudio – especially if he had to carry his camera with him . . . Robin was up for a race too, but he's younger than me and much fitter. In fact, Robin looks like he could cope with the ninety-one storeys every day. But in the end Sunny suggested a local guy who worked in the building and ran the race every year.

'That's cool,' I said (feeling slightly worried now). 'If he's a regular competitor that will make for more of a race.'

His name was Hon-Nein Peng and when I found him he was doing his warm-up exercises in full running gear. He was an incredible ninety-two years old, his head shaved to a bristle and a Confucius-style goatee clutching his chin. He greeted us with a smile.

I couldn't believe it: the guy looked so trim and fit, he made my cycling buddy of the other day look like a schoolboy.

'My God, Hon,' I said, 'you look so young. What's your secret? Cigarettes, whisky, wild, wild women?'

'My friends think I look about seventy,' he said, 'maybe sixty-five. There is no secret though, not really. I think it's just down to meat and skydiving.'

'Meat and skydiving?'

'Uh-huh. I don't eat vegetables, never have. I just eat lots of meat, go running and swimming and every now and again I jump out of a plane.'

'Right . . . Tell me, Hon, how many times have you run up the ninety-one flights of stairs?'

He held up six fingers. 'Once to practise then five times racing.'

'How long does it take?'

'Twenty-seven minutes.'

Like a couple of good old boys we warmed up – lots of chest pumps and stretches, a bit of toe-touching, the whole routine punctuated by the odd macho grunt.

Then he beat me.

Of course he did. I wasn't about to embarrass a ninety-two-year-old skydiver, was I?

Back on terra firma I received a text from a biker and internet blogger called M13, who had heard that we were coming to Taipei. I really wanted to meet him . . . as did the local police, apparently. They think he's responsible for organising illegal road races and he is something of a thorn in their side. He sent us a video clip where he's in deep conversation with a roadside dummy – one of the mechanical flag-wavers that the council use whenever there are roadworks. He never takes off his crash helmet for fear of being identified – you could call him the Stig of Taiwan. At the end of the video a construction worker in a hard hat comes and drags him away.

He sounded like a lot of fun, though I wasn't sure about road racing. A track would be good, particularly when he mentioned I could borrow a 1000 cc motorbike. Anyway, the plan was to meet in the early hours of Saturday morning and it was all very covert. M13 sent us some GPS coordinates and a time to rendezvous and that was it. He promised us a day of mayhem and madness so of course we said we would be there.

Mayhem and madness was pretty much what we got. I was up at 4.30 a.m. and was not feeling confident at all. In fact, it was more than that: I was feeling distinctly uneasy and that's not good when you're planning a bike ride. I've had that kind of feeling a few times in my life – waking up early with a nagging sensation that something was wrong. Unfortunately that's often how things have turned out.

I remember one Sunday morning when I met up with my friends for a bit of a blat. On a country lane south of London somewhere, I came round a tight bend too quickly and lost it. I went flying across the road and collided with a wooden post. I was knocked out and woke up with torn ligaments in my shoulder and arm. On another, far more serious occasion, a good friend of mine overcooked a similar corner, ran across the road into the bushes and caught a piece of wire across the throat. He was killed instantly.

So it was with a certain degree of trepidation that I punched in the GPS coordinates M13 had given. I really did not know much about this guy. He sounded like a lot of fun, but taking the decision to hook up with anyone you don't really know is always a leap of faith.

The coordinates were for a place called Lungtan in Taoyuan County, known locally as the Temple on the Lake. By the time we found it, a group of pretty serious-looking sports-bike riders had gathered. It was not even 5.30 a.m., and yet further along the road some people were taking part in an early morning aerobics lesson.

Not long after we arrived, M13 showed up wearing a full-face helmet with a home-made ski-mask underneath. I'd been worried he would suggest some kind of illegal racing but fortunately he told us he'd planned an hour's ride on a mountain road and then some time on a track. He had arranged a Kawasaki street-fighter for me – a nice bike, easy to ride and very responsive. They also had a full-face helmet, so I looked the part and was good to go. The other riders were young guys in race leathers, most of whom had well-worn knee-sliders.

'So what's the road like?' I asked M13. Though he wouldn't say where he was from, he spoke with a strong Canadian accent and we were able to communicate fluently in English.

'Gorgeous. Tight and twisty, although it's not that fast. We'll go up into the mountains, stop at a café, then come back here again for the track.'

It sounded great, although I was still feeling pretty nervous. These boys looked as though they liked nothing better than getting their knee down, and the last time I had been on this kind of ride was the day my friend was killed. I told myself to chill out, that you can't not do things just because something might happen. That's ridiculous. If you lived life like that you would never step outside your front door. Life is there to be grabbed by the scruff of the neck.

The problem with riding in groups is that things can get out of hand. Whether we like to admit it or not, competition among sports-bike riders is fierce and roads can turn into impromptu race tracks. It's a macho thing where it's all about how much wear you have on the very edge of the tyre, how scraped up your knee-sliders are and whether you can keep up. Sometimes people ride beyond their capabilities and that's when accidents happen. These days, when I want a speed fix, I go to the track where you can ride as fast as you like and there is no traffic coming the other way.

I just could not shake this feeling of trepidation and as if to confirm my fears I heard a siren blare suddenly further up the road. A few moments later, two black-and-white police cars pulled up and this really stroppy-looking cop climbed out of the first one. He was wearing a flak jacket, combat boots and a baseball cap, looking more like a paramilitary than a copper. He was not happy.

Obviously he hated bikers. His face was the colour of beetroot and when he saw both Claudio and Robin with cameras he really went off on one. It was fortunate we had Sunny there to interpret.

'Stop recording,' he told us. 'You're not allowed to film here.'

That was bullshit. We were doing nothing wrong. We had the correct filming permits and this was a free country. In fact, we were under no restrictions whatsoever. Robin moved to a discreet distance, but he kept on filming.

This copper was typical of some men when they step into a uniform – they think it gives them the right to bully people.

He did not let up. Twice I assured him we were doing nothing wrong, but he still kept on. He demanded that Claudio give him his passport, but there was no way Claudio was going to do that. Again we told him we had permission to film. But he kept on about the passport, waving his arms around and telling us to switch off the cameras. Keeping the camera rolling and his passport safely in his pocket, Claudio retreated to the other side of the road.

We made it clear we hadn't filmed the copper's face but we were not going to stop filming altogether. If he wanted to make an exhibition of himself, that was up to him.

When he realised that we would stand our ground whatever he threatened, he changed his tune. He was no longer asking for passports; now he wanted a piece of paper stating categorically that we would not show his face.

The argument went on and on and by now the bikers were standing around looking pretty bored. In the end we signed a piece of paper for the cop and he seemed satisfied. With a final sneer in Claudio's direction, he got in the police car and left.

'Jesus,' I said to M13, 'is it always like that?'

'Not always, but most cops don't like bikers. They hate the big bikes particularly, and it's only been a couple of years that big bikes have even been legal in Taiwan.'

'I heard that. So what did you do before?'

'Before they were legal? People imported them illegally. There were about twenty thousand big bikes on the street and none of them had licence plates. If you rode in a large group the cops would leave you alone because it was just too much hassle for them to pull you over. If you were on your own, though, you flew straight through red lights because, if you stopped, a cop might jump out and whip your ignition keys away. The worst thing that could happen was they took your bike.'

Thankfully big bikes were legal now, and we were finally on our way. I tried to find out a little more about M13 but he was reluctant to talk about himself, other than referring to his 'moto-blogging', as he called it. He said he was the first person to put a camera on his crash helmet and film his rides for the internet. He also reckoned he was the most popular guy on YouTube when people were looking for bike videos. He was married to a Taiwanese girl and was fluent in Chinese, but that was all he was going to say.

Initially at least, I made sure we were riding sensibly. Claudio was two-up on one of the bikes so he could film, and that moment with the Gestapo had done nothing to ease the knot of tension in my stomach.

M13 told me that he rode with lots of different groups. Many times he would be riding along on his own and a bunch of bikes would come past and he would hook up with them. They would stop for a coffee or something and exchange phone numbers. That was the brotherhood – the oneness of spirit that's the same in Taiwan as anywhere else in the world.

Gradually I began to unwind. I loved this bike and before long I started doing my usual thing of messing about, one foot on the seat, riding side-saddle and popping a couple of second-gear wheelies.

Half an hour into the trip, however, I came down a hill and round a corner to see one of the riders lying spread-eagled in the middle of the road. My heart was in my mouth. A couple of other bikes had stopped already and two guys were running around looking pretty panicked. We pulled over right away.

That bad feeling had been right again, and seeing that guy prostrate was just a little macabre. Somehow he had overcooked the corner and I hoped to God he was all right. At first it looked pretty bad – he was lying so still on the road. But as we got closer he started to move his limbs, and instinctively I knew there was nothing seriously wrong. You can just tell – I've been down the road a few times myself and you know when you're badly hurt. This guy was shocked from the fall and he was hurting all right – a bit bruised and battered – but he was basically okay.

Someone phoned for an ambulance and while we were waiting for it to arrive we learned what had happened. The rider hadn't misjudged the corner; he had been side-swiped by another bike that took the bend more quickly and clipped him as he went by. It was enough for him to lose control and he'd been flipped off.

Two medics arrived and stabilised his neck and left leg before loading him onto a stretcher. He would be all right, but his bike was damaged and that was all he really cared about. It's the same with any biker. When you have a spill, all you can see is your beloved bike cart-wheeling down the road and the only thought in your head is how much it's going to cost. His bike wasn't too bad – the fairing was scuffed, the rear-set foot-pegs were bent out of shape and one of the mirrors was hanging off, which might be a bit expensive. He had been taping his ride on video and he said that we could use the crash footage if we wanted . . . but it would cost. That was a good sign – lying there with the medics taping him up, his business head was working and he was already thinking of ways to raise the funds to get his bike fixed. He was out of luck, though, because we weren't about to pay for any footage.

The accident had put a dampener on the whole ride, and a couple of the guys had already gone back to Taipei. We discussed it with M13 and decided to abort the mountain road and head straight for the track.

The Lungtan speedway track wasn't far from where we had first met up. It was a bit of a shit-hole, if I'm brutally honest, very small and tight and the run-off areas were poor. The safety barriers were just banks of painted tyres and I was conscious that I had no leather trousers. We soon discovered that this was the only standard race track in the whole of Taiwan. They hold novice races here as a way of trying to combat the illegal street races we had heard about.

Like I say, I had no proper leathers, and I hate going on a track without them. I was wearing jeans but they wouldn't give me much protection if I came off. They found me some strap-on knee-sliders, but it wasn't enough to give me total confidence. I did a couple of sighting laps, found the racing line and settled into a rhythm. But I couldn't lean the bike over as far as I would like and kept scraping the foot-pegs. As the laps unravelled I did manage to get a bit of a lick on, I suppose; Claudio filmed it and told me afterwards that M13 said he had trouble keeping up.

I spent half an hour messing about with the other guys before taking a breather. It was an incredibly hot day – the sun was a fireball and the cement absolutely baking. Once I'd had a drink and a bit of a sit-down in the shade, I raced a girl called Jessica on a scooter. She beat the pants off me. She did have a full-on racing-spec machine, mind you, with sticky tyres, a massive carburettor and a racing exhaust. I had a stock scooter and even with a head start she completely annihilated me.

Robin shook his head sadly. 'I filmed you on the Dakar and you never looked better. Just three years later and you're beaten by a girl on a scooter.'

Yeah. Thanks for that, Robin . . . Ignoring him I turned my attention to an Alfa Romeo. I took part in a short car race with two other guys and then Sam Kue, the track champion, took me out in his Mitsubishi drifter. I'd seen drifting – guys sliding cars around a race track – on TV, but actually being in the car was something else.

Sam was in his element: 'Number one, baby!' he kept telling me. 'Number one!'

Spinning the steering wheel, he smoked the tyres all the way from the pit lane to the first corner then all around the track. I loved it, it was an amazing experience. Thrown from side to side at every turn, I was screaming like a girl.

What a way to say goodbye to this great country. I loved the place, particularly on this last day, and after a couple of laps in the Mitsubishi – very hot but very happy – I jumped in the van for the drive back to Taipei.

18

The Land of the Rising Sun

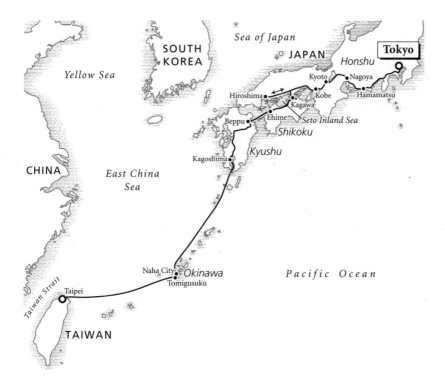

JAPAN IS OFTEN CALLED the Land of the Rising Sun. The phrase comes from the name the Japanese gave their country – Nippon-Koku, which means 'sun-origin'. Sun or rain, I was really looking forward to this last leg of the trip. I had been to Japan once before, but that was just a brief visit to Tokyo twenty years ago. This is the motorcycling mecca of the world, and I couldn't wait to get to grips with all the amazing bikes they have out here. Amazingly enough, the only motorbikes being ridden in Japan prior to the Second World War were imported – none of the Japanese manufacturers pre-date 1945. Given that they now dominate the world market, it's an incredible achievement.

As planned, we made the crossing from Taiwan on a cruise ship, which, despite my reservations, turned out to be a great opportunity to unwind after the rigours of overland travelling. We spent the evening in the company of a bunch of ladyboys, who dressed me up in pink and insisted I join them for the Ms Universe Bingo Pageant. It was like being in panto, only these guys took it extremely seriously. I wasn't quite ready to play Widow Twanky just yet, but I've always had a thing for lingerie, so I joined in with the fun. Robin and Claudio caught every detail, of course, and I'm convinced they plan to use it against me. I reckon they'll wait till I'm invited to the Bulldog Bash by the Hells Angels or something, then bring it out as a slide show. Anyway, in the spirit of adventure I braved the pageant and afterwards I spent far too many hours in the casino. Claudio's alcohol consumption was as sensible as ever, but the same cannot be said for Sam and Robin. Suffice to say that by the time the sun was rising, three of the party were nursing hangovers.

The cruise ship docked on the island of Okinawa, in the middle of the East China Sea. Japan is made up of more than six thousand islands, although the four largest – Honshu, Hokkaido,

Kyushu and Shikoku – account for 97 per cent of population, which currently stands at 128 million. The metropolitan area of Tokyo alone is home to 30 million.

Okinawa. The very name has a resonance – for many this is where the Second World War really ended. Since then, of course, Japan has risen from the ashes and, despite its recent economic problems, it is still the world's second-largest economy.

We had seen a lot of Japanese influence throughout this trip, and most of it related to the war. We had learned all about the invasion of the Philippines from Alex, the museum curator in Tacloban, visited two memorials to General MacArthur and, before that, we'd been told about the attack on Horn Island. And now I was walking through the tunnels under the Japanese naval HQ in Tomigusuku.

Our Japanese translator Masato had now joined us, but my guide through the tunnels, a local historian called Kei Kodawa, spoke excellent English. He told me that the Battle of Okinawa was the most intense in Japanese memory; indeed, such was the ferocity of the US bombardment that they refer to it as the 'typhoon of steel'. It began on 1 April 1945 and eighty-two days later the Japanese finally surrendered.

Okinawa is only 340 miles from mainland Japan and its capture was a major Allied objective. It was from here that the Allies planned to launch their final assault; it was to be a springboard from which to attack Tokyo. As it turned out, that final assault was not necessary. The Soviet Union formally declared war on Japan in August 1945 and then the atomic bombs were dropped on Hiroshima and Nagasaki.

I had been in similar tunnels in Vietnam on the last trip, but these were noticeably more sophisticated. Okinawa is sixty-four miles long and about eighteen miles wide, and when the Japanese 9th Division was sent to the Philippines, the troops left to defend the island had to change their strategy. Ultimately that task fell to Colonel Hiromichi Yahara. He knew the fire power of the Allies – how many ships they had and how many men – so he worked out a plan that concentrated his forces in the southern part of the island. Strategically this area was vital, and Yahara believed it was more easily defendable.

The region was littered with caves and natural tunnels, and that gave Yahara an idea. As soon as the 9th Division moved out, he ordered the construction of an underground network of tunnels big enough to move the entire 32nd Army. It was a monumental undertaking and had to be completed in time to combat the attempted invasion. With no mechanised tunnelling equipment, labourers from the civilian population completed the job with nothing more than picks and shovels. The command cave for the 32nd Army lay 160 feet below Shuri Castle, and the naval command was here at Naha City. Shuri Castle had stood since the fourteenth century but was destroyed in the fighting. Today it's a very grand, very red building that was rebuilt in 1958.

With thirteen hundred warships in Okinawan waters, the Allies landed their ground forces on 1 April 1945. By then the Japanese were underground, though, so initially the American marines met with little resistance. But that changed quickly and the subsequent fighting was as intense as any they had encountered. For two months battle was waged, with the marines finally securing the area around Shuri on 31 May.

While the ground forces that landed on Okinawa were American marines, a quarter of the planes used in the air bombardment were provided by the British Pacific Fleet, a combination of British, Canadian and ANZAC forces. Their primary mission was to provide air cover against Japanese kamikaze attacks.

The Allies attacked the naval base, which was commanded by Rear Admiral Minoru Ota, on 4 June 1945. Ota turned his 200 mm anti-ship rockets on to the lines of US marines to devastating effect. The battle was bloody and brutal, but on 11 June the Americans finally took the base. At that point Ota, along with 175 of his men, committed mass suicide by blowing themselves up in the tunnels. Kei showed me the farewell message the admiral had written on the wall. I could see his writing clearly and it was all the more poignant when juxtaposed with the deep scars in the rock created by blasts from the hand-grenades.

Kei introduced me to a survivor, a man called Yoshitaka Agarie, who was in the Japanese navy and had been in the tunnels. He wasn't with Ota, but he talked about hiding in the tunnels when the formal surrender came. All they had to drink was what they could lick from the condensation that formed on the ceiling. He told me that the temperature underground had been more than 90 degrees Fahrenheit with 100 per cent humidity. He said that the Japanese army could be brutal, not just in their treatment of the enemy but to their own ranks. He described his personal experience in the navy quite differently, however, saying it was more like a family.

In vivid detail, Agarie explained how in the aftermath of the surrender the Japanese army officers not only took their own lives but tried to persuade the civilian population to do the same. People were told that if they allowed themselves to be captured and taken to prison camps, the men would be castrated and the women raped. Hiding out in the hills around the base, Agarie saw some people captured and he followed them to the prison camp. He had no plans to commit suicide; he was a man desperate to live. He spent a couple of days watching the camp to see if the propaganda was true. It wasn't. Not only did he see no evidence of cruelty, he thought the Americans treated their captives with some respect.

Having seen the camps for himself, Agarie went into the mountains around Naha and tried to convince the people not to kill themselves, but to surrender to the Americans. He was sure they would be well treated. Most people followed his lead, so when the war was over the rebuilding process could begin.

To be here sixty-four years later was extremely moving. It was also a complete culture shock after the last few days in Taiwan, messing about on motorbikes.

Above ground once more, I thanked Kei for his tour then took a taxi back to Naha City. The cabbie's name was Daisu, but he called himself Dice, and he took me on an impromptu guided tour. The Ryukyu Islands, of which Okinawa is the largest, have been inhabited in some form or another for centuries, and back in the 1800s they were referred to as Luchu, which is more of a Chinese name.

Dice showed me the downtown area of Naha City and the *shotengai*, or public market, at Makishi, famed for its meat and fish. We visited some local shops and he suggested I try a nice glass of snake's blood wine. I obliged him, but couldn't stomach more than a sip. I'd had enough of all that in Taiwan. Leaving the market area, Dice took me to a shop where they supplied traditional wedding clothes. As I'm already married I had no idea why I was there, but spotting Sam lurking I wondered if this was another of his attempts to get me dressed up as a woman. I needn't have worried; there was no dress and no make-up this time. Instead they dressed me in the traditional robes of a Japanese gentleman. First came a white undergarment, similar to a karate jacket, then they wrapped my waist in a pink sash, before slipping on the kimono and hat. I considered my appearance in the mirror; I could have been Tom Cruise in a scene from *The Last Samurai*. Well, almost.

Outside the shop a couple of guys in weird-looking masks thrust some leaflets at us. They had seen the camera and were talking to Dice and gesticulating. I couldn't understand what they were saying, but Dice explained they were wrestlers who were performing later, and they wanted to know if I fancied doing a bit of training with them. I was up for that. I was up for wrestling as well, but they told me that although their performance was sort of slapstick, they did throw each other around and I really could get hurt. They gave us directions to the gym, and once we were there I joined in with a few back flips and forward rolls. Later we looked in on the performance itself and they were right – it was slapstick. Two guys in costumes – one green, one yellow – reminded me of the Flowerpot Men. The moves were clearly choreographed, but the kids loved it and I have to admit it was very entertaining.

Japan was full of surprises – colourful masks and concoctions. Okinawa is steeped in the kind of history that leaves a lasting impression. I couldn't get those tunnels out of my mind, trying to imagine Admiral Ota scrawling his farewell message on the wall before he and his men pulled the pins on their hand-grenades.

Early the following morning we took a ferry to Kyushu, the most southerly of the four large islands and home to thirteen million people. Kyushu is green, mountainous and very beautiful. It's also a hotbed of tectonic activity. When you think about Japanese volcanoes you tend to think of Mount Fuji, straddling the shores of Lake Kawaguchi. But Fuji's last eruption was in 1708. The most active volcano in Japan is Mount Aso on Kyushu.

We were due in Hiroshima on 6 August for the peace ceremony, so we took the next train north from Kagoshima to Beppu, where we were due to catch a fishing boat.

It had occurred to me a few times since we left Sydney that the scenery in each country we visited seemed quite similar. I suppose it was bound to – we were on islands in the tropics and they were lush, wet and mountainous, not to mention hot. In many ways Kyushu was no different, but from the windows of the train it seemed more spectacular than other places we'd seen. Mount Aso, for example, sits at the head of the most stunning valley, and the steam rising from the crater is so white against the blue sky it looks like low cloud.

Beppu is famous for its *onsen*, or hot springs. Aside from Yellowstone National Park in the US, it is home to the largest volume of naturally hot water anywhere. There are thousands of springs and many public hot baths throughout the city. Beppu is lodged between the mountains and the sea, and the architecture is very different from what we had seen in Taiwan. Here the buildings seemed sort of flatter – they were still tall, but not skyscrapers. And they were tiered, almost as if someone had taken each complete storey on a trowel and laid it on top of the one below so it overhung. It gave the city a really traditional, authentic feel. It was also teeming with people in its narrow streets, with the shops all squashed against each other. They say it's quite a spiritual place, but with so many people coming here to bathe in the hot springs, it was also pretty touristy.

Of course, I wanted to try the springs too, as well as a hot mud bath. I had my pick of places – there was the Pond of Blood, a large pool where the steam is so thick and red you can't see the surface of the water, or Sea Hell, a cleft in the palm trees that, from above, looked more like Mount Aso's crater than a hot spring. It was a tough decision, but I settled on the former.

The mountain range that forms the backdrop to the city is the Takeshi Tsurumi, which is where Japan's population of macaque monkeys lives. It was fairly obvious why the Japanese liked to come here – the relaxing hot springs, the wildlife in the mountains . . . not to mention the museum they've set up in honour of the town's sex industry.

We didn't make it there, which is a shame, because I'm told there is a very nice display of samurai warriors in various clinches with the local geisha. I did manage to get my clothes off, however . . . in the mud bath. There is nothing like it for soothing the muscles after three months on the road.

Three months – was that what it had been? No wonder I was itching to get to Tokyo.

Revitalised by the mud, I got my gear together and headed for the harbour, where I hoped the fishing boat to Shikoku would be waiting. Given the difficulty we had had with boats so far, you can understand my concern. But thankfully the boat was there – a one-man affair owned by a fisherman who promised we would not only catch fish as we made the crossing, but would eat whatever we caught. That sounded good, so with our bags loaded we left Kyushu and headed across the strait for the coast of Shikoku.

To the west now was the Seto Inland Sea. Like a smaller version of the Med, it's almost entirely enclosed by the combined land mass of Kyushu, Shikoku and Honshu.

This was my kind of crossing. The water was calm, there were no monsoons or typhoons to contend with and the air was rich with the tang of salt. With a certain amount of anticipation, I set about trying to catch lunch. I'm no fisherman, but I had a feeling that things were finally going my way. I was sure the Boorman boat curse had finally been banished, and nothing was going to spoil this.

I landed a fish, but it was so ugly, so fat and boss-eyed, I couldn't think of eating it. Neither could my host and fortunately he was able to catch a much better-looking one. I asked him how best to cook it. I was thinking garlic and herbs, a slice of lemon perhaps, and some bread and balsamic vinegar.

'No,' he said, 'we will make sashimi.'

Contrary to popular belief, sushi doesn't always contain raw fish. It's based on vinegared rice and garnished with other bits and pieces, including raw and cooked fish. Sashimi is the sliced raw fish. The word literally means 'pierced body'. Once upon a time restaurants would pin the fish tail and fin to the slices so the customer was able to identify what kind of fish they were eating.

We didn't bother with that. We just sliced the fish as you're supposed to, served it with soy sauce and a little wasabi paste, then ate it with the sun beating down and the sound of the inland sea lapping at the gunwales. Who knows, maybe I'll make some kind of sailor yet . . .

After this very pleasant interlude we landed at the port of Ehime on Shikoku, where we headed straight for the station. The boat had been fantastic, so it was something of a letdown to clamber onto a fairly grotty local train, changing twice on our way to Kagawa.

Shikoku is the smallest of the big four islands. The southern half is extremely mountainous with almost no flat land at all. In fact, they breed a wolf-like dog called a shikoku (strangely enough) specifically for hunting in the mountains. One day I would love to come back and spend a few days camping, but sadly it was soon time to move on. From Kagawa station we hitched a lift on a truck that took us to Honshu via the Kobe–Awaji–Naruto Expressway, and I have to say I saw nothing of it, not the road or the bridge or the seaway below, because by the time we got into Kobe it was four o'clock in the morning.

After a few hours' sleep, I spent the morning looking around Core Machine, a Triumph custom shop in Kobe. The owner told me he only really got into motorbikes after using one to deliver food to people made homeless by the Kobe earthquake in 1995. He could get to places that other vehicles couldn't and the respect he developed for the machine gradually evolved into a passion for bikes and his own custom shop. The quake was the worst to hit Japan since 1923 – four and a half thousand Kobe citizens were killed.

I found his story really inspiring. I could just imagine him on some old bike with panniers and top box, picking his way through the rubble to get vital supplies to the survivors.

Knowing that I was making for Kyoto that night, he offered me the loan of a bike. It helped confirm my gut feeling that I had been right to end the trip in Japan. At heart I am a biker, bikes are what I do and I like to begin and end each trip on one. As I had hoped, there had been a few more along the way on this journey, and there would be at least one more before we finished. I would ride into Tokyo on a bike, alone this time, and perhaps that was how it should be.

The motorcycle culture in Japan is totally different from anywhere else in the world. Despite being a relatively recent development, it's become ingrained in the society. The competition between the big four manufacturers – Honda, Yamaha, Suzuki and Kawasaki – is intense. Honda won six world titles in a row, from 1994 to 1999 (an amazing five on the trot by Mick Doohan, riding their 500 cc two-stroke). They won another three times (2001–03) with Valentino Rossi, before he defected to Yamaha (with whom he has since won another three titles). The rivalry is everything and it filters down to the street bike market, with the big models changing every couple of years. For a long time the Honda Fireblade was God, then the Yamaha R1 and after that the Suzuki GSXR 1000. Right now it seems to be the R1 again, with their new generation of cross-plane crankshafts. I knew all about the factories – the big four brands and how they had come to dominate the world market – but I knew less about were the smaller outfits, the bespoke chopper builders, and hopefully before we left I'd be able to rectify that.

On Sunday I would be taking the train to Nagoya to meet up with Taka, a Japanese kid who works for Dare Jennings at Deus Ex Machina in Sydney. I'd spoken to Taka in Dare's shop and it turned out he would be in Japan at the same time as us, so he offered to be my guide for a couple of days. He knew the bike scene in Japan as well as anyone, and for the last few days of this journey that would be a real bonus.

We hooked up at Nagoya station, before taking the bullet train to a bike fair at Hamamatsu down by the coast. The train isn't actually called the 'bullet' in Japan; it is the Shinkansen, which means 'new trunk line' and refers to the track itself but has become synonymous with the trains. Four different rail companies run four different areas, and – this being Japan –

each is as efficient as the others. Generally you find six trains running every hour. Since 2003 they have been 'maglev' (magnetic levitation) trains, which were first used in Shanghai. In the most recent speed tests, they surpassed 360 miles an hour.

Hamamatsu is a sprawling city on a flat plain known as the Mikatahara Plateau, about fifty miles due east of Nagoya. The Shinkawa River runs through the downtown area, and was so straight it looked more like a canal to me. Taka and I spent the day taking in the bike fair – it was a Kawasaki event with lots of stalls, a few stunts being performed and people selling everything from leathers to bike parts to bike memorabilia. Most of the bikes on display were second-hand sports bikes, but then racing is in the blood here and the All Japan Superbike Championship is very competitive. Having someone with me who was as into bikes as Taka made all the difference. Not only could he interpret, but he shared my enthusiasm.

Japan was turning out just as I had hoped. It was bikes, bikes and more bikes and I could not think of a better way of edging towards Tokyo. In fact, the whole trip had been a blast. Together with Lucy and Liz back in London, Sam had worked really hard setting this up and both Robin and Claudio had gone above and beyond to make sure we covered everything. The three of them had been brilliant – great company and always coming up with interesting suggestions and new ideas every step of the way.

The following day – a Monday – Taka suggested we check out just how diverse the biking culture is. I was all for that. First off he took me to a shop selling second-hand bike clothes, then across town to Stuntgear, a small shop that sells everything from crash cages to handlebars and stunt stays. The owner was a very cool guy called Keisuke and he was more than happy to show me around. If you're into making your bike as trick as it gets, Stuntgear is the place: they can alter the subframe of your bike to cope with the more outrageous stunts and they sell all the protective clothing you could want. It's heaven for the would-be stunt rider.

We mentioned we'd been to the bike fair in Hamamatsu and

Keisuke told us he was riding down there himself tomorrow. He planned to stay the night with one of his friends and I was more than welcome to join him if I fancied it. I had nothing planned for tomorrow, so I told Keisuke I'd be glad to ride with him.

It was just perfect: riding a V Max with a mad-keen guy like Keisuke. These were great roads. Lake Hamana, just west of the city, was a basin of crystal water, and from some vantage points you could see the slopes of Mount Fuji. I was absolutely in my element now.

We spent that night having a barbecue with Keisuke's friend Suzuki and in the morning another of his mates came over in a Nissan QX56 Infiniti that he had imported from the United States. I had never seen or heard anything like it: the paintwork, the sound system, it was awesome. The guy's nickname was Jack Hammer and his Infiniti had started life as a people carrier, although virtually nothing but the basic shape was recognisable now. It was custom-painted a lurid, Kermit the Frog kind of green, with massive tyres and chrome wheels. The whole boot section was devoted to the sound system: there must have been eight speakers back there. There were more speakers in the front doors, which Jack had redesigned so they tilted up instead of opening outwards. He had fitted a hydraulic suspension system that at the flick of a button would lift the front or back or both. Under the bonnet was a 5.7-litre V8; the head cover was painted the same fluorescent green as the rest of the car. I asked him how much he had spent on it and he reckoned about $200,000. God, I thought, you could buy a house for that.

Before we returned to Nagoya I had to say goodbye to Taka. He had been the best tour guide and I would really miss him. Having met him in Sydney where it all began, and then hooking up again in Japan where it was coming to an end, it was a personal way to wrap things up for me. I gave him a hug and told him to tell Dare I'd be back, then I climbed into the green monster so Jack could drive me to Zero Engineering.

The guy who owns the Zero name is Japanese but lives in San Francisco. There is a very particular style to their bikes and an artistic philosophy that goes with it. In a quiet suburb of Nagoya we found the nondescript-looking workshop run by a long-haired aficionado called Kosaki. There was no smoked-glass showroom and no massive sign. Instead the place was given away by the number of old Harleys parked outside. I cannot speak highly enough of these bikes and as I jumped down from the green beast I was tingling with excitement.

I first came across Zero when I was riding the Pacific Coast Highway with Peter Fonda, just before Ewan and I left on *Long Way Down*. We stopped to take a look at a Heroes and Legends bike fair, where some of the Zero creations were being exhibited. We're talking Samurai choppers, whose trademark look is stretched and low and rakish. Over the years they have perfected their own goose-neck frame that gives the whole bike a narrow appearance that is both classic and futuristic. Zero talk about the engine and transmission being the heart of a motorcycle, but to find its soul you have to look at the frame.

As I say, they're not merely motorcycles, they are works of art. Kosaki works with the customer to get an idea of the kind of thing they want, and then his creative juices kick in. Before he begins, he has visualised the finished bike in his head – there are no technical drawings.

It's hard to describe just how good Kosaki is without actually seeing the bikes in the flesh: each one is lovingly brought to life and the incubation period is at least three months. He's doing well if he completes three bikes in a year; hardly surprising when every part is hand-crafted.

The workshop was full of motorbikes and, spotting one in particular, I asked Kosaki to bring it out. This was classic Zero, very long and very low with café-racer-style clip-on bars and a 'suicide' gear change – that is, a foot-operated clutch and a hand-operated gear stick. The suicide part is the fact that you have to take your hand off the bar to change gear. The bike was painted gun-metal grey with the tank hand-beaten and incorporated into the frame. The engine came from a completely reconditioned 1938 Harley Davidson. When Kosaki fired it up, it thumped away as only a V twin can. I didn't dare ask to ride it – this was a customer's bike and what with the suicide shift and everything, even if he had let me I really did not want to risk dropping it.

I was fascinated by how Kosaki worked, and asked him where

he found his design ideas. He said that after seventeen years it was a mish-mash of experience. He would take something from this bike and something else from another, then something else again from yet another. That way there was an element of all the bikes he'd ever built in every new one. I liked the concept, it gave the development process a wonderful sense of continuity. Kosaki personified the Japanese motorbike culture, something that is as instinctive in people as getting up and eating breakfast. These guys live and breathe their motorbikes – they aren't mechanics, they're artists, pure and simple.

Back in the Infiniti, Jack took me to the bullet train for the trip to Hiroshima. I had been waiting for this moment ever since I'd set foot on Okinawa – tomorrow was 6 August, the sixty-fourth anniversary of the day they dropped the bomb. A peace ceremony had been arranged in the Memorial Park and the President of Japan would be attending. We would be there, of course, but before the official ceremony I wanted to get a feel for the place, so we had got in touch with a local guide, a lovely woman named Tomoko Nishizaki.

The actual memorial is known as the Genbaku Dome (or Atomic Bomb Dome) and is the remains of the building that took the primary impact of the bomb. Designed by Czech architect Jan Letzel, it was originally built to house the Hiroshima Commercial Museum and was completed in 1915.

It is now a UNESCO world heritage site – something that caused a lot of controversy when it was declared in 1996. The Chinese weren't happy and neither were the Americans, who pointed out that it was not Japan but the countries they attacked that suffered the worst casualties of the war. But Hiroshima is where nuclear weapons were used against mankind for the first time, and because of that it will always be remembered.

The whole affair was steeped in controversy, not least because of what happened to the USS *Indianapolis*, the ship that delivered crucial parts for the bomb. After it made the delivery, the *Indianapolis* was hit by a Japanese torpedo off the Philippines and it sank inside twelve minutes. Three hundred crewmen went down with it, and of the nine hundred remaining men who went into the sea, only 321 survived. Their mission had been so secret that no one realised they were late to their destination, so it was four days before any search teams went out. By then almost six hundred men had succumbed to dehydration and exposure, many of them eaten by sharks. To this day it's the biggest single loss of life in US naval history.

It's hard to describe how I felt being at Hiroshima, particularly the day before the anniversary. There is an aura about the place that is like nothing I have ever felt before or am likely to feel again. The river passes under the T-shaped Aioi Bridge, which had been the Americans' actual target. The Genbaku Dome perches on the headland – roofless, grey stone walls that are partially collapsed, empty windows, exposed steel struts that are all that's left of the dome. A permanent and very vivid memorial to the day they dropped the first atomic bomb.

Walking the pathways with Tomoko, it was impossible not to sense the terrible history imprinted in every stone. We paused for a moment in silence as she pointed to the bridge.

'That was the target,' she told me. 'But instead of hitting the bridge, the bomb detonated above the dome itself. It was eight-fifteen in the morning.'

Listening to her, I found myself thinking back to the museum in Tacloban and the stories of Japanese occupation. I thought about MacArthur promising he would return, the image of him rising from the sea. I thought back to Okinawa and the mass suicide in the tunnels. In silence again I stared at the dome – empty and sombre, jarring with the brilliant sky above. I tried to imagine how it must have been that day. The mushroom cloud, the ash and smoke and the unbelievable heat. I imagined the buildings collapsing and how people must have thought the world had ended.

Tomoko took me to the statue erected to the memory of Sadako Sasaki – a young girl holding a folded paper crane. Sadako was two years old when the bomb fell and had been at home with her mother, a mile from the dome. Initially she showed no signs of having been affected at all. She wasn't burned, she hadn't been struck by anything, she was one of the lucky ones. Only perhaps she wasn't. Nine years later she developed what the doctors thought was a chicken pox rash on the back of her neck. That was in November, and by the turn of the year she had purple spots on her legs. Sadako was diagnosed with leukaemia, though her mother referred to it as 'an atom-bomb disease'. In February 1955 she was taken into hospital and given less than a year to live.

Her best friend Chizuko Hamamoto came to visit her in hospital. Chizuko had a piece of gold paper which she fashioned into a little crane using origami. Sadako didn't understand what she was doing, so Chizuko told her about the zenbazuru. In Japan the crane is one of several creatures believed to have mystical powers, and there is an old story that anyone who folds one thousand paper cranes – or a zenbazuru, as all the tied-together cranes are called – will be granted one wish.

Tomoko explained that the full story is told in a book called *Sadako and the Thousand Paper Cranes*, where it is said that after her friend's visit Sadako set about trying to fold enough cranes to be granted her wish to be well again. She reached 644 before she died. To honour her memory, her friends then folded another 356 and all one thousand were buried with her.

On 6 August we attended the peace ceremony as planned, listening to the various dignitaries and paying our respects. One survivor gave his testimony, and although he spoke in Japanese, we were all touched by the sentiment. But it was the memory of the little girl folding her paper cranes that will stay with me the most.

After such an emotional couple of days I wanted to have a little down-time, so the next day Sam suggested a bit of paragliding on Mount Fuji. I made a couple of phone calls and had soon arranged a tandem jump from high up on the mountain. It sounded like great fun – already I'd been on the lava flow at the foot of one volcano, so why not go up in the air above another? I had visions of gliding two-up right over the crater, but by the time we got there the weather had closed in. We could no longer see the summit and that made flying too dangerous. The instructor was waiting for us on the south side of the mountain, however, and although the tandem was out of the question, he said I could try a jump from the training hill on my own.

He asked if I'd paraglided before and I said I had – twenty-five years ago. But I hadn't forgotten anything, luckily, and once I was kitted up with the harness and chute ready to inflate, I noticed the only difference was a sort of airbag pouch dangling from my behind. It was designed to protect your spine if you came in hard; it hadn't been available when I'd last had a go. The others thought it looked hilarious and Claudio made sure he got a close-up.

'Very nice, Charley,' he said. 'Very fetching.'

'Really? You don't think my bum looks big in it?'

The instructor was a cool guy. He told me he came to work on an XJR 1300 sit-up-and-beg Yamaha. We talked bikes for a bit, but I was ready to fly and he took some time reminding me how to steer the chute with the twin handles. It works a lot like a kite – you pull on one handle to go left and on the other to go right. Not difficult at all. He watched while I practised and when he was satisfied I wasn't going to kill myself, it was time to fly.

Now the adrenaline was pumping. With the chute inflated he ran me right to the edge and pushed me off. The next thing I knew I was paddling the air with my feet, the exhilaration of take-off stopping the breath in my throat. I was floating, I was flying. I was an eagle, a hawk, I was a *hayabusa* – a Japanese falcon. It was fantastic. Four times I steered my way to the ground before going back for more. I love flying. I mean, it doesn't love me that much, we've established that, but I really love the idea of it. Since the Philippines I had decided I might like to buy an ultralight, but this – this was the freedom of the very air itself.

So far I had been to Stuntgear, seen the fantastic machines they create at Zero Engineering and arranged for the loan of a rat bike from Bratstyle to ride into Tokyo. But before I finished my biking tour of Japan, there was one other outfit I had to see.

Jene Choppers is one of the oldest and most famous independent bike companies in the country. We found the workshop in the small town of Fujikawaguchiko-machi, which is little more than a petrol station and a couple of shops close to Mount Fuji. Turning off the main road, we trundled down a gravel track to a large warehouse and a whole stack of motorbikes. I love what Zero do, but I'd seen these Jene bikes on the internet, and there was something about the used, sort of unfinished quality that sets them apart. The guy behind Jene Choppers is Norio Nida and, together with his wife Hyoko, he has run the business for about six years.

The bikes are unique – real choppers with extended forks and ape-hanger bars. When I say there is a used quality to them, I mean they look as though, come rain or shine, they're ridden every day. Some choppers are so much polished chrome you know they only come out on the odd sunny Sunday.

Norio explained that the chopper culture had grown up because of the American influence in the country. These days it was so easy to import frames and old engines from California that more and more people were going for the individual retro look. But this doesn't even begin to describe what Norio manages to achieve with his designs.

He is another artist, a genius really. He takes everyday items and somehow manages to incorporate them in the detail of his motorbikes. He showed me one superb creation where the tail-light was housed in a drinking gourd, one of those Arabian-style water bottles that are made of leather. This was stainless steel with little perforations in the back. The linkages for the hoses were brass, he had skulls set into fuel tanks and one bike had a suicide gear-shifter in the shape of a knight's mace. The Jene logo would appear between the bars. One even had a chain linkage for the clutch.

The closer I looked, the more detail I could see. It blew me away – in all my years being around motorbikes, I have never seen anything that comes close. There was even a tiny brass knuckle-duster that Norio had hand-crafted and used to decorate an oil cap.

The workshop just reeked of motorbikes – the ethos of what this amazing man was doing permeated the atmosphere. I was in an artist's studio with tools, benches and pieces of machinery. The crank cases and pistons, the individual frames – it was like a canvas waiting to be completed. Using a lathe-style compressed-air hammer, Norio demonstrated how he shaped the metal for petrol tanks with a series of small dents. It was painstaking work, the tiny dents then smoothed between a pair of metal rollers. Just to convince myself how difficult it actually was, I had a go, and in no time the perfectly shaped skin was marred with a huge bruise and all I could do was apologise to Norio for my ineptitude. This was precision engineering at its best.

What I really liked about the place was that it was family-run. Hyoko was every bit as enthusiastic as her husband and told me she has a 50 per cent say in what Norio is doing. He said she has the knack of seeing the solution to a problem when he doesn't even know there is a problem. They introduced me to their thirteen-year-old daughter Inai, and I had to ask her what her school friends thought about her dad building choppers for a living. With a smile she told me they just thought he was cool.

He was. Norio personified cool, calm and collected. I loved what he was doing here; it was different from anything I'd seen on my travels.

His bikes take six months to build and cost around $35,000. I asked Robin and Claudio what kind of hand-built car you could buy for the same money. There aren't any, and the thing about a Jene bike is that each one is unique. If you spent the money on one today, you could ride it for ten years and it would still be worth what you paid for it. Norio can spend three months just reconditioning an engine. He strips it back to nothing and then builds it up anew. He works as closely with his customers as they do at Zero.

He told me his favourite bike was a low-slung hardtail called FTW. Black with a short wheelbase and slash pipes and what looked like a Harley-style springer set of forks, it is the only bike Norio has built where he and the customer envisaged exactly the same thing. There was no divergence of opinion and they finished up with precisely what they had both wanted.

I was dying to ride one of these beauties and, taking my life in my hands, I popped the question. Norio looked at me as if I'd grown another head. Then he grinned. 'Of course you can ride one.'

Thank you, God, thank you, thank you.

He lent me an old-style full-face helmet and wheeled out a serious black beauty before bringing out his own gold bike, the one with the knuckle-duster. Then we set off for a spin around Lake Kawaguchi. With the lake on one side and the foothills of Mount Fuji on the other, riding alongside this amazing artist on one of his incredible creations . . . Well, I was in my absolute element. Biker heaven.

I don't think I've ever slept as well as I did that night. I dreamed of a black bike with a skull and crossbones, riding mile after mile of perfect blacktop on an empty highway.

Waking refreshed and happy, I set off for Yokohama, which lies just south of Tokyo. This is Japan's most prominent port and, as with many port cities, it has a large foreign population. There are some 75,000 Chinese and Koreans, with some Filipino and a few Brazilian nationals too. The area became a base for foreign trade when Commodore Matthew Perry turned up in 1853 with a fleet of American ships. His mission was to persuade the Japanese to start opening their ports for commerce, and a local shogun named Tokugawa agreed. He and Perry signed the Treaty of Peace and Amity and Yokohama eventually grew into the international port it is today.

We had lunch in one of the Maid Cafés that are prevalent in this part of the country. It's not quite what it might sound, although when it was first mooted I'll admit my ears pricked up. These are theme restaurants that have been going since about 2000, and are closely linked with manga and anime comic books. They represent a slice of Otaku culture, a section of society that's fixated on video games and animated stories. In pixie dresses and knee-high boots, the 'cosplay' girls who served us really did look as though they had stepped out of a video game. (Cosplay is an abbreviation of costume play.) It's really not my thing, but just as when I'd taken part in the ladyboy pageant, I was happy to join in the spirit of the occasion. Masato, our translator, told the girls I was a global biking megastar (well, that's what I told her to say anyway . . .).

That night we saw a more traditional side of Japanese culture when we attended a samurai performance. Watching the actors, I was reminded of the Mongolian warrior's costume we kept on display back at the office in London. Ewan and I had bought it at an auction a year or so after we finished *Long Way Round*. Since then I'd raced the Dakar and Ewan and I had ridden through Africa. Twice now I'd bumbled my way across the world by any means I could. But this was the last night and tomorrow I would ride into Tokyo. I had been to Okinawa, I had seen the dome at Hiroshima and I'd ridden some of the best motorbikes money can buy. It had been absolutely amazing, and as the performance ended I admit I was a little choked up.

I was still feeling emotional when I woke the following morning and went down to the street where my bike was waiting – a classic, grey and black Japanese rat lent by the custom-bike shop Bratstyle. It was Sunday 9 August, the last day of the journey.

There was a stillness in the air as I swung a leg over the saddle. The bike was fitted with a motor from a 1940s Harley Davidson, and firing her up the V-twin rumble was unmistakable. Adjusting the chinstrap on my helmet, I checked the mirrors and pulled away from the kerb, heading for the Rainbow Bridge.

Tokyo lay in a haze of sunlight that seemed to shimmer across the skyscrapers. Perched on the low-slung, hardtail seat, all I could hear was the throb of the engine thumping away beneath me.

The final few miles of another journey. The last few months rolled through my head like a movie – Sydney and the convoy, and before that my aunt's funeral in Cornwall, where I had voiced my hopes and fears to my dad. I wondered how he was. I wondered how my mother was. It wouldn't be long now and I'd be with Olly, Doone and Kinvara. I couldn't wait.

I could feel a few tears welling. Changing down, I switched lanes to pass a car, then rocked back again. I felt strangely uncomfortable, almost claustrophobic, with the seething metropolis ahead of me. This was the hi-tech capital of a country that just sixty years ago had been crushed beyond belief.

In my mind's eye I could visualise the ruins at Hiroshima, the statue of Sadako. I could hear the voice of the survivor as he told his story. I was in Okinawa as Ota wrote his farewell message.

And in the same moment I was on Leyte, as MacArthur strode up Red Beach.

And yet here I was on a rat bike, riding into Tokyo. Not so long ago I had been lying on the banks of a swollen river in Papua New Guinea waiting for the water level to go down. I'll never forget that day. It was as basic as life got – a fast-flowing river with no way to get across other than to wait. I remember thinking that the lifestyle there felt totally alien to me, even after all the sights I've seen on my travels – the thatched houses, women suckling pigs and remote tribes in distant mountains, where the rite of passage to manhood was the stuff of life itself.

To go from that – a basic yet rewarding way of life – to this mass of concrete and neon was mind-boggling. The immensity of everything I'd seen and the fact that the journey was over suddenly got to me. The world seemed to close in – the bay below, the buildings, the lights of the Rainbow Bridge.

What had happened to Brendan, who gave us a ride up to Brisbane in his beaten-up Mitsubishi? Where had his travels taken him? What was happening in Gapun, the tiny Papuan village where Don was trying to preserve an ancient language? What would happen to Emilio and the other street kids in Manila? I had met so many amazing people on this journey.

Riding across the bridge to Tokyo, I could see highland villages smothered in cloud. I could see women walking pigs on leads, like I would walk my dog. I could see men, their teeth stained with betel-nut juice, their machetes blocking the road.

Pulling over, I sat with the bike burbling away in neutral and stared at the city ahead. There was so much more to do, so many other places still to see. I adjusted my helmet, kicked the bike into first gear and pulled back onto the bridge.

Winding on the throttle now, I crossed the bridge and was in the city. I was among the skyscrapers and glass, the concrete and unlit neon. It struck me that I was still in the jungle, only instead of palm trees and muddy rivers it was glass buildings and spotless tarmac. It was exactly where I had planned to be when we set out eighty-one days earlier. Boorman on a bike, blasting into the city!

On and on I rode, two kilometres, three, four, before finally I came to Shibuya Crossing, deep in the heart of the city. This was the centre of everything – shopping, entertainment, nightlife. Even now some of last night's revellers were still spilling from various nightclubs.

Five roads converged here and as I slowed for a zebra crossing, the old Harley was coughing and snarling and a bunch of kids, still half cut, were looking on as they leaned against each other in a collective effort to remain upright.

Suddenly I was laughing: they reminded me of the bunch of drunks we'd encountered at the river crossing. Pulling up, I stopped the bike and climbed off. In that moment the relief just seemed to hit me, the euphoria of bringing it all to a close. The kids were gawping now as halfway across the street I stopped to consider the five roads leading in five different directions.

Quietly, I lay down. Right there in the middle of the zebra crossing. Arms stretched, I lay on my back and looked up at the sky. An intersection that gave me five separate options; it seemed a good place to stop. Before I had a chance to consider it further, one of the kids staggered over and looked down at me. He was followed by another and another, all of them still reeling with drink, breathing the fumes all over me.

'Are you all right, mate?' one of them slurred.

I looked up at him with a grin. 'Yeah, I'm fine,' I said. 'Thanks for asking.'

Appendix

Route Details

Country	Day number	Day	Date	From
AUSTRALIA	1	**Monday**	18-May-09	Deus Ex Machina Motorcycles, Sydney
				MacKillop Park Freshwater Reserve
				Fraser Beach
	2	**Tuesday**	19-May-09	Wingham
				Wauchope
				Macksville
	3	**Wednesday**	20-May-09	Nymboida Coaching Station
				Coutts Crossing General Stores
	4	**Thursday**	21-May-09	The Arts Factory
				Moggill
	5	**Friday**	22-May-09	Watts Bridge Airfield, Cressbrook, near Brisbane
				Maryborough Airfield
				Maryborough Military and Colonial Museum
				Maryborough West train station
				Rockhampton train station
	6	**Saturday**	23-May-09	Rockhampton Aero Club
				The Old Station
				The Old Station
	7	**Sunday**	24-May-09	Waverly Creek Reserve rest area
	8	**Monday**	25-May-09	Cairns
	9	**Tuesday**	26-May-09	Cairns, Royal Flying Doctor Service of Australia
	10	**Wednesday**	27-May-09	Cairns

To	Transport	Notes	Section mileage	Total mileage
MacKillop Park Freshwater Reserve, Harbord, Manly	Kawasaki W650 motorbike	With Dare Jennings and other Deus riders	18	18
Fraser Beach	Kawasaki W650 motorbike	In convoy with Dare Jennings, Deus riders, Wayne Gardner, Daly Waters boys and others	84	102
Australia Inn, Wingham	Triumph Thruxon rat-style motorbike	With Dare Jennings	134	236
Wauchope, New South Wales	Triumph Thruxon rat-style motorbike	With Dare Jennings	47	283
Macksville	Diamond T truck	With Mark, owner	67	350
Nymboida Coaching Station	Oshkosh truck	With Stan, owner	99	449
Coutts Crossing General Stores, Nymboida	Holden V8 Commodore car	Lift with Joel and Tatum, travellers	12	461
The Arts Factory Backpackers' Lodge, Byron Bay	evMe electric car	With Phil Coop from evMe	111	572
Moggill	Mitsubishi Magna SE car, a.k.a 'The Millennium Pigeon'	Lift with Brendan, backpacker	109	681
Watts Bridge Airfield, Cressbrook	Ford VA Falcon (ute)	With Clint from Supermarine Aircraft	60	741
Maryborough Airfield, Queensland	Supermarine Mark 26B Spitfire	With Rick, Super-marine pilot	112	853
Maryborough Military and Colonial Museum	Replica 1952 MG-TD	With Ron Stephenson, owner	2	855
Maryborough West train station	Ferret Scout Car	With Graeme Knoll, from Maryborough Museum	5	859
Rockhampton train station	Tilt train		237	1,096
Rockhampton Palm Motor Inn	Toyota Avalon Taxi		4	1,100
The Old Station	Cessna 185, plane	With Rob, owner of The Old Station	35	1,135
The Old Station	Horse (Wallie)	Mustering cattle with Helen from The Old Station		1,135
Waverly Creek Reserve rest area	Ford BF XLS, HSV Maloo and VZ 55 Holden (utes)	With Cameron, Ronnie and Ben, ute owners	144	1,279
Cairns	Ford BF XLS, HSV Maloo, VZ 55 Holden (utes)	With Cameron, Ronnie and Ben, ute owners	557	1,836
Cairns		REST DAY		1,836
Pormpuraaw	Beechcraft/Catpass 250 Plane	With Emma, RFDS pilot	691	2,527
Mossman	Suzuki DRZ400 E; Suzuki DRZ250 and KTM	With David Williams of Fair Dinkum Tours; night at Karnak Farm with Diane Cilento	96	2,623

Country	Day number	Day	Date	From
	11	**Thursday**	28-May-09	Mossman
				Field opposite Lions Den, Helenvale
	12	**Friday**	29-May-09	Lions Den Hotel, Helenvale, near Wujal Wujal Cooktown Airfield
				Lizard Island
				Rio Tinto mine, Weipa
	13	**Saturday**	30-May-09	Weipa Airfield
				Bamaga Airport
				Seisa Dock
				Horn Island
	14	**Sunday**	31-May-09	Thursday Island
	15	**Monday**	1-Jun-09	Thursday Island
				Thursday Island Horn Island port
PAPUA NEW GUINEA	16	**Tuesday**	2-Jun-09	Horn Island
				Daru Port Moresby
	17	**Wednesday**	3-Jun-09	Wagi Valley Transport, Lae
	18	**Thursday**	4-Jun-09	Goroka
				Goroka General Hospital
				Mount Sion School for the Disabled
				Arikayfa village
				Recourse centre for Disabled
	19	**Friday**	5-Jun-09	VSO Lodge, Goroka
				Komunive Village

To	Transport	Notes	Section mileage	Total mileage
Lions Den Hotel, Helenvale, near Wujal Wujal	Suzuki DRZ400 E; Suzuki DRZ250 and KTM	With David Williams	48	2,671
Field opposite Lions Den, Helenvale	Zero electric motorbikes	With Phil from Zero		2,671
Cooktown Airfield	Modified Toyota Land Cruiser	Lift with Max	11	2,682
Lizard Island	Twin-engined Beechcraft Duchess	With Graeme Normington, Marine Surveyor	56	2,738
Weipa Airfield	Twin-engined Beechcraft Duchess	With Graeme Normington	280	3,017
Rio Tinto mine, Weipa	Caterpillar Dumper truck	With Lynn Olsen, from Rio Tinto		3,017
Bamaga Airport	Twin-engined Beechcraft Duchess	With Graeme Normington	130	3,147
Seisa Dock	Truck	With Brett, tinnie instructor	5	3,152
Horn Island	Cairns Custom Craft (tinnie)	With Brett	21	3,173
Thursday Island	Standby-vessel	With Ben and Rob, boat operators	1	3,175
Thursday Island		Visit to Ina Mills, local singer		3,175
Pearl Island Seafoods Crayfish factory, Thursday Island	Toyota Hilux 4x4	With Greg Wright, from Pearl Island Crayfish Factory	1	3,176
Horn Island	Ferry		1	3,177
Horn Island Airfield	Van	With Lachlan 'Lockie' Winkler	1	3,178
Daru	Aero Strike Commander 500s twin engine	With Will, pilot from charter company	123	3,301
Port Moresby	Plane	Commerical flight	273	3,574
Lae	Plane	Commerical flight	192	3,766
Goroka	Westen Star truck	With Koi, driver	165	3,931
Goroka		VSO visit to Goroka General Hospital with Marcel Pool		3,931
Mount Sion School for the Disabled	Toyota 4x4 Rural outreach vehicle		5	3,936
Arikayfa village	Toyota 4x4 Rural outreach vehicle		4	3,940
Recourse centre for Disabled	Toyota 4x4 Rural outreach vehicle		3	3,943
Lahamenegu Coffee Factory	Toyota 4x4 Rural outreach vehicle	With John Leahy, owner of coffee factory	1	3,944
Komunive Village	Toyota 4x4 Rural outreach vehicle	Mud men visit	12	3,956
VSO Lodge, Goroka	Toyota 4x4 Rural outreach vehicle	Mumu at VSO Lodge with Marcel	12	3,968

Country	Day number	Day	Date	From
	20	**Saturday**	6-Jun-09	Goroka
	21	**Sunday**	7-Jun-09	Betty's Lodge, Mount Wilhelm Bundi Junction
	22	**Monday**	8-Jun-09	Madang
	23	**Tuesday**	9-Jun-09	Madang Boroi Jetty Kasimak
	24	**Wednesday**	10-Jun-09	Gapun
	25	**Thursday**	11-Jun-09	Kasimer (house down the swamp from Gapun) Angoram
	26	**Friday**	12-Jun-09	Wewak
	27	**Saturday**	13-Jun-09	Aitape
	28	**Sunday**	14-Jun-09	Vanimo
	29	**Monday**	15-Jun-09	Vanimo Port Moresby
INDONESIA	30	**Tuesday**	16-Jun-09	Singapore Jakarta
	31	**Wednesday**	17-Jun-09	Down town Makassar Central Station, Makassar Dywa Terminal, Makassar Maros Watansoppeng
	32	**Thursday**	18-Jun-09	Sengkang Palopo Masamba

To	Transport	Notes	Section mileage	Total mileage
Betty's Lodge, Mount Wilhelm	Yamaha WR 450 F motorbike	With Daniel, from Lae dirt bike club	88	4,056
Bundi Junction	Yamaha WR 450 F motorbike		55	4,111
Nancy Sullivan's house, Madang	Toyota Land Cruiser	With Emmanuel, owner	86	4,197
Madang	Bitamu Security Services vehicle, Nissan Vanette	With Norbert Belele, from Bitamu Security Services	0	4,197
Boroi Jetty	Public Motor Vehicle (PMV)		132	4,329
Kasimak, via Watam Village	Dinghy	With Milson, owner	27	4,356
Gapun	Walk		1	4,358
Gapun		Day in village with Don Kulick, linguistic anthropologist, and Samson, village leader	0	4,358
Angoram	Charley and Claudio in motor canoe, Sam and Robin in dugout canoe	With Melchio and Margaret, canoe owners	43	4,400
Wewak	PMV Toyota Dyna		57	4,457
Aitape	Toyota Dyna truck	With Ben Keri, owner	103	4,560
Vanimo, via Sissano	Motorboat	With Rainbubus family	79	4,639
Wutung (Border PNG and West Papua)	Rental Hilux car	Border closed	21	4,659
Port Moresby	Dehavilland Dash 8 Turbo Prop Plane	Commerical flight	621	5,280
Singapore	Plane	Commerical flight	3067	8,347
Jakarta	Plane	Commercial flight	557	8,904
Makassar, South Sulawesi	Plane	Commercial flight	868	9,772
Central Station, Makassar	Becak (tricycle rickshaw)	With Nanharman, driver	2	9,774
Dywa Terminal, Makassar	Pete-pete (local Makassar Suzuki bus)	With Idris Dewa, bus driver	11	9,784
Maros	Pete-pete (local Makassar Suzuki bus)		35	9,819
Watansoppeng	Ojek (motorcycle taxi)		14	9,833
Sengkang	Small pick-up truck Suzuki Carry 1.5	With Eddy and Joyle, owners	40	9,873
Palopo	Mercedes Colt, bus		159	10,032
Masamba	Pete-pete (local South Sulawesi Suzuki bus)		48	10,080
Cendana Putih	UNICEF truck	With Coco from UNICEF	15	10,095

Country	Day number	Day	Date	From
	33	**Friday**	19-Jun-09	Cendana Putih
				Cendana Putih
				Palopo
	34	**Saturday**	20-Jun-09	Siguntu
				Lemo
				Kete Kesu
	35	**Sunday**	21-Jun-09	Makale
				Parepare
	36	**Monday**	22-Jun-09	Ujung Lero
	37	**Tuesday**	23-Jun-09	Mamuju
	38	**Wednesday**	24-Jun-09	Palu
				Palasa
	39	**Thursday**	25-Jun-09	Gorontalo
	40	**Friday**	26-Jun-09	Minauna Village
	41	**Saturday**	27-Jun-09	Manado
PHILIPPINES	42	**Sunday**	28-Jun-09	Singapore
				Manila
	43	**Monday**	29-Jun-09	Davao City
				Mintal
				Wildredo's catfish restaurant
				Los Amigos
				Salumay, Davao
				Malaybalay City
	44	**Tuesday**	30-Jun-09	Monastery of Transfiguration
				Del Monte Farm
				Del Monte Plantation

To	Transport	Notes	Section mileage	Total mileage
Cendana Putih		UNICEF project. Fitting water filtration system at Waniasri and Sumarna's home		10,095
Palopo	UNICEF truck		37	10,132
Siguntu village, Rantepao	Small pick-up truck Suzuki Carry 1.5		33	10,165
Lemo	Becak (tricycle rickshaw)	At traditional funeral	7	10,172
Kete Kesu	Yamaha motorbike	Visiting burial grounds with Luther	16	10,189
Makale	Toyota Dyna 1.5PS truck		25	10,213
Parepare	Harley-Davidson motorbike	With Onny	82·	10,295
Ujung Lero	Traditional fishing boat	Delivering ice to restaurant in Ujung Lero	2	10,297
Mamuju	Toyota Land Cruiser 40 Series		152	10,449
Palu	Local bus		257	10,706
Palasa	Toyota Hilux, government vehicle		128	10,834
Gorontalo	Mitsubishi Colt Mini-Van (support vehicle)		212	11,046
Minauna Village, North Sulawesi	Suzuki Thunder 125 cc motorbike	With Minto, Dal and Ivan, local bikers; night camping on beach	126	11,172
Manado	Suzuki Thunder 125 cc motorbike	With Dal and Ivan	101	11,273
Singapore	Plane	Commercial flight	1461	12,734
Manila, Philippines	Plane	Commercial flight	1492	14,226
Davao City, Mindanao	Plane	Commercial flight	610	14,836
Mintal, Davao City	Jeepney	With Ray, fruit and vegetable delivery man	9	14,845
Wildredo's catfish restaurant	Habal-habal (motorbike taxi with a side car)		4	14,849
Los Amigos	Local bus		10	14,859
Baganihan, Davao	Local bus		31	14,890
Malaybalay City	Local bus		104	14,994
Monastery of Transfiguration, San Jose town, Malaybalay	Motorbike taxi	Tour of coffee plantation with Father Adag	1	14,995
Del Monte Farm, Manolo Fortich	Daihatsu multi-cab	Tour of pineapple plantation	31	15,026
Del Monte Plantation	Del Monte Mitsubishi pick-up		7	15,033
Del Monte Tinning Factory	Monte FUSO 10-wheeler pineapple truck		27	15,060

Country	Day number	Day	Date	From
	45	**Wednesday**	1-Jul-09	Ferry Terminal, Lapasan, Cagayan de Oro
				Benoni Pier, Camiguin
				Agoho, Camiguin
	46	**Thursday**	2-Jul-09	Agoho, Camiguin
				Balbagon Pier, Mambajao, Camiguin
				Jagna Port
				Tagbilaran Port
	47	**Friday**	3-Jul-09	Lahug, Cebu
				CNT Restaurant
				Pier 3 Cebu City Port
				Ormoc Pier
				Carigara
	48	**Saturday**	4-Jul-09	Tacloban
				Red Beach
				Basey
	49	**Sunday**	5-Jul-09	Calbayog
				Looc ferry terminal
				Matnog
				Headquarters of 3rd Scout Ranger Battalion
				Legazpi City
	50	**Monday**	6-Jul-09	Mount Mayon
				Cagsawa Ruins, Daraga, Albay

To	Transport	Notes	Section mileage	Total mileage
Benoni Port, Camiguin	Sea Cat catamaran		60	15,120
Agoho, Camiguin	Daihatsu multi-cab		14	15,134
White Island, Camiguin	Banca (local outrigger canoe)	With Benjamin, local fisherman	1	15,135
Balbagon Pier, Mambajao, Camiguin	'The Mariner' (modified Kawasaki motorbike with passenger cabin)		6	15,141
Jagna Port, Bohol Island	Super Shuttle Ferry		37	15,178
Tagbilaran Port	Bohol Police Patrol Vehicle (Toyota Vios)	With Justine (translator) and Ramon, local police officer	15	15,193
Mactan Naval Base, Cebu Island	Philippine Navy Fleet Patrol Gunning Boat	With Peter, captain	29	15,222
CNT Restaurant	Motorbike tricycles with bamboo-style polyethylene covers	Race to restaurant with Manny and Andi, tricycle owners	2	15,224
Pier 3 Cebu City Port	Motorbike tricycles with bamboo-style polyethylene covers		1	15,225
Ormoc Pier, Ormoc, Leyte	Aboitiz Super Cat (Double-hulled Catamaran vessel)	With Jasper Nacinta, captain	71	15,296
Carigara	Delivery truck	With Jon-Jon and Bernard, delivering batteries	11	15,307
Tacloban	'Banig' Taxi	Dr Rusty Balderian's woven bamboo covered tuk-tuk, runs on coco-bio-diesel, made from cooking oil	7	15,315
Red Beach, Palo	Motorbike tricycle with sidecar	Visit to General MacArthur memorial	2	15,317
Basey, Samar	Jega Spider Cab	Across the San Juanico Bridge	5	15,322
Calbayog	2GO Delivery Truck	With Rommel, delivery man	90	15,412
Looc ferry terminal, Allen	Scrap metal pick-up lorry	With Ronnie 'the scrap metal guy'	9	15,421
Matnog, Sorsogon	Ferry		9	15,430
Headquarters of 3rd Scout Ranger Battalion, Philippine Army, Barangay Rangas, Juban	Ambulance of Kabalikat-Bicol Province Rescue Ambulance Service	With '01' from Kabalikat-Bicol Ambulance Service	8	15,438
Mount Mayon Volcano Observatory, Lignon Hill, Legazpi City	3rd Scout Ranger Battalion vehicle	To visit Ed Laguerta, local vulcanologist	4	15,443
Legazpi City	Double decker jeepney		0	15,443
Cagsawa Ruins, Daraga, Albay	ATV/Quad bikes	With Mr Chan, local councillor	2	15,445
Camsur Watersports Complex, Pili, Camarines Norte	Yamaha X1 110 Scooter	With X3M scooter club	8	15,453

Country	Day number	Day	Date	From
	51	**Tuesday**	7-Jul-09	Camsur Watersports Complex
				Calauag, Quezon
				Lopez train station
				Lopez sports centre
	52	**Wednesday**	8-Jul-09	Unisan Farm, Quezon
				Bus terminal, Lucena
				Sarao Jeepney Factory
	53	**Thursday**	9-Jul-09	Malate, Manila
	54	**Friday**	10-Jul-09	Makati City, Manila
	55	**Saturday**	11-Jul-09	Handlebar Bar and Grill, Manila
	56	**Sunday**	12-Jul-09	Angeles City
				Subic Bay Freeport, International Airport
	57	**Monday**	13-Jul-09	Yacht Club, Subic Bay
				Subic Bay Freeport, International Airport
TAIWAN	58	**Tuesday**	14-Jul-09	Manila
				Hong Kong
	59	**Wednesday**	15-Jul-09	Kaohsiung Bus Terminal
				Kenting
	60	**Thursday**	16-Jul-09	Surf shop, Kenting Beach
	61	**Friday**	17-Jul-09	Formosa Boulevard station, Kaohsiung
				Spring travel Vehicles, Kaohsiung, Taiwan
	62	**Saturday**	18-Jul-09	Fo Guan Shan Monastery
				Hsin-Hua
				Tainan City
				Chiayi City train station
				Chiayi city centre Post Office

To	Transport	Notes	Section mileage	Total mileage
Calauag, Quezon	Yamaha X1 110 Scooter	With X3M scooter club	9	15,462
Lopez train station	Skate (railroad trolley)	With Justine and her husband, Webster	4	15,466
Lopez sports centre	Jeepney	To see cock-fighting	2	15,468
Unisan Farm, Quezon	Farm truck	To visit home of Filipino senator, Suarez, and his son Jet	2	15,470
Bus terminal, Lucena	Farm truck	Delivering two goats with Jet	1	15,471
Sarao jeepney factory, Las Piñas City	Stretched 'Hammer'	The Filipino version of a Hummer	12	15,483
Malate, Manila	Sarao jeepney	With Ed Sarao, co-owner of factory	2	15,486
Binondo, Manila		UNICEF project. With Butch, visiting street kids		15,486
Makati City, Manila		REST DAY		15,486
Big Hat Bar, Angeles City	Harley-Davidson motorcycles	With Mad Dog Motorcycle Club	52	15,538
Subic Bay Freeport, International Airport	Ultra Light Airplane RANS S-12, X-AIR Max Air Drifter	With Terry, pilot	28	15,566
Yacht Club, Subic Bay	Taxi		3	15,569
Subic Bay Freeport, International Airport	Taxi		3	15,572
Manila	Support Vehicle		68	15,640
Hong Kong	Plane	Commercial flight	698	16,338
Kaohsiung, Taiwan	Plane	Commercial flight	394	16,732
Kenting	Public bus		74	16,806
Surf shop, Kenting Beach	VW Surfer Van	Surfing day with Afei	1	16,807
Lotus Lake, Kaohsiung	Support Vehicle	Dragon-boating with American World Games team	74	16,881
Spring travel Vehicles, Kaohsiung, Taiwan	Kaohsiung MRT Metro train (tube)		1	16,882
Fo Guan Shan Monastery	Yamaha Scooter		14	16,896
Hsin-Hua, Tainan	Package delivery truck	With Lo Bo-Ya, delivery man. Lunch at Ango's cricket farm and restaurant	35	16,931
Tainan City	Motor tricycle	Fruit delivery vehicle	10	16,941
Chiayi City train station	Bullet train		45	16,986
Chiayi city centre	Shuttle Bus		1	16,987
Sheng Le tea farm, Chiayi County, Alishan	Post Office van	Tour of tea plantation with Lo Hsiu-Mei	32	17,019

Country	Day number	Day	Date	From
	63	**Sunday**	19-Jul-09	Sheng Le tea farm
				Fenchihu Mountain train station
				Chiayi City train station
	64	**Monday**	20-Jul-09	Sun Moon Lake
				GIANT bike shop Shueishe
				Puli bus station
	65	**Tuesday**	21-Jul-09	Meifeng farm lodge
	66	**Wednesday**	22-Jul-09	Taroko Train Station
				Suao train station
				Jhuangwei Hsuehshan Tunnel depo
				Highway 5 Highway Patrol HQ
	67	**Thursday**	23-Jul-09	Lhongshan Metro Station, Taipei
				Taipei Main Station
				National Central University
				Sanyang Industry Co
	68	**Friday**	24-Jul-09	Taipei
	69	**Saturday**	25-Jul-09	Central Taipei
				The Temple on the Lake
	70	**Sunday**	26-Jul-09	Central Taipei
				Keelung Port, Taiwan
JAPAN	71	**Monday**	27-Jul-09	On cruise
	72	**Tuesday**	28-Jul-09	Naha, Okinawa
	73	**Wednesday**	29-Jul-09	Naha Port, Okinawa
	74	**Thursday**	30-Jul-09	Kagoshima

To	Transport	Notes	Section mileage	Total mileage
Fenchihu Mountain train station	Tea delivery truck	With Lo Hsiu-Mei's son, Chan-Kjao	3	17,022
Chiayi City train station	Alishan mountain train		25	17,047
Sun Moon Lake	Plumber's van	With Yang, plumber. Camping at Sun Moon Lake with Ling and Chen	65	17,112
Shueishe port	Fishing boat	With Yang	2	17,114
Puli bus station	GIANT mountain bike	With Tim, cyclist	10	17,123
Meifeng farm lodge	Public bus		51	17,174
Taroko Gorge	Yamaha 250 motorcycle	With Clint, Sam, Joseph and Li Jane-Liu, dirt bikers	42	17,216
Suao train station	Local train	Trip to cold springs	50	17,267
Jhuangwei train station	Local train		12	17,279
Highway 5 Highway Patrol HQ	Hsuehshan Tunnel support truck		29	17,308
Taipei 101 tower, Taipei	Highway Police patrol vehicle (BMW)	With Warrant, police officer	6	17,313
Jhongli Main Station, Taoyuan County (Taipei Main Station)	Taipei Metro train		1	17,314
National Central University, Jhongli City	Local train	To see motorbike powered by compressed air, with Allen, 'mad professor'	25	17,339
Sanyang Industry Co (SYM) in Hsin-Chu	Taxi	Visit to scooter factory with Yang, SYM overseas marketing manager	10	17,349
Taipei	300 cc SYM scooter		35	17,384
Taipei	Taxi around city	Visit to Taipei 101	2	17,386
The Temple on the Lake, Lungtan, Taouan County	Taxi		2	17,388
Lungtan Racetrack, Taouan County	Kawasaki Z1000, Alfa 156 and Mitsubishi Drifter (around the track)	With 'M13'	3	17,391
Keelung train station	Train		19	17,410
On cruise	SuperStar Libra Star Cruises		0	17,410
Naha Port, Okinawa, Japan	SuperStar Libra Star Cruises		383	17,793
Naha, Okinawa	Velo Taxi	Visit to Tomigusuku tunnels with local historian Kei Kodawa	1	17,794
Kagoshima Ferry Port, Kagoshima, Kyushu	Ferry		417	18,211
Kurume	Local trains		147	18,358

Country	Day number	Day	Date	From
	74	**Thursday**	30-Jul-09	Kurume
	75	**Friday**	31-Jul-09	Beppu
				Ehime train station
				Kagawa train station
	76	**Saturday**	1-Aug-09	Core Machine, Kobe City
	77	**Sunday**	2-Aug-09	Kyoto train Station
				Nagoya train station
	78	**Monday**	3-Aug-09	Hamamatsu
	79	**Tuesday**	4-Aug-09	Tenpaku-ku Shimada Monastery, Nagoya
				Paradise Road Custom, Meitouku district, Nagoya
	80	**Wednesday**	5-Aug-09	Shizuoka
				Shizuoka
	81	**Thursday**	6-Aug-09	Hiroshima
				Hiroshima
	82	**Friday**	7-Aug-09	Shizuoka
	83	**Saturday**	8-Aug-09	Mount Fuji
	84	**Sunday**	9-Aug-09	Yokohama

To	Transport	Notes	Section mileage	Total mileage
Beppu	Moto Guzzi V7 (750 cc) or Hesketh	Visit to hot springs	78	18,436
Yawatahama port, Ehime, Shikoku Island	Fishing boat		55	18,491
Kagawa train station	Train		143	18,634
Kobe City	Deco truck		77	18,710
Kyoto	Custom Triumph motorbike from Core Machine		46	18,757
Nagoya train station	Shinkansen (bullet train)		84	18,841
Suzuki Biking Event, Hamamatsu, Shizuoka Island	Taka's brother's Volvo	With Taka, from Deus Ex Machina	27	18,868
Nagoya	Taka's brother's Volvo	Visit to Stuntgear shop with Taka	0	18,868
Paradise Road Custom, Meitouku district, Nagoya	Ford Model T (customized)		2	18,870
Hamamatsu City, Shizuoka	ESXR 1000 Sports bike		67	18,937
Zero Engineering	Nissan QX56 Infiniti truck	Lift to Zero with Jack, owner of Nissan and tour with Kosaki, owner	1	18,938
Hiroshima	Shinkansen (bullet train)	Visit to Genbaku Dome with guide, Tomoko Nishizaki	421	19,359
Hiroshima		Peace ceremony	0	19,359
Shizuoka	Shinkansen (bullet train)		421	19,780
Mount Fuji	Jene chopper	Tour of Jene Choppers with Norio Nida, owner	47	19,827
Yokohama	Otaku Style Itasha cars/ Anima cars	Visit to Maid Café	64	19,891
Tokyo (Shibuya crossing)	Bratstyle motorbike		20	**19,911**

A Message from Charley

Right to the Edge: Sydney to Tokyo By Any Means was about getting to know people and places in far off and often exotic lands, where cultures, traditions, beliefs and languages all differ from mine and from each other. These differences are often marked, but more noticeable still are the great similarities that we share; similarities that are nowhere more evident than in the children I was fortunate enough to meet.

On this trip I spent time at UNICEF projects in Sulawesi and Manila in my role as UNICEF Ambassador. I was reminded again that all children have the most extraordinary capacity for joy and for love, that they can be amazingly tenacious, resilient and resourceful, wonderfully playful and infuriatingly cheeky. But not every child has the same opportunities and the lottery of where and when a child is born can determine whether they have clean water, enough food to eat, a school or doctor to go to and even family or friends to care for them.

It is a truth (and not just because it was agreed by governments in the 1989 UN Convention on the Rights of the Child) that all children, in every corner of the world, have the same rights – to be educated, to be healthy, to be heard and treated fairly, to have a childhood. The greatest promise we can make to children is to ensure these rights are protected.

Yet many millions of children are still being denied their rights. Children, in numbers sometimes too great for us to grasp, are dying through easily preventable diseases. Millions more face discrimination, violence, abuse and exploitation, while too many others are burdened by desperate poverty.

We must never forget the child behind the statistics, or be daunted by the size of the task ahead. If we are to keep to our promise of a better life for every child we must be louder, stronger, bolder, more furious and more committed than ever before.

Whenever I have the privilege of visiting UNICEF projects, I am always aware that the work I am seeing is only made possible by the amazing generosity of UNICEF supporters – the schoolboy back in England who pledges his pocket money for a month; the mother who puts on running shoes for the first time and runs a marathon to raise money; the company that commits to help UNICEF build and equip a healthcare centre. UNICEF relies entirely on such voluntary donations.

By supporting UNICEF you become the bricks and mortar, the life-saving vaccination, the training, the knowledge and the expertise, the emergency shelter, the clean water, the caring hand, the protector of all children and their rights. You are helping children not only just to survive but also to thrive.

To find out more, visit www.unicef.org.uk/byanymeans

unicef

UNICEF is the world's leading organisation working for children and their rights. We work in more than 190 countries to build a world fit for children.

The UN Convention on the Rights of the Child (1989) underpins all of our work. UNICEF is the only children's organisation that is recognised in the Convention. We work tirelessly to protect and promote children's rights.

Our practical programmes help meet every child's right to be healthy, to be educated, to be treated fairly, to be listened to, and to have a childhood free from adult responsibilities. We work with governments and communities to help them keep their promise to fulfil children's rights.

Child survival
UNICEF is the world's largest supplier of mosquito nets and vaccines for children. We also save many children's lives by ensuring clean water, nutritious food and health care for mothers during pregnancy and birth.

Education for all
UNICEF works to realise every girl's and boy's right to quality basic education. We help build schools and classrooms, recruit and train teachers and provide education supplies.

Unite for Children, Unite against AIDS
UNICEF helps prevent the mother-to-child transmission of HIV, procures medicine for children with HIV, prevents HIV infections among young people and protects children orphaned by AIDS.

Protection for vulnerable children
We also protect children vulnerable to violence, abuse and exploitation, especially child soldiers, street children, trafficked children and child labourers.

Leader in emergencies
With a permanent presence worldwide, UNICEF responds rapidly wherever and whenever a disaster strikes, providing humanitarian relief for children caught up by war or natural disasters.

You and UNICEF
The rights of many millions of children are being denied: children still die of easily preventable causes, still lack protection, education, food, shelter and clean water, and still face poverty and discrimination. Much remains to be done.

We need your help to protect the rights of every child. UNICEF relies entirely on voluntary donations to fund our work. The smallest donation can make a decisive difference to the life of a child.

Campaign, donate or raise money to help UNICEF keep the promise of a better life for every child.

Log on www.unicef.org.uk/byanymeans
Call 0844 801 2414
Email helpdesk@unicef.org.uk

If you are outside the UK there are still many ways you can support UNICEF. Please visit www.unicef.org to find out more.

Sharing skills
Changing lives

VSO is an international development charity that tackles global poverty by using the skills, commitment, and enthusiasm of individuals from around the world.

Professionals with backgrounds in education, health, and business work with local colleagues to improve the public services and employment opportunities that lift many thousands of people out of poverty. Volunteers share their professional expertise so that when they return home, their skills live on in more confident and capable local professionals.

VSO volunteers are involved in a range of different activities from training teachers and health workers to teaching women farmers how to establish a small business. It does not cost individuals anything to volunteer with VSO and they are provided with return flights, basic accommodation, and an allowance for essential living costs.

Young people can also get involved in with VSO through Global Xchange. Global Xchange is a six-month exchange programme, which gives 18–25 year olds from different countries a unique opportunity to live and work together, to develop and share valuable skills, and to make a practical contribution to community development projects.

VSO also encourages individuals to think global but act local by getting involved in development issues from their own communities. We've helped hundreds of supporters with talks and exhibitions, action days and theatre productions, on issues ranging from fair trade to women's equality. By raising awareness of development issues close to home our supporters are helping to tackle prejudice and misunderstanding about other people and cultures.

VSO is a charity in need of funds and there are a number of ways to support us including regular giving, Volunteer Linking schemes, fundraising events or by becoming a corporate partner.

To get involved with VSO, overseas or in the UK, visit www.vso.org.uk or call + 44 20 8780 7500

Royal Flying Doctor Service

The furthest corner. The finest care.

For locals, as well as for those travelling and working in rural and remote Australia, the Royal Flying Doctor Service (RFDS) plays an integral role in their safety and provides a true sense of security should life present challenges beyond their capacity to manage.

Every day across Australia, the RFDS treats more than 717 patients. In order to reach these patients, RFDS aircraft must fly the equivalent of 25 round trips to the moon every year.

While emergency aeromedical retrieval and inter-hospital transfers remain a primary duty of the Flying Doctor, the organisation also provides an extensive network of primary health care services such as mental health, indigenous health, children's health and women's health at a range of clinic locations across Australia.

On his latest adventure, Charley visited Pormpuraaw, a remote indigenous community where the RFDS provide a primary health care clinic. Charley also visited the RFDS Cairns Base, the largest RFDS base in Australia, where he witnessed first hand the lifesaving work of the Service when an aircraft landed with a seriously ill patient.

Across Australia, 50 aircraft fitted with lifesaving medical equipment and staffed by pilots, doctors and nurses are on standby twenty-four hours a day, 365 days a year. With each aircraft costing around AU$7 million, the RFDS is constantly challenged to raise enough money to cover the costs of aircraft replacement.

You can make a lasting difference by donating to the Flying Doctor.

To find out more information or to donate log on to www.flyingdoctor.org.au

Acknowledgements

Olivia, Doone, Kinvara and the whole Boorman clan

Russ Malkin

Production Staff
Lisa Benton, Sarah Blackett, Ollie Blackwell, Kirk Douglas, Rob Drake, Jeff Gulvin, Corin Holmes, Sarah Lawrence, Liz Mercer, Stephanie Newman, Hannah Palmer, Claudio von Planta, Robin Shek, Samuel Simon, Lucy Trujillo, Rhian Williams

With Special Thanks To
Aboitiz Transport System, Inc. – 2GO, Afei, Andy Klepp, Angeles City Flying Club, Armed Forces of the Philippines, AST, BBC, BBC Worldwide, Ben Dickenson, Berthy Joris, Betty Higgins, Bianca Graham, BMW Motorrad Japan, Bob McTavish, Brad Kennerley, Brendan Barry, Brett Petersen, Cameron Russell, CamSur Watersports Complex, Pili, Camarines Sur Province, Christian Storms, Coboo Designs, Conrad Leach, Core Machine, Councillor Celoy Chan of Legazpi City, Crank, Dare Jennings, Darren Loveday, Decont, Dedy Karya, Del Monte Philippines Inc., Deus Ex Machina, Diane Cilento, District Head of Luwu Utara, HM Luthfi A. Mutty, Don Kulick, Ed Sarao at Sarao Jeepney Factory, Ela Motors, Emmanual Yama, eVme, Fair Dinkum Bike Tours, Fo Guan Shan Monastery, Fuji Q Highlands, Gabriel Ellis, Girlie Linao, Global Events and Expeditions, Graeme Knoll, Graeme Normington, Hachette, Hammer Factory, Head of the Luwu Utara Planning Board, HM Nur Husain, Hermes Hawe, Hills Balfour Synergy, Humphrey Smith, Indonesian Embassy, London, Inky Nakpil, Intomedia, Jaclyn Meier, JAL Airlines, Jene Chopper, John and Chana Graham, John and Cynthea Leahy, John Tamoy, Joyce at Rainbubus, Justine Espina, Kabalikat-Bicol Provice Rescue Ambulance Service, Kentec Mail and Courier Service, Luther Rape, M13, Mad Dog Motorcycle Club, Marcel Pool, Mark Johnson, Maryborough Military Museum, Masato Yamada, Mayor Noel Rosal of Legazpi City, McMurdo, Media Insurance, Mick Golden, Mon Takada, Monastery of the Transfiguration, Mr Takamine at Bratstyle Motorbike, Nancy Sullivan & Associates, Nicki Chung, Nokia, Objective, Ocean Adventure, Subic Bay, Philippines, Onny Gappa, Paradise Road Custom Cars, Pearl Island Seafoods, Peter Boyd, Peter Jackson, Philippine Department of Tourism, London, Philippine Embassy, London, Philippine Institute of Volcanology and Seismology (Phivolcs), Philippine Navy, Pilgrims Group, Papua New Guinea Embassy, London, Professor Huang, Qantas, QR Tilt Train, Richard Darwood, Richard Mohr, Rio Tinto Alcan, Robert Buleka of National Film Institute, Robert Kirby, Ronald Windsor, Royal Flying Doctor Service (RFDS), Saltmarsh PR, Sanyang Industry Co. (SYM), Shimaguchi Tetsuo, Sky Trans, Songline Cruises, Sony, Stan Newman, Steve Loveday, Stuntgear, Sueme,

Sunny Han, Supermarine Aircraft, Superstar Libra Cruises, Taipei 101, Taipei Grand Formosa Hotel, Taiwan Tourist Board, Takayuki Aoyama, Team X3M Naga Scooter Club, Tenpaku-ku Shimada Zen Buddhist Monastery, The Arts Factory Backpackers Lodge, The Cambridge Hotel, Sydney, The Hilton Hotel, Cairns, The Hilton Hotel, Tokyo, The Lions Den Hotel, The Old Station, Tomoko Nishizaki, Hiroshima Film Commission, Tourism Australia, Tourism New South Wales, Tourism Queensland, Tourism Tropical North Queensland, UKTV, UNICEF, Universal, VSO, Yasu at Frontend Magazine, Zero Engineering, Zero Motorbikes.

Picture Credits

Picture credit	Page reference
Oliver Blackwell	12 (both images)
Sunny Han	26 (bottom image)
Brad Kennerley	2 (bottom image)
Claudio von Planta	5 (top image), 10 (bottom image), 11 (top image)
Robin Shek	1 (bottom image), 4 (both images), 5 (bottom image), 8 (bottom image), 13 (bottom image), 15 (top and middle images), 16 (bottom image), 19 (top image), 24 (bottom image), 29 (middle image), 31 (top image)
Sam Simon	1 (top image), 2 (top image), 3 (both images), 6 (both images), 7, 8 (top image), 9 (both images), 10 (top image), 11 (bottom image), 13 (top image), 14 (all images), 15 (bottom image), 16 (top image), 17 (both images), 18 (both images), 19 (bottom image), 20 (all images), 21 (both images), 22 (both images), 23 (both images), 24 (top image), 25 (both images), 26 (top image), 27 (both images), 28 (both images), 29 (top and bottom images), 30 (both images), 31 (bottom image), 32 (bottom image)
Masato Yamada	32 (top image)

Would you like to become an Adventure Travel Writer?

If reading about Charley's adventures has inspired you, we'd like to bring you the opportunity to follow in his footsteps and head to Queensland, Australia, to have 'The Best Adventure in the World' – and write all about it!

Tourism Queensland, Big Earth and the *Independent* have created an amazing competition for one budding writer to win the opportunity to travel to Queensland and write about his or her experiences for the *Independent*. Full details on how to enter the competition are available at

www.experiencequeensland.com/travelwriter
(closing date for entry 31 December 2009).*

Queensland, Australia provides plenty of inspiration for adventurers of all levels, with much to explore: dive in one of the natural wonders of the world, the Great Barrier Reef, scattered with over 900 islands and cays; sail around the magnificent Whitsunday Islands; visit the world's most ancient rainforest; take a 4WD to Australia's tip at Cape York or around the world's largest sand island, Fraser Island; encounter incredible wildlife and nature; learn more of Aboriginal history and culture; head to Queensland's vast Outback with incredible national parks, local characters, dinosaur trails and much more . . .

Discover more about Queensland at www.experiencequeensland.com

For inspiration on adventures in Queensland, visit www.islandreefjob.com and read the travel blog written by Ben Southall, who secured Tourism Queensland's 'Best Job in the World'!

To help you plan your next big adventure visit www.bigearth.co.uk

Follow the travels of 6 adventurers at www.independent.co.uk/gapyear

This is a competition run by Tourism Queensland. Submissions should follow website guidelines and should not be sent to the publisher.